"Information through Innovation"

Introduction to the AS/400

Robert W. Janson

*Florida Community College
at Jacksonville*

boyd & fraser publishing company

Senior Acquisitions Editor: James H. Edwards
Production Manager: Peggy J. Flanagan
Production Services: Nancy Benjamin, Books By Design, Inc.
Compositor: Gex, Inc.
Interior Design: Sally Bindari, Books By Design, Inc.
Cover Design: Kevin Meyers
Manufacturing Coordinator: Tracy Megison
Marketing Manager: Eileen Pfeffer

 © 1994 by boyd & fraser publishing company
A Division of South-Western Publishing Co.
One Corporate Place • Ferncroft Village
Danvers, Massachusetts 01923

 International Thomson Publishing
boyd & fraser publishing company is an ITP company.
The ITP trademark is used under license.

 This book is printed on recycled, acid-free paper that meets
Environmental Protection Agency standards.

All rights reserved. No part of this work may be reproduced or used in any form or by any means — graphic, electronic, or mechanical, including photocopying, recording, taping, or information and retrieval systems — without written permission from the publisher.

Names of all products mentioned herein are used for identification purposes only and may be trademarks and/or registered trademarks of their respective owners. South-Western Publishing Co. and boyd & fraser publishing company disclaim any affiliation, association, or connection with, or sponsorship or endorsement by such owners.

Manufactured in the United States of America

Library of Congress Cataloging-in-Publication Data

Janson, Robert W.
  Introduction to the AS/400 / Robert W. Janson.
    p. cm.
  Includes index.
  ISBN 0-87709-262-1
  1. IBM AS/400 (Computer) I. Title.
QA76.8.I25919J36 1994   93-34422
004.1'45--dc20   CIP

1 2 3 4 5 6 7 8 9 10 DH 7 6 5 4 3

Brief Contents

Detailed Contents

Preface

One of the most common questions I hear from new computer students is "What courses should I take to get a job?" One of the most common laments of data processing managers is "Where can I get qualified AS/400 programmers?" Between these two questions is a lack of educational programs and materials to train new computer programmers and operators on the AS/400. Much has been written about the AS/400, and a great many books, manuals, and magazine articles cover just about every conceivable topic on it. None of these materials, however, are geared toward the beginning student. Often, they assume a knowledge of advanced computer science principles or familiarity with a large, multiuser computer environment.

This book has been written for the beginning computer student. The purpose is to introduce the student to the AS/400's application development environment and provide a hands-on approach to the major AS/400 utilities. After studying this text, the student should be ready to take an introduction to AS/400 programming class. This text was written with the assumption that the reader has taken an introduction to computers course and therefore is familiar with personal computers. It has also been assumed that the reader is familiar with the most common PC software packages—word processing, database, spreadsheet—and has had some exposure to operating system functions such as copying a file and formatting a disk. All screen references and exercises are for Version 2 Release 2 of the AS/400 operating system.

To all those reading this book and exploring the AS/400 for the first time, I hope you find the subject as interesting and fun as I have. If you have any suggestions or questions please feel free to write to me care of the publisher.

I'd like to thank my wife, Brenda, and my parents for their never-ending confidence in me. I also am grateful to my noncomputer-oriented friends for listening to me even though they were bored.

Robert W. Janson
Jacksonville, Florida

System Overview and Architecture

1

Overview

This chapter starts off with a brief definition and discussion of minicomputers and their role in a data processing organization. Some history regarding the origins and evolution of the AS/400 will then be covered followed by an explanation of the major hardware and software components of the AS/400 and how these components interact. A more detailed look at the major functions of the AS/400 operating system follows. Finally, the screens and menus that allow a user to sign on and access the various AS/400 functions and utilities are explained.

After finishing this chapter, you will understand:

- What a minicomputer is
- The AS/400's major hardware and software components and how they interrelate
- An operating system's major functions and the OS/400 utilities that provide these functions

You also will be able to:

- Sign on to the AS/400
- Use the on-line help facility
- Access AS/400 functions through the menu system

What Is a Minicomputer?

Minicomputers are generally considered medium-sized computers. (By medium sized I do not mean between 5'6" and 5'10", 150 to 175 lbs.) They are between microcomputers and mainframe computers in terms of processing speed, storage space, and number of users that can be supported at once. The terms *minicomputer*, *microcomputer*, and *mainframe*, however, are fuzzy descriptions. Before a computer is classified as one of these, it does not have to perform at a certain processing speed or have a minimum storage capacity. In fact, the smallest minicomputers are often less powerful than the biggest microcomputers, and the high-end minicomputers are more powerful than many of the smallest mainframes. There is considerable overlap at the extremes of all three categories, and in general, a wide range of capabilities can be found within each category. Another fact that adds to the fuzziness of these definitions is that the speed and storage capacity of all computer categories are increasing every year. What was considered a minicomputer in the early 1980s is within the range of most microcomputers today. By the end of the decade, it will probably be in the range of laptops. The current generation of minis are performing at what was considered mainframe speed ten years ago.

An organization might choose a minicomputer over a microcomputer or a mainframe for several reasons. First, a microcomputer simply may not be fast enough or have the storage capacity to support the required processing. Another limitation of micros is the number of users they can support at the same time. Many of them lack the power to run many programs at once. Mainframes, of course, have all the capabilities of a mini, but they cost more, require specialized personnel to set up and maintain, take up more space, and often need special environmental conditions (temperature control, water lines, and so on).

AS/400 History

The AS/400 is IBM's latest minicomputer. In "IBM language," it is referred to as a midrange computer. (Presumably, they chose the term *midrange* because it sounds less diminutive than *mini*. And rightfully so because very little is mini about the AS/400.) Its high-end models provide incredible processing and storage capacity, and its software incorporates the latest advances and techniques to provide an efficient, easy-to-use, and seamless user environment. The AS/400 did not, however, spring up from the ground in this new and radical state. It has a long parentage and offers differing degrees of compatibility with previous generations of IBM minicomputers.

A brief family history of the AS/400 (Figure 1.1) starts off with the introduction of the System 3 (S/3) in July 1969. The AS/400's great-grandpappy was IBM's first entry into "low-end" systems. Its processing capabilities would be in today's micro range, but for its day, it did offer some technological advances. For instance, it used a punch card that was one-third the size of traditional punch cards but held 120 percent of the data. Punch cards had been the same for 40 years prior to this advancement—an eternity compared to the turnover rate of most computer technology today.

FIGURE 1.1
The AS/400 Family Tree

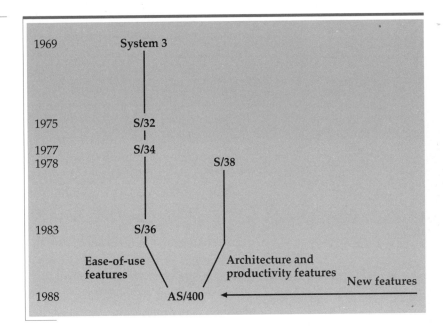

In January 1975, the next member of the S/3X family was introduced—the S/32. It also featured the latest computer capabilities, such as allowing users to enter commands directly from a keyboard and a display screen that could show 240 characters (6 rows of 40 characters). Main memory size for the S/32 was 32K, and it had a 13MB fixed disk.

The next generation came only two years later, in April 1977. The S/34 supported multiple workstations (printers and terminals) and could handle up to eight local users at a time. It had 256K of main memory and a 13MB fixed disk—storage sizes that are exceeded by almost all microcomputers sold today.

The S/38, announced in October 1978, was the next machine in the family, but it represented a change in architecture. It was a step forward, in terms of hardware, from the previous generation, with 32MB of memory and 14GB of disk, but more important, it was geared specifically for application development. Its utilities and user interface were built to help facilitate the software development process. Today, this may sound pretty logical, but at the time, it was a major change in outlook. Computers were normally built for maximum performance. Usability was a secondary issue at best. This change marked the realization that a computer's ease of use was as important as its processing speed. (A faster passenger plane could be built, but if it were so complicated that only a few people could fly it, what good would it be to the airlines? The same realization came to computer manufacturers. More usable computers would be more valuable to businesses.)

Meanwhile, development continued on the S/34 architecture. The S/36 was introduced in May 1983 and eventually contained 7MB of memory and 1.4GB of disk and could support up to 72 local workstations.

In June 1988, IBM announced the AS/400 computer family (AS stands for Application Systems). The AS/400 was an expansion of the S/38 architecture but also provided application program compatibility with the S/36. The AS/400 family also differed from the S/3X family in several significant ways. It offered much more compatibility across machines within the family. Programs created on one model of the AS/400 could be transferred and run on any other AS/400 system without any changes. This was not the case for programs developed on the S/36 and S/38. Each had a different architecture that prevented the sharing of programs. The AS/400, of course, offered a great improvement in performance. The high-end models of the AS/400 offered three times the performance of the largest S/38 and five times that of the largest S/36. This improvement was achieved through faster processors, more storage, and better fixed-disk systems (more about this later in the chapter).

The AS/400 is also easier to use than its predecessors. It is billed as a "plug-and-go" system (plug it in and start working). An example of a plug-and-go feature is that the operating system can come pre-loaded on the system. Users do not have to perform or wait for an operating system installation. All screens and menus that an AS/400 user would be exposed to have been developed with ease of use in mind. For instance, they are all supported by an extensive on-line help facility that is consistent in appearance and function. Also, a computer-based tutorial resident on the AS/400 can quickly get a new user up and running.

Software Architecture

There are three categories of software on the AS/400 (Figure 1.2):

Licensed Internal Code (LIC)

Operating system software

Application software

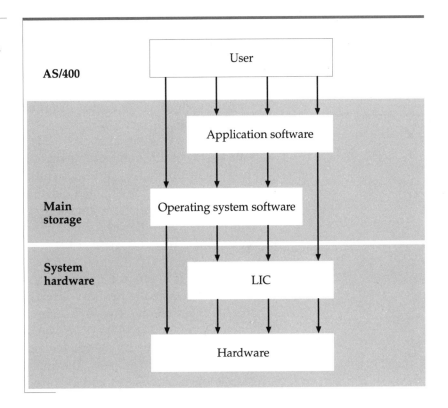

LIC. The deepest layer of software, the Licensed Internal Code (LIC), is an IBM-supplied set of programs that provide the database, security, communications, and other essential AS/400 functions. Users never interact directly with the LIC, and it cannot be changed by programmers or system operators. It is such an integral part of the system that it is not even considered to be running "on" the machine. The LIC is considered part of the machine itself. (To update the LIC, read-only chips must be replaced.)

The LIC programs provide the majority of the hardware interface and form a buffer between the application programs and the hardware specifics. Any changes to the hardware necessitate corresponding changes in the IBM-supported LIC, not the user's application programs. Buffering the application programs from any future hardware changes eliminates a whole category of possible maintenance costs.

Another advantage provided by the LIC is that by putting functions such as database and communications into the LIC their performance is enhanced. In addition, any time that would normally be spent installing and setting up the software is eliminated. Most database and communications software are independent of the operating system and, therefore, must be installed and set up separately from the operating system. This is not the case on the AS/400.

There are some limitations, however, caused by embedding these functions so deeply in the machine. Because the code cannot be changed or affected via program parameters, the user loses some measure of flexibility or control over the system environment.

Operating System Software. This middle layer of software performs many of the mundane system housekeeping tasks and manages the system's resources. It also includes common operating system functions, such as copying and deleting files. These functions can be invoked by application programs, from a menu, or directly by entering commands at the keyboard. These operating system commands are known as *control language* (CL).

Application Software. This top layer of software performs user tasks and acts as the primary interface between the user and the AS/400. Application software includes system-supplied functions like OfficeVision/400 or PDM (Program Development Manager), purchased software such as a CASE tool or a payroll system, and specialized user-developed systems. The application software can execute or call the operating system and LIC programs. Most of the time, users work with the application programs and screens to execute functions on the AS/400.

AS/400 Models

Like all computer systems, the AS/400 has input, output, and processing devices. Three basic system units (processing devices) are the core of all AS/400 models: the 9402, 9404, and 9406. (A smaller system unit has been reclassified as an entry system, rather than a midrange system.)

The 9402 and 9404 are the smaller of the three systems and run off normal electrical outlets (110 volts). They come in several different models that can support a varying number of workstations (under a hundred for the 9402 and up to several hundred for the 9404). Each model is contained in a single chassis that can fit under your desk (if you have a space 14 inches across, 26 inches high, and 30 inches deep).

The 9406 also has several models but is rack mounted rather than contained in a single box. The rack is similar to an empty stereo cabinet. Any AS/400 component can be added to it. This provides flexibility regarding system configuration, allows for growth within the rack, and lets systems grow through the addition of more racks of components.

All models can be expanded. They have expansion slots and adapters for peripheral equipment (printers, fixed disks) that can increase system capacity and functionality. The 9406 can support thousands of workstations.

Hardware Architecture

The AS/400 uses multiprocessors and two internal storage areas to improve system performance. (Figure 1.3 diagrams the hardware components and their relationship to one another.) The speed at which a computer operates depends heavily on the speed of its processors, the speed at which data can be transferred from main storage to the processor, and the amount of work being performed. The AS/400's hardware architecture addresses each of these key performance issues.

To increase the efficiency of work performed on each of the system components, the AS/400 employs many processors, each built for specialized functions. These specialized processors perform their subset of functions much faster than the general-purpose processor could, and they actually decrease the amount of work the system processor must perform. This multiprocessor architecture enables each instruction to execute faster, decreases the amount of work the system processor must perform, and minimizes the bottlenecks that could occur owing to the single-threadedness of a uniprocessor architecture. Multiple processors also permit simultaneous processing, which can sometimes decrease the elapsed time it takes to complete a task even if the total time remains the same. If the operating system breaks a 60-second task down into three 20-second tasks and distributes the work to several processors, the total task will be completed in less time.

FIGURE 1.3

Hardware Components and Their Relationship to One Another

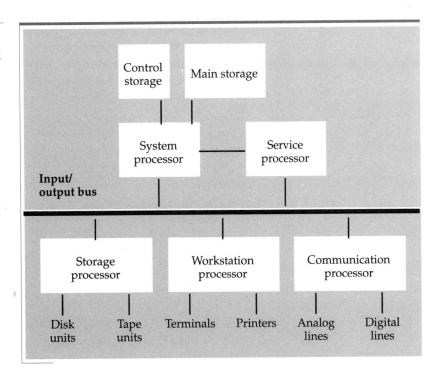

The AS/400 also stores instructions and data in a specialized memory area called *control storage*. This specialized memory and the data pathways that link it to the system processor provide the capability to transfer data faster.

Further, the system architecture allows larger amounts of information to be stored and transferred. The AS/400 hard-disk system provides greater capacity than previous systems, and data can be transferred faster and in larger blocks over the specially designed *input/output bus*.

Through the use of specialized components and the coordination of work by the AS/400 operating system, a considerable performance increase has been achieved over previous minicomputers.

Hardware Components

System Processor

Essentially, the system processor is the core of the AS/400. It executes the program instructions and performs all math calculations. It can move information 32 bits at a time, that is, it has a *word size* of 32 bits. It also supports 48-bit addressing. All computers store the location of data in an address. The size of the address dictates how many storage spaces the processor can uniquely identify. For instance, if there were only one-digit house numbers, you could uniquely address only ten houses on a street (assuming you could give the number 0 to a house). The same holds for a computer: The more bits it can use for addresses, the more storage it can uniquely label and access. With 48-bit addressing, the AS/400 is able to have 2 to the 48th power, or 281 trillion, unique addresses. This addressing capacity is quite sufficient for most users and is even larger than that of most IBM mainframe computers. However, the architecture of the AS/400 allows future computers to use 64-bit addressing, thereby providing the AS/400 family of computers with a lot more room to grow.

Main Storage

All programs and data that the system processor is currently executing are contained in main storage. As mentioned earlier, all information is stored in 32-bit words. Information can travel from main memory to the system processor 32 bits at a time. In addition to the 32 bits, several added *check bits* are sent whenever data is transferred. These check bits help in error detection. If one of the 32 bits is wrong, the AS/400 operating system can read the check bits, determine which bit has been altered, and correct it. This error detection and correction feature not only ensures data accuracy but also cuts down on the time consumed by resending information.

Control Storage

Control storage is a high-speed memory area containing the most often used LIC instructions. All program and operating system instructions are converted into simple LIC instructions. These instructions, in turn, are executed by the processor's electronic circuits. Rather than having the instructions kept in secondary storage and, when needed, transferred to main memory, the AS/400 developers created this specialized storage area (either 4K or 8K in size) for the most frequently used commands. The system processor can access control storage directly. However, control storage is not large enough to store all the LIC instructions. Some LIC instructions are stored in an *auxiliary storage pool*. This is a fancy name for a disk storage area where less frequently used LIC instructions are kept. If a required instruction resides in the auxiliary storage pool, access must be made through the slower disk device, and the instructions copied to and then read from main memory. This process, of course, is slower than the processor accessing control storage directly.

Input/Output Bus

The input/output (I/O) bus is the internal circuitry that provides the high-speed transfer of data between the system processor and the I/O processors. Only one information transfer at a time can occur on the bus. Some of the larger AS/400 models can support multiple buses and thereby allow simultaneous transfers of data. Multiple buses increase the overall system communication rate.

I/O Processors

All I/O devices attached to the AS/400 are managed by the I/O processors. Each processor has separate responsibilities and tasks that are performed simultaneously and in coordination with the system processor. I/O processors free the system processor from having to perform any external device communications work. The system processor can start new jobs while the I/O processors deal with the much slower external devices. Each I/O processor is linked to the I/O bus, which enables communication with the system processor.

Service Processor

The service processor is a specialized processor that constantly monitors system performance. The system operator can communicate directly to the service processor through the AS/400 control terminal. When the operator "brings up" the system (performs an *initial program load*, or IPL), he or she is actually requesting a function controlled by the service processor. The service processor also helps the operator with error detection and reporting.

A Look at the Internal Workings

By this time, you might be saying, "How in the world does this collection of software and hardware all fit together?" Let's walk through the hardware and software activity that would occur if you were operating a spreadsheet application on the AS/400.

Assume that the spreadsheet application has already been loaded into main memory, its initial blank spreadsheet has been displayed, and it is waiting for information from the terminal.

1. As a key is pressed on the keyboard, the workstation sends the appropriate electronic impulses over the cable to the workstation processor (one of the specialized I/O processors).

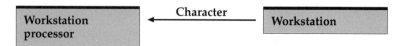

2. The workstation controller translates the impulses into a character or a function code, which is then stored in a buffer area. If it is a character, electronic impulses for a "display character" command are sent by the controller back to the workstation. The workstation will receive and decode the signal and display the specified character. All this is done without bothering the main processor or using any of the software layers. Each specialized processor has its own codes and instructions that it can perform independently of the system processor and the operating system. (This is typical of a multiprocessor architecture.)

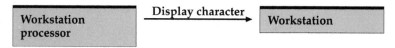

3. The workstation controller will continue to do this until the user requests a function that the workstation controller cannot perform, such as pressing the ENTER key after typing a formula in a spreadsheet cell. The ENTER key tells the workstation controller to interrupt the main processor.

4. The workstation controller sends the data over the I/O bus to the system processor (Figure 1.4). The system processor, following instructions that were translated into LIC communication instructions, verifies that all data has been transferred accurately. An operating system program is activated that controls execution of the spreadsheet program.

FIGURE 1.4

Communication Between the Workstation Processor and the System Processor

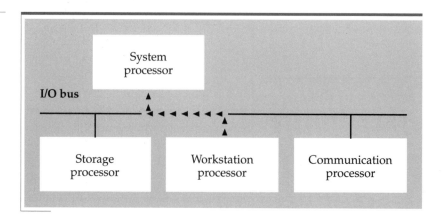

5. The operating system program tells the system processor which application program instructions to execute and makes the new information, from the workstation, available.

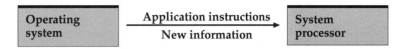

6. The application instructions (spreadsheet) tell the system processor how to perform the calculation. The application will also dictate that the new data be sent to the workstation display.

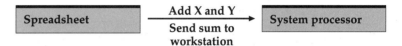

7. The operating system instructs the system processor to send the data to the I/O processor. The I/O processor sends the new cell value to the workstation, where it is displayed.

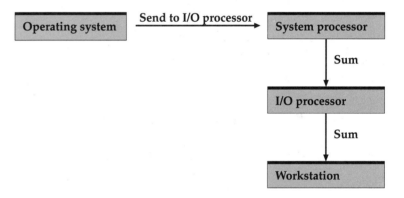

8. The application program is reactivated and told that the data has been sent to the workstation (a). The application program tells the system processor that it is finished and to call when the next set of information is available (b). The operating system receives the message (c) and starts processing other tasks.

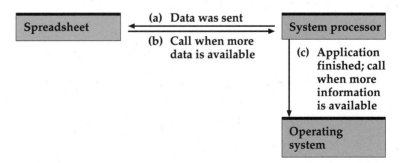

9. The process begins again when the workstation sends data to the I/O processor.

OS/400

Just like all operating systems, the AS/400 operating system is a set of programs that perform a variety of system tasks. Some common functions of an operating system are to:

- Create and maintain userids
- Provide security
- Initiate programs
- Manage multiple programs
- Provide communication among system devices
- Manage external and internal storage

Some tasks are done continually behind the scenes (such as checking security before access to a file is allowed), whereas others can be invoked by both users and application programs (such as running a program).

Executing Operating System Functions

Application programs communicate with the operating system and the LIC through an *application program interface* (API). There are IBM-supplied APIs for many of the AS/400 system functions, and the operating system is no exception. OS/400's API is a set of operating system commands (CL commands) that can be issued directly by application programs. These commands allow the application programs to interact with the LIC and the computer hardware through operating system programs. By using the API, the applications are further buffered from any hardware changes. If hardware changes require reconfiguration of the system, changes to the LIC, or even operating system program changes, the API commands would stay the same. Thus, all application programs can continue running on the new hardware with no changes or recompiling.

Users can execute a wider range of operating system functions directly by either typing in CL commands or stepping through a series of menus and screens to execute the operating system functions. Usually, AS/400 beginners prefer the menus and screens because they don't have to memorize commands, parameter keywords, and their syntax. At the same time, the screens serve as good learning tools by clearly showing all available options and values. As you gain more familiarity with the individual CL commands, paging through the prompt screens will seem time consuming, and executing commands from the command line will become the preferred method.

Application programs also have access to this larger subset of operating systems functions. CL commands can be grouped into programs. A programmer can create a *control language program* (CLP) that contains CL commands that are not part of the API, that is, commands that cannot be executed directly from within an application program. An application program, written in any one of several higher-level programming languages, can then call this CLP.

The AS/400 also allows data to be passed between application programs and CLPs. In this way, application programs can control the execution of operating system functions based on program parameters and use the results of the system commands in further processing. In essence, the programmer can expand or enhance the operating system's API by creating CLPs and having application programs call them. We cover CL in more detail in later chapters.

OS/400 Major Functions

In the remainder of this chapter, we cover four major areas of the AS/400 operating system:

Storage management and database support

Communications support

Systems management

Application development utilities

In later chapters, we discuss in detail several of the database and application development utilities, as well as one aspect of communications, PC Support. The following sections give a look at the unique approach that the AS/400 has taken toward these functions and provide an overview of the various options offered.

Storage Management and Database Support

The operating system and the LIC work together to provide:

- One common view of all storage
- An object-oriented approach toward stored information
- A built-in relational database management system and a variety of data management utilities

The AS/400 employs a unique addressing technique called *single-level storage*. From a user's or an application's point of view, all storage is the same. There is no differentiation in addressing between main memory and disk storage. All storage locations use the same addressing scheme. In addition, the location of information on specific physical devices is totally handled by the operating system. (Unlike a PC, where the user must specify the particular drive, or a mainframe, where the storage device address must be supplied, the AS/400 manages all the physical storage "behind the scenes.") This feature greatly simplifies the programmer's job. The programmer does not have to keep track of where the data physically resides or change programs based on physical moves. The programmer and the application programs are buffered from most physical aspects of storage management.

Another unique storage feature is the way the operating system treats all stored information. All stored entities (programs, files, documents, source code, etc.) are considered independent, equal *objects*. The three primary programming objects are *libraries*, *objects*, and *members*. A library is created to hold objects and usually acts as an index or a directory for related objects. Objects can contain compiled programs and file definitions. Some objects can be made up of members. Members contain information such as source code and data.

The beauty of the operating system's object management is that many of these different objects can be accessed and managed with the same commands. (There are a variety of objects and members, which we will explain in much greater detail in Chapter 2.)

Creating a Database. For creating databases, the AS/400 offers a series of tools. *Data Description Specifications* (DDS) is a data definition language that allows the user to define data structures and individual data fields. DDS, in keeping with the overall object-oriented approach, allows users to also define edit functions that will be stored with the data. In traditional, nonobject-oriented programming, application programs that receive data from users contain auditing and editing routines. (For example, is the data being provided an integer between 1 and 9999?) With the AS/400, these rules regarding the data are defined and included with the data definition at the time of file creation. All information concerning the object is stored with the object. If there are database changes (for example, a data field is expanded to include two decimal places), the audits, edits, and file definition have to be changed only in the DDS code. Programmers avoid searching through all the application programs that could possibly use this data, changing the edits and audits for the ones that do use the data and then recompiling the programs.

This object-oriented approach—that data objects contain data, as well as all information related to that data, rather than the traditional approach, in which files contained the data and programs contained the data structure and value-checking routines—is a great time saver and increases data integrity by simplifying the edit and audit functions.

Interactive Data Definition Utility (IDDU) is a menu-driven alternative to DDS. It allows users to define database structures through a series of menus and prompts. (IDDU actually generates DDS code.) IDDU is very easy to understand and use; however, it is not flexible and does not have the full power of DDS.

SQL/400 (SQL stands for Structured Query Language), a separately purchased program, also allows data objects to be created. SQL is an industry standard set of commands to create and manipulate data. SQL/400 commands can be embedded directly into AS/400 application programs or executed on-line through the interactive SQL utility. SQL/400, though letting you create databases, also creates other supporting objects that carry some extra storage and processing overhead. For instance, when a data object is being updated or deleted, many of these supporting objects also have to be modified.

Inputting Data. Once the database has been defined, there needs to be a way to load data into it. Once again, the AS/400 offers a variety of methods. Interactive SQL allows users to add data from the keyboard. The user needs to know only the command and the data structure in order to load new records. Interactive SQL is good for loading small amounts of data. A large quantity of data would quickly become a burden to enter, and the chance for error would increase greatly.

The AS/400 also offers a unique data entry package called the *Data File Utility* (DFU). Invoking DFU against a data member creates a simple application program. This program has a basic input screen and logic that allow users to enter values for the data elements. Each entry field is the maximum length as defined in the data definition, and all defined edits and audits are performed. The advantage of DFU is that the user does not have to remember any commands or the data structure. The DFU program prompts for the correct data elements from an easy-to-read screen.

Often, data entry is more complicated than simply loading data elements. Adding information to one group of data requires updating in another file. (For example, processing the sale of a corn dog requires the inventory quantity, which resides in the inventory member, to be decreased and the total sales dollar amount, which resides in the sales member, to be increased.) Neither SQL nor DFU can ensure that the updating between data members is done correctly or is done at all. An application program, with the correct logic, would have to be written to ensure that all the files are updated correctly. The AS/400 supports many higher-level programming languages that can perform this task.

Viewing Data. There are several ways to view data: interactive SQL, individual application programs, or an AS/400 utility called *Query*. Query provides an easy and quick way to define a request to view data in a database. It provides screens that prompt for files and field names and, if requested, will show all files that are available to be viewed. There are also a variety of selection criteria and logic operations that can extract a subset of data or combine data from multiple sources. Query also gives extensive control over the format and style of the output and some basic report calculations. Data display programs created by Query can be saved and rerun at any time.

Interactive SQL also allows the creation and storage of information requests. However, it does not offer all the format control of Query and nowhere near the control of writing a report program.

Application programs provide total control over data selection and format. Any intricate processing or complex calculations should be handled with specialized application programs.

Communications Support

The AS/400 can communicate with both intelligent workstations (PCs) and mainframes (IBM and non-IBM). Hardware such as connectors, controllers, and the communication processor allow the AS/400 to physically link to common communications lines such as token ring, V.35, and 232/V.24. Of course, providing communication between different computers is not as simple as stringing some wire between them. Once the AS/400 is integrated into a communications network, software is needed to support the *protocol* (the syntax, or "grammar," of communication between devices) of the network. The AS/400 operating system supports a variety of communication methods (token passing, bisync, sdlc, async, X.25) and fully supports IBM's overall communications strategy, *SNA* (Systems Network Architecture).

Once the connection is made, the AS/400 does not abandon the user and his or her network needs. Several features of the OS/400 help manage the network once it has been established. Some of the key network management functions supported are problem tracking and determination, network configuration, and software distribution among AS/400s, mainframes, and PCs.

AS/400 and Mainframe Communications.

Several mainframe interface functions are provided in OS/400. For instance, OS/400 provides the ability for AS/400 workstations to function as mainframe terminals. OS/400 also lets 3270 terminals (mainframe terminals) and the mainframe operator's terminal access the AS/400 as if they were AS/400 terminals. This means that network operators and mainframe programmers can interact with an AS/400 as if they were directly linked. Were there network problems, the network operator, from the mainframe operator's terminal, could issue commands to determine the source of the trouble. If the network problems required AS/400 program changes, new AS/400 programs could be written and installed from the mainframe and host operator's terminal. Enabling mainframe operators to interact with all AS/400s in the network avoids having program changes keyed in or loaded from tape at each AS/400 on the network.

The AS/400 also provides the ability to interchange various objects such as documents, files, and electronic mail between the mainframe and the AS/400.

AS/400-to-AS/400 Communications.

OS/400 also supports communication between different AS/400s on the same network. OS/400 allows users to send documents and nondocument objects such as data members, messages, and programs between AS/400 systems. Both of these functions are part of *SNADS* (Systems Network Architecture

Distribution Services), which must be present and configured on all systems. (*Configuring* means setting up routing tables, defining system addresses, and declaring system parameters for each machine on the network. Configuring should be done by the systems programmer or network manager when the machine is first added to the network.)

AS/400 and PC Communications. The AS/400 also provides support for using personal computers as intelligent workstations. With *PC Support* software, a PC can function as an AS/400 terminal. PC Support, working with OS/400, also provides communication, data transfer, and data sharing between the AS/400 and PCs. For instance, data can be transferred from AS/400 files and sent to the PC, programs on the PC can run against the data, and then the updated data can be sent back to the AS/400.

Systems Management

The larger a system gets, the more complex its management becomes. In a multiuser system environment, some of the systems management tasks include:

- Allocating system resources among jobs
- Controlling job execution
- Creating and maintaining userids
- Security
- Performance monitoring
- System backup and recovery

The AS/400 operating system was designed to make systems management as easy as possible. All systems management tasks can be performed through a series of menus and screens that prompt for information regarding how the system is to run or parameter data for functions the system is to perform. These systems management tasks start with bringing the system up in the morning and can end with shutting the system down at night. In between, systems operators and administrators use systems management functions to create and define userids, restore lost files from transaction journals, and establish parameters for performance data gathering. In addition, systems management allows the operators to perform tasks such as partitioning and allocating main memory for specialized or shared usage, mass copying objects for backup purposes, or setting up jobs to run at specific dates and times.

Application Development

The AS/400 supports the following programming languages:

RPG

COBOL

C

PL1

Pascal

BASIC

REXX

SQL

FORTRAN

The AS/400 also supports CL programming for executing operating system tasks and traditional programming tasks, such as accessing a database and manipulating data.

The AS/400 has a series of application development tools (utilities and programs) that simplify and speed up software development. *PDM* (Program Development Manager) provides a menu system that ties many of the application development functions together. For instance, copying files and members is a commonly used programmer function. (Programmers often want a copy of production data for testing a new program, or they will copy a current program member and use it as a base for a new program because the old program contains code that is needed in the new program.)

Files can be copied by typing in a CL command and specifying the names of the files to copy to and from, in the correct order and with the necessary keywords, according to the command's syntax rules. Alternatively, PDM could be used to provide a screen of all files, the file could be selected from the list supplied, and the user would provide the name of the new file. PDM would build the correct CL command and submit it to be executed. With PDM, knowledge of each command's syntax is not required. PDM menus also provide access to the following tools:

- *SEU* (Source Entry Utility) provides a full-screen editor for programmers to create application programs. The editor has many of the same functions as a word processing application, such as insert, delete, and search. It also supplies some specialized functions for programmers, such as a prompt for programming language commands. A *command prompt* is a fill-in-the-blanks display, where a command's parameter values can be entered. A programmer would specify the command to be entered and press F4. SEU would then display the command prompt.

  SEU also provides on-line syntax checking. As the programming language code is entered, the validity of each line is checked. The programmer does not have to wait for a compiled listing of the program to get error messages. The on-line syntax checker responds with error messages when the source code is entered into the file.

- *SDA* (Screen Design Aid) helps programmers design and create screens and menus. Normally, this is a long and tedious task requiring exact specification of where on the screen each text segment or data element is to appear. With SDA, programmers can simply move the cursor to any area of the screen and type in the text they want to appear. SDA is also integrated with the AS/400's database. If a database field is specified on a screen, SDA will retrieve the field characteristics—size, decimal versus integer, and so on—from the database and allocate the needed space on the screen. Further, screen creation with SDA is interactive: As changes are made to the screen specifications, SDA will show the effect at the display station where the programmer is working. SDA is also fully supported by on-line help.

- *APF* (for Advanced Printer Functions) provides specialized printing capability. It provides different print fonts, generates graphs, prints bar code labels, and so on.

Another development tool available is the *Interactive Debug Facility*, or simply DEBUG, which lets the programmer control and monitor the execution of application programs. For instance, a program can be set to stop executing at a particular line number. While the program is stopped, the programmer can check the program's progress by displaying the value of individual program variables. DEBUG also allows the user to change these values. These designated stopping points are called *breakpoints*. There is also a trace function that records the line-by-line execution of a program.

Accessing and Navigating the AS/400 Menus

To access the AS/400 from a workstation, bring up the AS/400 Sign On screen (Figure 1.5). (How to bring this screen up depends on your particular system and network configuration. If necessary, see your systems support representative for help.) At this screen, enter your unique *userid* and *password* in the fields to the right of the strings of periods that follow the words User and Password. The password will not appear on the screen. (This prevents someone from seeing the password and gaining unauthorized entry into the system.) Press ENTER.

Under a basic system configuration, the AS/400 Main Menu screen should be displayed (Figure 1.6). If the Main Menu screen is not displayed, simply type **go main** at the command line. (The command line is in the lower left-hand portion of the screen. Notice the symbol ===> and the underscores to the right of it. The underscores mark the location of the command line. CL commands can be typed there.) The go main command instructs the AS/400 to display the AS/400 Main Menu screen. The go command is just one of many shortcuts that the AS/400 offers users to access its screens and functions faster.

FIGURE 1.5

```
                              Sign On

                                    System. . . . . .:
                                    Subsystem . . . .: QINTER
                                    Display . . . . .:


             User . . . . . . . . . . . .  _____
             Password . . . . . . . . .
             Program/procedure. . . . . .  _____
             Menu . . . . . . . . . . . .  _____
             Current library. . . . . . .  _____







                              (C) COPYRIGHT IBM CORP. 1980, 1991.
```

FIGURE 1.6

```
 MAIN                      AS/400 Main Menu
                                                      System:
 Select one of the following:

        1. User tasks
        2. Office tasks
        3. General system tasks
        4. Files, libraries, and folders
        5. Programming
        6. Communications
        7. Define or change the system
        8. Problem handling
        9. Display a menu
       10. Information Assistant options
       11. PC Support tasks

       90. Sign off

 Selection or command
 ===>_____
     _____
 F3=Exit  F4=Prompt  F9=Retrieve  F12=Cancel  F13=User support
 F23=Set initial menu
 (C) COPYRIGHT IBM CORP. 1980, 1991.
```

Users not familiar with all the screens and their functions can select a screen option that describes the type of function or object with which to work. For instance, if a user wanted to copy a file but was not sure which screen provides that function, he or she could read the options available on the AS/400 Main Menu screen and pick one that seems to fit. If the user were trying to copy a file, for instance, option 4, Files, libraries, and folders, would seem to be the logical choice. To select that option, the user would type the option number at the command line and press ENTER.

Selecting an option will bring up either another menu (with further function or object options) or a data screen where the user must supply information in order for the function to be executed. In the case of option 4, `Files, libraries, and folders`, another menu would appear. At that menu, the user would specify the type of object with which he or she wished to work by selecting another menu option. That would lead the user to another submenu and another option selection (this time, `to work with files`). Finally, a data entry screen would be displayed where the user would have to specify the particular file with which to work. The `Work with files` screen would then be displayed. This screen provides the copy function option that the user originally set out to find.

As we mentioned, a faster way to execute a system function (and bypass all intervening screens) is to enter the correct CL command and press ENTER. This method directly activates the appropriate system program and performs the function. The drawback to this method is that all the needed command parameters must be entered according to the command syntax. As you become more familiar with the AS/400, you will rely less on the menus and more on the CL commands. However, in the beginning, the menu system is a lifesaver.

Using On-Line Help

Another key ease-of-use and learning feature of the AS/400 is the extensive on-line help facility. From any AS/400 screen, the user can press F1 for *contextual help*, which gives an explanation of the purpose of the screen being viewed and the options or functions that can be chosen. For instance, pressing F1 at the `AS/400 Main Menu` screen will display the `AS/400 Main Menu - Help` screen (Figure 1.7). When `More...` appears in the bottom right-hand corner of the screen, it means there is further information on the screen. Press PAGE DOWN to scroll through the information.

Also notice that the bottom two lines on every AS/400 screen define the active function keys for that screen. This is a feature found throughout the system and is just one more aspect of the common user interface that makes the AS/400 so user friendly. However, some screens cannot fit all the active function keys within those two lines. If that is the case, press F24 to scroll through the other function key definitions within the two-line area.

Another use of contextual help is to find more information about system messages, which can be sent for various reasons. For instance, an incorrect CL command will result in an error message. Or, as is more often the case, if programs are executed, the system sends informational messages regarding the status of the submitted jobs. Given the limited space available on screens, sometimes the messages are not very clear about the seriousness of the error or its repercussions. An easy way to get more information on these system messages is through contextual help. Move the cursor to the message and press F1 to display a help screen that:

- Explains the message in greater detail
- Gives possible reasons for the message
- Suggests actions to resolve the problems

FIGURE 1.7

```
 MAIN                        AS/400 Main Menu
 .......................................................................
 :                       AS/400 Main Menu - Help                       :
 :   The AS/400 Main (MAIN) menu allows you to select the general task :
 :   you want to do.                                                    :
 :                                                                      :
 : How to Use a Menu                                                    :
 :                                                                      :
 :   To select a menu option, type the option number and press Enter.  :
 :   To run a command, type the command and press Enter. For assistance:
 :   in selecting a command, press F4 (Prompt) without typing anything.:
 :                                                                      :
 :   For assistance in entering a command, type the command and press F4:
 :   (Prompt). To see a previous command you entered, press F9         :
 :   (Retrieve).                                                        :
 :                                                                      :
 :   To go to another menu, use the Go to menu (GO) command. Type GO   :
 :   followed by the menu ID, then press the Enter key. For example, to:
 :                                                             More... :
 : F3=Exit help   F10=Move to top  F11=Search index   F12=Cancel       :
 : F13=User support F14=Print help                                     :
 :.......................................................................:
```

If it still is not clear, message help will often refer to other functions within the system or the system manuals where further information is available.

A second type of help is *index search*, which provides information on topics specified by the user. Pressing F11 at any help screen will bring up the Search Help Index screen (Figure 1.8). At this screen, the user types in the topic or phrase to be searched for and presses F5. For instance, Figure 1.8 is requesting further information about PDM. Pressing F5 after typing **pdm** will result in a listing of all topics concerning PDM (Figure 1.9).

To display the topic, type **5** under the Option heading to the left of the topic title and press ENTER. The text can also be printed by typing **6** next to the Topic title and pressing ENTER.

To exit the help facility (or any screen except the original one displayed at sign-on), press F3. To end the AS/400 session, type **SIGNOFF** at any screen's command line and press ENTER.

FIGURE 1.8

```
                      Search Help Index

Index Search allows you to tell the system to search for specific
information. To use Index Search, do the following:

  1. Type the phrase or words to search for.

  2. Press Enter.

When you press Enter, the system searches for topics related to the
words you supplied and displays a list of topics found.

If you press Enter without typing anything, the system displays a list
of all available topics.


Type words to search for, press Enter.
  PDM _____

F3=Exit help  F5=All topics  F12=Cancel  F13=User support
```

FIGURE 1.9

```
                      Main Help Index for AS/400

Type options, press Enter.
  5=Display topic      6=Print topic

Option  Topic
   _       Find string using PDM (FNDSTRPDM) command
   _       PDM (programming development manager)
   _       Start programming development manager (STRPDM) command
   _       Work with libraries using PDM (WRKLIBPDM) command
   _       Work with members using PDM (WRKMBRPDM) command
   _       Work with objects using PDM (WRKOBJPDM) command




                                                         Bottom
Or to search again, type new words and press Enter.
  PDM _____

F3=Exit help  F5=All topics  F12=Cancel  F13=User support
```

Summary

The AS/400 is a combination of many of the latest hardware and software features available today. By using a multiprocessor architecture, a bigger word size, and high-speed storage, the AS/400 has been able to make a major performance improvement over its S/3X ancestors. The AS/400 is also geared toward application systems and has many utilities and functions that speed up the development, modification, and day-to-day running of user applications.

The AS/400 is relatively easy to use. By making many system decisions for the customer, the AS/400 architecture has decreased and simplified the system functions a user needs to perform in order to maintain the AS/400. The developers have also "pushed" the system software closer to the hardware, thereby creating efficiencies that few operating systems can match. The flip side of the coin is that there is a certain lack of control over how the system functions and an inability to perform some fine-tuning that is normally available to system programmers on mainframe systems.

Another usability feature is the variety of ways that users can access and use the AS/400's functions. The menu system, on-line help, and APIs each provide a different method for users to access and execute the functions they need. Each tool by itself is a considerable improvement over previous generations of mainframe and minicomputer software. Together, they represent a new standard.

LAB EXERCISE

In this exercise, you will use the on-line help facility. Specifically, you will use index search to find information on specific topics and message help to diagnose a bad command.

1. Sign on to the AS/400.

2. From any screen, press F1 to invoke help.

3. Press F11 to select the index search option.

4. Type the first item in review question 1 (source entry utility) and press ENTER.

5. Print the first topic by selecting option 6.

6. Perform steps 3 through 5 for the other utilities in Review Question 1.

7. Exit help by pressing F3.

8. At the command line, type an incorrect command (for example, STRMDP) and press ENTER.

9. Move the cursor to the message at the bottom of the screen.

10. Press F1 to invoke message help.

11. Notice the error message's unique message ID and the possible reasons that the error occurred.

12. Print the error message by pressing F1, the Print or Print Screen key.

REVIEW QUESTIONS

1. Describe the types of functions provided by the following utilities:

Source Entry Utility

Program Development Manager

contextual help

index help

2. The AS/400 supports many programming languages. What language is used most often to develop applications on the AS/400?

3. What are the three types of software on the AS/400? Give a short description of each.

4. What is single-level storage management?

5. Describe the functions of the following AS/400 hardware components:

    control storage

    I/O processor

    I/O bus

    service processor

6. What is an API? Give an example of an AS/400 API.

7. What does LIC stand for? What functions does it provide?

8. Define the relationship between libraries, objects, and members.

9. What are some of the differences between mainframe, minicomputer, and microcomputer systems?

10. What advantages do multiprocessor computer systems have over single processor systems?

DISCUSSION QUESTIONS

1. You are trying to convince a customer to buy an AS/400. The customer, however, is concerned about the amount of time it will take to develop new application programs for the AS/400. What application development tools does the AS/400 provide, and how do they help speed up the development process?

2. Communication between computers is a growing issue. Discuss the AS/400's capabilities regarding communication with mainframe and PC systems.

3. Discuss the issues a company must address when deciding whether to buy a mainframe, minicomputer, or microcomputer system to handle its computing needs.

4. Explain why it is increasingly important that computer systems be easy to use. Discuss the features that make the AS/400 user friendly.

PDM and SEU

2

Overview

PDM and SEU are two utilities that provide easy access to common programming functions used heavily during system development and maintenance. Creating, copying, deleting, and updating files as well as creating, editing, and compiling programs can be easily accomplished through a series of menus, screens, and line commands provided by these programming tools.

This chapter covers some of the basic functions provided by PDM, explains how to create and execute programs, and includes a step-by-step walkthrough of the PDM screens and individual SEU line commands.

After finishing this chapter, you will understand:

- The relationship between libraries, objects, and members on the AS/400
- The functions available through PDM
- The capabilities of SEU

You also will be able to:

- Access and navigate the PDM screens
- Create, edit, and compile a program member

Objects and Their Organization

All information on the AS/400—programs, files, source code, printer definitions, and so on—is stored in libraries, objects, or members. PDM is the user-friendly interface to the operating system functions that create and modify programming-related information and store that information in libraries, objects, and members. CL (control language) commands can be issued directly to the operating system to perform the functions that PDM provides; however, the user has to remember the correct commands and their syntax. PDM, on the other hand, "hand holds" users through the process. By progressing through a series of menus, the user selects the type of work to be performed and specifies the parameters. Once the function is specified, the name of the library, object, or member can be entered on the appropriate screen. (Or the user can request a list of available libraries, objects, or members from PDM and select the object from the provided list.) This step-by-step process saves the user from having to memorize each CL command and its keywords.

As mentioned earlier, libraries are made up of objects, and some objects are made up of members. Other objects do not have members associated with them. A hierarchy, or ownership relationship, exists among libraries, objects, and members—a member must be in or belong to an object, and all objects belong to a library (Figure 2.1). When an object is referenced, the library it belongs to must also be identified. When a member is referenced, the member's "owning" object and library are needed to clearly identify the member.

FIGURE 2.1

The Hierarchical Relationship Among Libraries, Objects, and Members

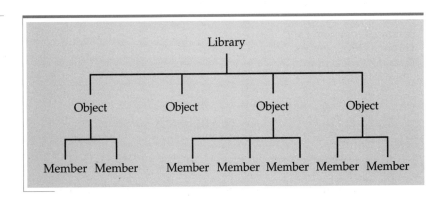

Libraries

Libraries are used to group related objects. A library can be thought of as a directory. Since all programs and data files are contained within either an object or a member, libraries are often used to group related programs and data. For instance, it is much easier to locate a payroll program or file if all payroll programs and files are stored in the same library.

Often, with large applications, there are also multiple copies of the same program. The copy being used day to day by the user is called the *production copy*. If the program is being modified or enhanced, the programmer creates and updates a *development copy*. All initial testing—successfully compiling the program, trying to get the program to execute without an abend (abnormal end), and so on—is also performed against the development version. Once the program can be normally executed, a *test copy* is created from the development copy. The test copy is executed using test data that simulates the production data. After the logic of the program is successfully tested, the test version will be copied to create the new production version.

Having three versions of a program can make a programmer's life quite confusing. If there are three versions of every program, how do you remember which program is which? Imagine if there are hundreds or thousands of programs.

Libraries can help. Three libraries can be created: development, test, and production (Figure 2.2). An object and a member would be created in the development library to hold the development copy of the program. After the program is entered or changes have successfully been made to it, the program from the development library would be copied to the test library. If during testing, problems are uncovered, the programmer can go back to the development version and rework the program. Then, when satisfied, the authorized person can copy the program back to the test library. After the program has been thoroughly tested, a copy would be sent to the production library, where it would be available to the users.

FIGURE 2.2

Program Promotion Path Through Development, Test, and Production Libraries

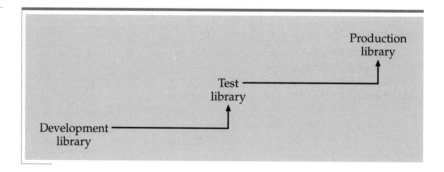

This is a common library organization for programs and data. Day-to-day, "real live" data is stored in production library data objects and members. A subset of the production data resides in the test library. This would spare the real data from any mistakes that might occur during testing yet would still provide test data that simulates the production environment. Finally, programmers would create and store data needed for initial testing in the development library. Using the three different libraries, there is never a question of which program is which. Further, it is easier to control who can access the production-level programs and data because they are all grouped together in one library.

Objects and Members

Objects and members contain all AS/400 programs and data. Their relationship, however, is not very straightforward. Each kind of object or member has a different relationship to other kinds of objects or members. (The relationships are a little complex, but if you follow the text closely and study the diagrams, they should become clear.)

Objects are characterized by a *type* and sometimes an *attribute* (Figure 2.3). Objects can have types equal to a variety of values. Some of the more common ones are *FILE, *PGM, and *MENU. Obviously, a type describes the information stored in the object. An attribute further describes objects that have a type of *FILE and some other objects that are the result of compiling a *source code member*. (A program is an example of a type of object created from compiling a source member.)

Examples of attributes for objects with a type of *FILE are *PF-SRC* and *PF-DTA*. PF-SRC means the file is a source physical file (Object1 in Figure 2.3). Members in a source physical file contain *source code*, a series of program language commands or data definition statements. All the members in Figure 2.3 (Larry, Curley, and Shemp)

FIGURE 2.3

Relationship of Source Physical Files and Members

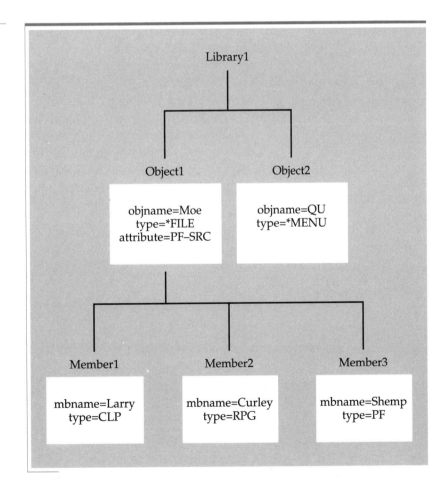

contain source code, which is why they reside under object Moe — a source physical file. PF-DTA means the file is a data physical file (Figure 2.4). Members belonging to a data physical file contain data.

Members are further classified by a *member type*. Member types and object types are different. The member type (CBL, CLP, RPG, PF) defines either the type of programming code contained in the member (COBOL, CL, RPG) or that the member is a physical file definition (PF) and contains DDS (*Data Description Specification*) statements, which define a file.

Members (such as Larry, Curley, and Shemp) in an object with an attribute of PF-SRC (such as Moe) contain source code instructions. Source code instructions are typed in by programmers and are "human readable." Computers cannot execute source code instructions; they execute machine language instructions. Compiling source code on the AS/400 converts source code into machine language instructions.

When a source code member is compiled, the system creates a new object and the compiled code is placed in it. (In some other computer architectures, this machine code would be called a *load module* or an *executable file*.) This new object, created by compiling source code contained in a member, has its type defined by the system as *PGM. Its attribute is dictated by the member type from which it was compiled. For instance, an object with an attribute of CLP (such as Object4, Larry, in Figure 2.5) is created when a member with type of CLP (Member1, Larry, in Figure 2.5) is compiled.

When a member with a type of PF (such as Shemp) is compiled, a new object is created and, in addition, a new member is created under the new object (see Figure 2.5, Object3 and Member4). The new object's type is defined as *FILE and its attribute is set to PF-DTA. The new member that is created does not have a type.

FIGURE 2.4

An Example of Source Physical and Data Physical Files

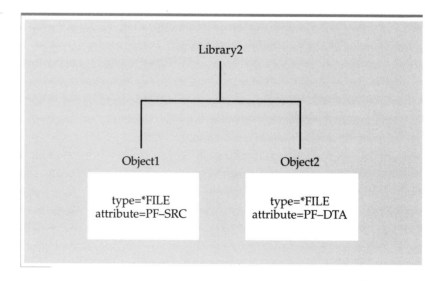

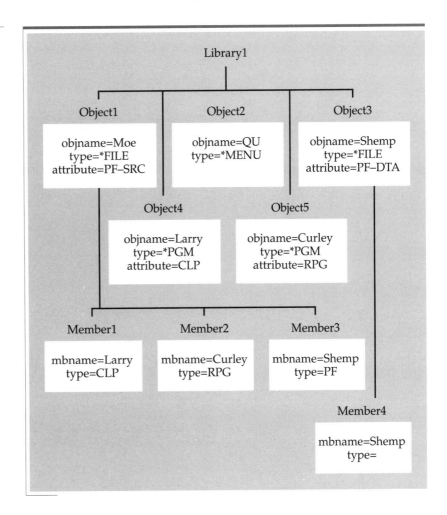

FIGURE 2.5
Results of Compiling Source Physical File Members

Using PDM to compile members Larry, Curley, and Shemp (which is not nearly as painful as some of the things Moe did to each of them) would result in three new objects and one new member (see Figure 2.5).

Object4 (Larry) is the result of compiling Member1 (Larry). Object5 (Curley) is the result of compiling Member2 (Curley). The third object and the fourth member, both named Shemp, were the result of compiling Member3, Shemp. The new object, Shemp, contains the machine language version of the file definition, and the new member will eventually hold the file's data. Notice also that Member4 has no type. Members belonging to a data physical file, by definition, contain data and have no type. From Figure 2.5, you can see all the naming conventions for the new objects and members and their associated attributes and types.

Starting PDM

As mentioned earlier, PDM allows users to create and manipulate objects. This includes creating all the programming objects just mentioned, entering program source code and data definitions, and compiling. In addition, PDM allows users to save, modify, and delete objects.

To start PDM from the AS/400 Main Menu (Figure 2.6), choose option 5, Programming, and press ENTER. This will bring up the Programming menu (Figure 2.7). From the Programming menu, select option 2, Programming Development Manager (PDM), and press ENTER. The PDM main menu (Figure 2.8) will appear.

FIGURE 2.6

```
MAIN                    AS/400 Main Menu
                                            System: CHICAGO
Select one of the following:

       1.  User tasks
       2.  Office tasks
       3.  General system tasks
       4.  Files, libraries, and folders
       5.  Programming
       6.  Communications
       7.  Define or change the system
       8.  Problem handling
       9.  Display a menu
      10.  Information Assistant options
      11.  PC Support tasks

      90.  Sign off

Selection or command
===>_____


F3=Exit  F4=Prompt  F9=Retrieve  F12=Cancel  F13=User support
F23=Set initial menu
```

FIGURE 2.7

```
PROGRAM                    Programming
                                            System: CHICAGO
Select one of the following:

       1.  Programmer menu
       2.  Programming Development Manager (PDM)
       3.  Utilities
       4.  Programming language debug
       5.  Structured Query Language (SQL) pre-compiler
       6.  Question and answer
       7.  IBM product information
       8.  Copy screen image
       9.  Cross System Product/Application Execution (CSP/AE)

      50.  System/36 programming

      70.  Related commands

Selection or command
===>_____


F3=Exit  F4=Prompt  F9=Retrieve  F12=Cancel  F13=User support
F16=AS/400 Main Menu
```

FIGURE 2.8

```
                 AS/400 Programming Development Manager (PDM)

      Select one of the following:

           1. Work with libraries
           2. Work with objects
           3. Work with members

           9. Work with user-defined options




      Selection or command
      ===>_____

      F3=Exit      F4=Prompt      F9=Retrieve      F10=Command entry
      F12=Cancel   F18=Change defaults
```

To access the AS/400 Programming Development Manager (PDM) menu from a screen other than the AS/400 Main Menu, type the CL command **STRPDM** at the command line and press ENTER.

The PDM main menu has options to work with libraries, objects, or members. Whenever one of these options is chosen, a screen will be displayed that asks for the library, object, or member with which to work. For identification of a member, the object and library names that it resides under are also requested. Members in different objects or different libraries can have the same name. If a member's library and object are not specified, the system will either use a default library and object name or search through the user's libraries and objects and select the first member that has the specified name. Unless the defaults are correct or the search order will yield the correct member, it's usually a good practice to fully describe the particular member by naming its library and object. The same holds for objects. When identifying an object, the library that contains the object should also be explicitly specified.

Creating Libraries and Objects

The AS/400 comes with many libraries already created, such as QGPL, which everyone is allowed to access. Objects and members can be stored in these general-purpose libraries; however, as applications grow and as work on the AS/400 becomes more complex, programmers and users discover a need for individual or restricted members and objects. These objects may contain text or programs that perform some specialized functions that are job related. Before these functions can be stored in members and objects, the members and objects have to be created. And before members or objects can be created, a library must exist to hold them.

To create a library, choose option 1, Work with libraries, from the AS/400 Programming Development Manager (PDM) menu (see Figure 2.8). The Specify Libraries to Work With screen (Figure 2.9) will be displayed. If the library was already created and a user wanted to work with it, he or she would type the library name at the library prompt (where the default value *ALL is located).

FIGURE 2.9

```
                    Specify Libraries to Work With

 Type choice, press Enter.

    Library . . . . . . .   *ALL_____   *LIBL, name, *generic*, *ALL,
                                        *ALLUSR, *USRLIBL, *CURLIB












 F3=Exit   F5=Refresh   F12=Cancel
```

To create a library, the user must progress to the Work with Libraries Using PDM screen. To access this screen, leave *ALL in the library name on the Specify Libraries to Work With screen and press ENTER. A list of all the libraries is displayed (Figure 2.10). Notice on the Work with Libraries Using PDM screen that *options* can be entered next to the libraries' names. These options direct the AS/400 to perform various functions, such as delete library or display library description, on the library.

The function keys are another way to perform library tasks. For our example, press F6 to create a library. Pressing F6 will result in the Create Library screen being displayed (Figure 2.11). At this screen, the name of the new library would be specified. For all examples in this book, it is assumed that each user has a seven-character userid, where the last two digits are a unique number, like INTRO99. For the new library name, enter the text **YOURLIB** followed by the unique two-digit number. For userid INTRO99, the library name would be YOURLIB99. The library name used in the examples will be YOURLIBXX, where XX is assumed to be the unique two-digit userid number.

FIGURE 2.10

```
                    Work with Libraries Using PDM

List type . . . . . . . *ALL_____  Position to . . . . . _____

Type options, press Enter.
   2=Change        3=Copy                   4=Delete  5=Display
   7=Rename        8=Display description    9=Save    10=Restore...


Opt  Library     Type        Text
__   QGPL        *PROD




                                                              More...
Parameters or command
===>_____
F3=Exit     F4=Prompt      F5=Refresh      F6=Create
F9=Retrieve F10=Command entry F23=More options F24=More keys
```

FIGURE 2.11

```
                    Create Library (CRTLIB)

Type choices, press Enter.

Library. . . . . . . . . . . . .  YOURLIBXX_  Name
Library type . . . . . . . . . .  *PROD       *PROD, *TEST
Text 'description' . . . . . . . *BLANK_____
_____




                                                              Bottom
F3=Exit  F4=Prompt  F5=Refresh  F10=Additional parameters  F12=Cancel
F13=How to use this display      F24=More keys
```

At the Create Library screen, descriptive text for this library can be entered. After specifying the new library, press ENTER. Pressing ENTER tells the system to start creating the new library. When the library is created, the Work with Libraries Using PDM screen will be redisplayed with a message on the second to last line saying Library YOURLIBXX created (Figure 2.12). To verify that the library was actually created, find YOURLIBXX on the list. (You may have to scroll down a list of libraries with PAGE DOWN to find it.)

Now that a library exists, an object can be created. From the AS/400 Programming Development Manager (PDM) menu (see Figure 2.8), choose option 2, Work with objects. This time the Specify Objects to Work With screen (Figure 2.13) will be displayed. On this screen, specify the library under which the new object will reside. For our example, we would type **YOURLIBXX** at the prompt and press ENTER. This will bring up all objects contained in the specified library (Figure 2.14). Since the library was just created, there would not be any objects listed. But objects can be created from the Work with Objects Using PDM screen. Pressing F6 will bring up the Create Commands screen (Figure 2.15). This screen lists options to create a multitude of different types of objects.

FIGURE 2.12

```
                    Work with Libraries Using PDM

    List type . . . . . . . *ALL_____     Position to . . . . . _____

    Type options, press Enter.
      2=Change        3=Copy                    4=Delete    5=Display
      7=Rename        8=Display description     9=Save      10=Restore ...

    Opt  Library   Type      Text

    __   QGPL      *PROD
    __   YOURLIBXX *PROD




                                                              More...
    Parameters or command
    ===>_____
    F3=Exit      F4=Prompt       F5=Refresh       F6=Create
    F9=Retrieve  F10=Command entry  F23=More options  F24=More keys
    Library YOURLIBXX created.
```

FIGURE 2.13

```
                    Specify Objects to Work With

    Type choices, press Enter.

       Library. . . . . . . . . . YOURLIBXX_ *CURLIB, name

       Object:
         Name . . . . . . . . . *ALL_____  *ALL, name, *generic*
         Type . . . . . . . . . *ALL_____  *ALL, *type
         Attribute. . . . . . . *ALL_____  *ALL, attribute, *generic*,
                                            *BLANK








    F3=Exit  F5=Refresh  F12=Cancel
```

FIGURE 2.14

```
                 Work with Objects Using PDM

Library . . . . . YOURLIBXX_  Position to. . . . . . . . _____
                              Position to type . . . . . _____

Type options, press Enter.
  2=Change         3=Copy      4=Delete    5=Display    7=Rename
  8=Display description        9=Save     10=Restore   11=Move ...

Opt  Object       Type      Attribute    Text

  (No objects in library)




Parameters or command
===>_____
F3=Exit       F4=Prompt         F5=Refresh       F6=Create
F9=Retrieve   F10=Command entry  F23=More options  F24=More keys
```

FIGURE 2.15

```
CMDCRT                 Create Commands

Select one of the following:

  Commands
      1.  Create Alert Table                         CRTALRTBL
      2.  Create APAR                                CRTAPAR
      3.  Create Authority Holder                    CRTAUTHLR
      4.  Create Authorization List                  CRTAUTL

      6.  Create BEST/1 Model                        CRTBESTMDL
      7.  Create Calendar                            CRTCAL
      8.  Create COBOL Program                       CRTCBLPGM
      9.  Create Configuration List                  CRTCFGL
     10.  Create C Locale Description                CRTCLD
     11.  Create CL Program                          CRTCLPGM
     12.  Create Class                               CRTCLS
     13.  Create Command                             CRTCMD
                                                      More...

Selection or command
===>_____

F3=Exit  F4=Prompt  F9=Retrieve  F12=Cancel  F16=Major menu
```

For this example, a file that will eventually hold a CLP (control language program) will be created. In the previous section on object types, we stated that all source code must reside in a member within an object with a type of *File and an attribute of PF-SRC (source physical file). Option 126 would create this type of object. (Paging down through the list of options will eventually result in the Create Commands screen, as shown in Figure 2.16, being displayed.) Typing **126** at the command line and pressing ENTER will bring up the Create Source Physical File (CRTSRCPF) screen (Figure 2.17). On this screen, enter the name of the new object, **CLOBJECT**, the library it will reside under, **YOURLIBXX**, and any descriptive text. After this is done, press ENTER. The system will start creating the new object. When it is complete, the `Create Commands` screen will reappear with a message at the bottom of the screen that says `File CLOBJECT created in library YOURLIBXX` (Figure 2.18). To verify that the object was created, go through PDM and get to the `Work with Objects Using PDM` screen for YOURLIBXX. It should display one object in that library, `CLOBJECT` (Figure 2.19), with an attribute of PF-SRC and a type of *FILE.

The next step is to create a member.

FIGURE 2.16

```
CMDCRT                    Create Commands
Select one of the following:

    116.  Create Save File                          CRTSAVF
    117.  Create Subsystem Description              CRTSBSD
    118.  Create Search Index                       CRTSCHIDX
    119.  Create Spelling Aid Dictionary            CRTSPADCT
    120.  Create SQL C Program                      CRTSQLC
    121.  Create SQL COBOL Program                  CRTSQLCBL
    122.  Create SQL FORTRAN Program                CRTSQLFTN
    123.  Create SQL Package                        CRTSQLPKG
    124.  Create SQL PL/I Program                   CRTSQLPLI
    125.  Create SQL RPG Program                    CRTSQLRPG
    126.  Create Source Physical File               CRTSRCPF
    127.  Create Session Description                CRTSSND
    128.  Create S/36 COBOL Program                 CRTS36CBL
    129.  Create S/36 Display File                  CRTS36DSPF
                                                        More...
Selection or command
===>126_____

F3=Exit   F4=Prompt   F9=Retrieve   F12=Cancel   F16=Major menu
```

FIGURE 2.17

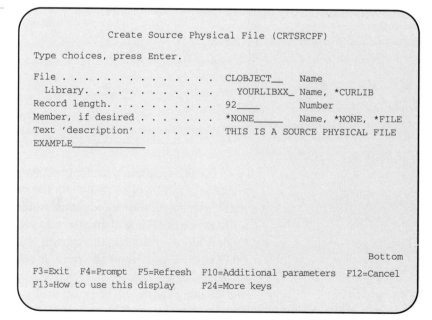

```
                Create Source Physical File (CRTSRCPF)

Type choices, press Enter.

File . . . . . . . . . . . . .   CLOBJECT__   Name
  Library. . . . . . . . . . .     YOURLIBXX_ Name, *CURLIB
Record length. . . . . . . . .   92____       Number
Member, if desired . . . . . .   *NONE_____  Name, *NONE, *FILE
Text 'description' . . . . . .   THIS IS A SOURCE PHYSICAL FILE
EXAMPLE_____




                                                          Bottom
F3=Exit  F4=Prompt  F5=Refresh  F10=Additional parameters  F12=Cancel
F13=How to use this display     F24=More keys
```

FIGURE 2.18

```
CMDCRT                    Create Commands

Select one of the following:

     116.  Create Save File                              CRTSAVF
     117.  Create Subsystem Description                  CRTSBSD
     118.  Create Search Index                           CRTSCHIDX
     119.  Create Spelling Aid Dictionary                CRTSPADCT
     120.  Create SQL C Program                          CRTSQLC
     121.  Create SQL COBOL Program                      CRTSQLCBL
     122.  Create SQL FORTRAN Program                    CRTSQLFTN
     123.  Create SQL Package                            CRTSQLPKG
     124.  Create SQL PL/I Program                       CRTSQLPLI
     125.  Create SQL RPG Program                        CRTSQLRPG
     126.  Create Source Physical File                   CRTSRCPF
     127.  Create Session Description                    CRTSSND
     128.  Create S/36 COBOL Program                     CRTS36CBL
     129.  Create S/36 Display File                      CRTS36DSPF
                                                          More...

Selection or command
===>_____

F3=Exit  F4=Prompt  F9=Retrieve  F12=Cancel  F16=Major menu
File CLOBJECT created in library YOURLIBXX.
```

FIGURE 2.19

```
                    Work with Objects Using PDM

Library . . . . . YOURLIBXX_   Position to. . . . . . . _____
                               Position to type . . . . . _____

Type options, press Enter.
  2=Change      3=Copy      4=Delete    5=Display      7=Rename
  8=Display description  9=Save    10=Restore   11=Move ...

Opt Object   Type   Attribute Text
__  CLOBJECT *FILE  PF-SRC    THIS IS A SOURCE PHYSICAL FILE EXAMPLE




                                                          Bottom
Parameters or command
===>_____
F3=Exit      F4=Prompt        F5=Refresh      F6=Create
F9=Retrieve  F10=Command entry  F23=More options  F24=More keys
```

Creating a Member

To create a member, choose option 3, `Work with members`, from the `AS/400 Programming Development Manager (PDM)` menu. This will display the `Specify Members to Work With` screen (Figure 2.20), which prompts for the library and source physical file that will contain the member. Type the previously created library and object names and press ENTER.

The `Work with Members Using PDM` screen (Figure 2.21) will be displayed. This screen lists all the current members within the file and provides a variety of member functions. To create a member, press F6. The `Start Source Entry Utility (STRSEU)` screen will be displayed. At this screen, the member name and type to be created would be specified. For our example, create a member called PGMMEMBER (Figure 2.22). Since a control language program is eventually going to be entered, the member type would have to be CLP. To find the values that can be entered in a prompt field, move the cursor to the field and press F4. A help screen will be displayed with all the valid values. Doing this for the source type prompt would result in Figure 2.23. The member type, CLP, could also be entered from this screen. Entering **CLP** and pressing ENTER would bring back the `Start Source Entry Utility (STRSEU)` screen with the source type prompt filled in. As can be seen in Figure 2.23, a variety of types are available. If after viewing the valid options, you are still unsure which to choose, move the cursor to the field and press F1 for a list of all the valid options and an explanation of each.

FIGURE 2.20

```
                      Specify Members to Work With

    Type choices, press Enter.

        File. . . . . . . . . . CLOBJECT__    Name, F4 for list

          Library . . . . . .     YOURLIBXX_  *LIBL, *CURLIB, name

        Member:
        Name . . . . . . . . .   *ALL_____  *ALL, name, *generic*
        Type . . . . . . . . .   *ALL_____  *ALL, type, *generic*, *BLANK










    F3=Exit   F4=Prompt   F5=Refresh   F12=Cancel
```

FIGURE 2.21

```
                    Work with Members Using PDM

File . . . . . .    CLOBJECT__
  Library . . . .      YOURLIBXX_    Position to . . . . .  _____

Type options, press Enter.
  2=Edit         3=Copy       4=Delete  5=Display  6=Print
  7=Rename       8=Display description  9=Save     13=Change text ...

Opt Member     Type        Text

  (No members in file)




Parameters or command
===>_____
F3=Exit       F4=Prompt        F5=Refresh        F6=Create
F9=Retrieve   F10=Command entry  F23=More options  F24=More keys
```

FIGURE 2.22

```
                Start Source Entry Utility (STRSEU)

Type choices, press Enter.

Source file . . . . . >  CLOBJECT    Name, *PRV
  Library . . . . . . >    YOURLIBXX  Name, *LIBL, *CURLIB, *PRV
Source member . . . . .  PGMMEMBER   Name, *PRV, *SELECT
Source type . . . . . .  *SAME_____  Name, *SAME, BAS, BASP, C...
Text 'description'. . .  *BLANK_____




                                                            Bottom
F3=Exit F4=Prompt F5=Refresh F12=Cancel F13=How to use this display
F24=More keys
```

After the member type has been specified and descriptive text entered, press **ENTER**. This will automatically invoke SEU, and the Edit screen (Figure 2.24) will be displayed. This screen allows the user to enter the program source code using SEU editing commands. We cover the SEU editing commads in another section, so for right now press **F3** key to exit the edit function. The Exit screen (Figure 2.25) will be displayed. This screen requires a confirmation that the member should be created. Entering **Y** at the Change/create

member prompt and pressing ENTER directs the AS/400 to create the
member. The Work with Members Using PDM screen will be displayed, and the newly created PGMMEMBER member with a type of
CLP will be listed (Figure 2.26).

FIGURE 2.23

```
                    Specify Value for Parameter TYPE

 Type choice, press Enter.

   Type . . . . . . . . . . . . . :   SIMPLE NAME
   Source type. . . . . . . . . .    *SAME_____

   *SAME                              DSPF
   BAS                                FTN
   BASP                               ICFF
   C                                  LF
   CBL                                MENU
   CICSCBL                            MNU
   CICSMAP                            MNUCMD
   CICSQLCBL                          MNUDDS
   CL                                 PAS
   CLD                                PF
   CLP                                PLI
   CMD                                PNLGRP
   DFU                                PRTF                          +

 F3=Exit F5=Refresh F12=Cancel F13=How to use this display F24=More keys
```

FIGURE 2.24

```
 Columns . . . :  1 71              Edit              YOURLIBXX/CLOBJECT
 SEU==> _____PGMMEMBER
 FMT **  ...+... 1 ...+... 2 ...+... 3 ...+... 4 ...+... 5 ...+... 6 ...+... 7
         *************** Beginning of data ********************************
 ,,,,,,
 ,,,,,,
 ,,,,,,
 ,,,,,,
 ,,,,,,
 ,,,,,,
 ,,,,,,
 ,,,,,,
 ,,,,,,
 ,,,,,,
 ,,,,,,
 ,,,,,,
 ,,,,,,
 ,,,,,,
         ***************** End of data *****************************************

 F3=Exit  F4=Prompt  F5=Refresh  F9=Retrieve  F10=Cursor
 F16=Repeat find     F17=Repeat change        F24=More keys
 Member PGMMEMBER added to file YOURLIBXX/CLOBJECT.                       +
```

FIGURE 2.25

```
                                    Exit

  Type choices, press Enter.

     Change/create member . . . . . . . N            Y=Yes, N=No
        Member . . . . . . . . . . . . PGMMEMBER_   Name, F4 for list
        File . . . . . . . . . . . . . CLOBJECT__   Name, F4 for list
         Library. . . . . . . . . . .   YOURLIBXX_  Name
        Text . . . . . . . . . . . . . CL_PROGRAM_ EXAMPLE_____
     Resequence member . . . . . . . . Y            Y=Yes, N=No
        Start . . . . . . . . . . . . 0001.00       0000.01-9999.99
        Increment . . . . . . . . . . 01.00         00.01-99.99

     Print member . . . . . . . . . N              Y=Yes, N=No

     Return to editing. . . . . . . . N             Y=Yes, N=No

     Go to member list. . . . . . . . N             Y=Yes, N=No



  F3=Exit   F4=Prompt   F5=Refresh   F12=Cancel
```

Manipulating Libraries, Objects, and Members

To perform a global operation on any of these objects, such as create, display, or delete, go through the Work with xxxxx screen (where xxxxx is libraries, objects, or members) and choose the appropriate function key or option to create, display, or delete.

As mentioned earlier, these options and functions can be executed directly from any system screen by entering the correct CL command on the command line. The correct command is often included at the end of a PDM screen's header enclosed in parentheses (see Figure 2.17). There is also a series of screens listing the types of CL commands and the commands themselves. These screens enable the user to zero in on the desired CL command by function, object type, and so on. We cover more about how to find and invoke CL commands in Chapter 3.

Starting SEU

As already shown, SEU is automatically invoked whenever a source physical file member is created. If the member has already been created, SEU can be activated to go back and edit the member. To invoke SEU, bring up the Work with Members Using PDM screen (see Figure 2.21) for the member to be edited. To the left of the member name type **2**, the Edit option, and press **ENTER**. The SEU Edit screen (Figure 2.27) will be displayed.

SEU can also be started by typing STRSEU at the command line on any screen. If no member is specified, the last member worked with will be used as the default.

FIGURE 2.26

```
                         Work with Members Using PDM

 File . . . . . .    CLOBJECT__
    Library. . . .   YOURLIBXX_          Position to . . ._____

 Type options, press Enter.
    2=Edit      3=Copy       4=Delete  5=Display 6=Print
    7=Rename    8=Display description  9=Save     13=Change text ...

 Opt Member    Type         Text
    __ PGMMEMBER CLP_____    CL_PROGRAM_EXAMPLE_____


                                                              Bottom
 Parameters or command
 ===>_____
 F3=Exit       F4=Prompt            F5=Refresh          F6=Create
 F9=Retrieve   F10=Command entry    F23=More options    F24=More keys
 Member PGMMEMBER added to file YOURLIBXX/CLOBJECT.              +
```

FIGURE 2.27

```
 Columns . . . :  1 71           Edit            YOURLIBXX/CLOBJECT
 SEU==> _____PGMMEMBER
 FMT **...+... 1 ...+... 2 ...+... 3 ...+... 4 ...+... 5 ...+... 6 ...+... 7
         **************** Beginning of data ***************************
         ******************* End of data ***************************




















    F3=Exit   F4=Prompt  F5=Refresh   F9=Retrieve   F10=Cursor
    F16=Repeat find       F17=Repeat change         F24=More keys
```

Using SEU

When a member is first created, it is empty. This is indicated by the
Beginning of data and End of data lines following each other on
the SEU Edit screen. SEU provides three different ways to execute
edit commands: issuing line commands; entering commands at the
SEU command line (the second line on the top left-hand side of the
screen) and pressing ENTER; or pressing function keys.

Line commands are entered to the left of the member line to be

worked on. For instance, to insert five blank lines in the member, type
I5 to the left of the `Beginning of data` line and press ENTER. The
result would appear as in Figure 2.28, which shows five blank lines preceded by ′ ′ ′ ′ ′ ′. As source code is entered on each line, the apostrophes will be replaced with line numbers. The line number area is where
line commands are entered. For instance, move the cursor to the fifth
line's line number area. Type a **D** over any of the apostrophes and press
ENTER. The member will now contain only four blank lines (Figure 2.29)
because the line command D deletes the line on which it is placed.

FIGURE 2.28

```
Columns . . . :  1  71              Edit            YOURLIBXX/CLOBJECT
SEU==> _____PGMMEMBER
FMT ** ...+... 1 ...+... 2 ...+... 3 ...+... 4 ...+... 5 ...+... 6 ...+... 7
          *************** Beginning of data *************************************
'''''''
'''''''
'''''''
'''''''
'''''''

          ****************** End of data ****************************************




F3=Exit  F4=Prompt  F5=Refresh  F9=Retrieve  F10=Cursor
F16=Repeat find      F17=Repeat change        F24=More keys
```

FIGURE 2.29

```
Columns . . . :  1  71              Edit            YOURLIBXX/CLOBJECT
SEU==> _____ PGMMEMBER
FMT ** ...+... 1 ...+... 2 ...+... 3 ...+... 4 ...+... 5 ...+... 6 ...+... 7
          *************** Beginning of data *************************************
0001.00
0002.00
0003.00
0004.00
          ****************** End of data ****************************************




F3=Exit  F4=Prompt  F5=Refresh  F9=Retrieve  F10=Cursor
F16=Repeat find      F17=Repeat change        F24=More keys
```

Moving Within a Member Using SEU

SEU provides a full-screen editor, meaning characters can be edited wherever they are located on the screen. Moving the cursor with the SEU editor is similar to most word processing applications. The arrow keys control movement within the member. The up and down arrow keys move the cursor between lines, and the left and right arrow keys move the cursor between characters on the same line. Further, when the bottom or top of a screen is reached, pressing the up or down arrow key will cause the lines to scroll.

To move around the program a little faster, type the following commands at the SEU prompt and then press ENTER:

To move to the top of the program:

• Type TOP (or T)

To move to the bottom of the program:

• Type BOT (or B)

There are also several special keys that allow a member to be traversed more than one line at a time:

To move back a page:

• Press PAGE UP (or SHIFT- ↓)

To move forward a page:

• Press PAGE DOWN (or SHIFT- ↑)

To move right in the member:

• Press F20

To move left in the member:

• Press F19

To move the cursor to the SEU prompt:

• Press F10

Entering Information

To add information to the member, move the cursor beneath the first asterisk in the Beginning of data line header and begin typing the source code or text. As shown in Figure 2.30, anything can be typed. When ENTER is pressed, however, SEU's interactive editor becomes apparent (Figure 2.31). When a line of program code is entered, the SEU editor checks the syntax of that line. If it is incorrect, the editor responds with a message at the bottom of the screen. In Figure 2.31, it is obvious that the line entered is not a CL command. The editor knows to look for CL commands because of the member type, CLP. The error message on the bottom of the screen states that the first "command" is not a valid

FIGURE 2.30

```
Columns . . . : 1 71              Edit            YOURLIBXX/CLOBJECT
SEU==> _____PGMMEMBER
FMT ** ...+... 1 ...+... 2 ...+... 3 ...+... 4 ...+... 5 ...+... 6 ...+... 7

        *************** Beginning of data ************************************
0001.00 THE RAIN IN SPAIN FALLS MAINLY ON THE PLAIN
0002.00
0003.00
0004.00
        ****************** End of data *************************************




F3=Exit  F4=Prompt  F5=Refresh  F9=Retrieve  F10=Cursor
F16=Repeat find     F17=Repeat change        F24=More keys
```

FIGURE 2.31

```
Columns . . . : 1 71              Edit            YOURLIBXX/CLOBJECT
SEU==>_____ PGMMEMBER
FMT ** ...+... 1 ...+... 2 ...+... 3 ...+... 4 ...+... 5 ...+... 6 ...+... 7
        *************** Beginning of data ************************************
0001.00 THE RAIN IN SPAIN FALLS MAINLY ON THE PLAIN
0002.00
0003.00
0004.00
        ****************** End of data *************************************




F3=Exit  F4=Prompt  F5=Refresh  F9=Retrieve  F10=Cursor
F16=Repeat find     F17=Repeat change        F24=More keys
Command THE in library *LIBL not found.
```

CL statement. Change the line to read STRPDM, which is the CL command to start PDM. When you press enter, no error message is displayed because this is a valid statement for a CLP member.

Prompting

Program code can also be entered using the prompt method. Prompting is a programmer's utility that facilitates source code entry. It can help find a command or, if the command is known, help with the syntax. To find a command, prompt (press F4) with no command specified. The prompt function will display a series of menus that allow the user to find the command. Once the command is chosen, the prompt will display a series of screens where the required and optional parameters can be entered. After the parameters have been specified and ENTER is pressed, the command will be inserted with the correct syntax at the line indicated. The prompt can be started by either pressing F4 or using an SEU line command.

To start the prompt using F4, move the cursor to the line where the command should be inserted and press F4. This will start the command search. The command can also be entered first—if it is already known—and then F4 pressed. This will result in a prompt screen, unique to that command, being displayed.

To activate the prompt through a line command, type IP—insert with prompt—in a line's number area. This will start the command search, and after all parameters are specified, the command will be placed on that line. If the line command prompt is used, the system will continue the prompt for the next line. This will continue until a blank line is entered.

The prompt screen displayed will depend on the type of member. Different programming languages have different requirements and commands, so there are quite a number of different prompt screens.

Editing a Member

Members can be edited by issuing several different line commands.
To insert a line:

* Move the cursor to the number area of the line where the new line is to be inserted.

* Type I and press ENTER.

If more than one line is to be inserted, type I followed by the number of lines to insert and press ENTER.
To delete a line:

* Type D in the number area of the line to be deleted, and press ENTER.

To delete multiple lines:

* Type DD in the number area of the first line to be deleted.

* Move the cursor to the last line to be deleted and type DD in its number area.

* Press ENTER.

The lines indicated by DD and all lines between the indicated lines will be deleted.

To copy or move a line:

- Type **C** (for copy) or **M** (for move) in the number area of the line to copy or move.

- Move the cursor to the new location for the line.

- Type **A** to copy or move the line *after* the line where the cursor is or type **B** to copy or move the line *before* the line where the cursor is.

- Press ENTER, and the line will be inserted.

To copy or move multiple lines:

- Type **CC** or **MM** in the number area of the first line to copy or move.

- Move the cursor to the last line to copy or move and type **CC** or **MM** in the number area of that line.

- Move the cursor to the new line and type **A** or **B** (for after or before).

- Press ENTER to complete the copy or move multiple lines command.

Other SEU Functions

SEU also allows the user to split the display screen and look at another member. (This function also lets users browse two other types of objects: spool files and output queues. We discuss these in Chapter 3.)

To browse another member:

Browse

- Press **F15**. This will bring up the `Browse/Copy Options` screen.

- Enter the member, file, and library names to be browsed at the `Browse/copy member`, `File`, and `Library` prompts (Figure 2.32).

- Press ENTER.

The SEU `Edit` screen will be redisplayed, but it will contain both the original member (in the upper half of the screen) and the browsed member that was specified (in the lower half of the screen), as shown in Figure 2.33.

The user can change the position of the "split line" by positioning the cursor and pressing **F6**. The split line will be moved to the line the cursor is on.

To exit the browse function:

- Move the cursor to the lower half of the screen and press **F12**.

FIGURE 2.32

```
                         Browse/Copy Options
Type choices, press Enter.
     Selection  . . . . . . .      1              1=Member
                                                  2=Spool file
                                                  3=Output queue

     Copy all records . . . . .    N              Y=Yes, N=No
     Browse/copy member . . . .    BROWSEMBR__     Name, F4 for list
         File . . . . . . . . . .    CLOBJECT__     Name, F4 for list
           Library  . . . . . . .     YOURLIBXX_    Name, *CURLIB, *LIBL

     Browse/copy spool file . .    PGMMEMBER_     Name, F4 for list
         Job. . . . . . . . . .     PGMMEMBER_     Name
           User . . . . . . . .      INTROxx___    Name, F4 for list
           Job number . . . . . .    *LAST_        Number, *LAST
           Spool number . . . . . .  *LAST         Number, *LAST, *ONLY

     Display output queue . . .    QPRINT____     Name, *ALL
         Library  . . . . . . . .    *LIBL_____    Name, *CURLIB, *LIBL

F3=Exit        F4=Prompt        F5=Refresh        F12=Cancel
F13=Change session defaults    F14=Find/Change options
```

FIGURE 2.33

```
Columns . . . : 1 71            Edit              YOURLIBXX/CLOBJECT
SEU==> _____  PGMMEMBER
FMT **  ...+... 1 ...+... 2 ...+... 3 ...+... 4 ...+... 5 ...+... 6 ...+... 7
        *************** Beginning of data ****************************
0001.00 STRPDM
0002.00
0003.00
0004.00
        **************** End of data *********************************

 Columns . . . : 1 71            Browse            YOURLIBXX/CLOBJECT
SEU==> _____  BROWSEMBR
        *************** Beginning of data ****************************
0001.00 /* THIS IS THE MEMBER BEING BROWSED */
0002.00 /* THIS IS THE MEMBER BEING BROWSED */
0003.00 /* THIS IS THE MEMBER BEING BROWSED */
0004.00 /* THIS IS THE MEMBER BEING BROWSED */
        **************** End of data *********************************




F3=Exit  F5=Refresh  F9=Retrieve  F10=Cursor  F12=Cancel
F16=Repeat find      F17=Repeat change         F24=More keys
```

Copying from Another Member

SEU also allows copying portions (or all) of one member into another. To copy from another member:

- Access the member to copy with the browse procedure.
- In the browse member, type **C** (or **CC**) to mark the line(s).
- In the original member, type **A** or **B** to mark the destination location.
- Press ENTER.

To copy all lines from another member:

* Type **Y** at the `Copy all records` prompt on the `Browse/Copy Options` screen.

* Press **ENTER**.

  In the original member, mark the "copy to" location.

* Press **ENTER**.

Exiting, Saving, and Printing Members

To exit SEU:

* Press **F3**. This will bring up the `Exit` menu (see Figure 2.25).

The `Exit` menu offers several options:
Exit and save the file with changes:

* Type **Y** at the `Change/create member` prompt.

* Press **ENTER**.

  Exit and not save the changes:

* Type **N** at the `Change/create member` prompt.

* Press **ENTER**.

  Exit and print out the file:

* Type **Y** at the `Print member` prompt.

* Press **ENTER**.

Compiling a Source Member

After exiting SEU, the `Work with Members Using PDM` screen will be displayed. As we mentioned earlier, all source code must be translated into machine language, and compiling is the procedure to do this.
To compile a member:

* Type **14** in the option field next to the member to be compiled. (To see other available options, press **F23**.)

* Press **ENTER**.

  If the member is being compiled for the first time, a message at the bottom of the screen will be displayed stating that the compile job has been submitted (Figure 2.34). If the member has been compiled before, the `Confirm Compile of Member` screen will be displayed (Figure 2.35).
  To compile a member:

* Type **Y** at the `Delete existing object` prompt to delete the program object that was the result of the previous compilation.

* Press **ENTER**.

  A message at the bottom of the screen will be displayed stating that the compile job has been submitted.

FIGURE 2.34

```
                    Work with Members Using PDM

File. . . . . . . CLOBJECT__
  Library . . . .                 Position to . . . . . _____

Type options, press Enter.
  2=Edit    3=Copy      4=Delete  5=Display  6=Print
  7=Rename  8=Display description 9=Save     13=Change text ...

Opt Member     Type      Text
__  PGMMEMBER  CLP_____  CL_PROGRAM_EXAMPLE_____


                                                            Bottom
Parameters or command
===>_____
F3=Exit       F4=Prompt          F5=Refresh         F6=Create
F9=Retrieve   F10=Command entry  F23=More options   F24=More keys
Job 040942/INTROxx/PGMMEMBER submitted to job queue QBATCH in library QGPL.
```

FIGURE 2.35

```
                    Confirm Compile of Member

The following object already exists for the compile operation:

  Object which exists . . . . . . . . . :  PGMMEMBER
    Library . . . . . . . . . . . . . . :    YOURLIBXX
  Object type . . . . . . . . . . . . . :  *PGM

  Member to compile . . . . . . . . . . :  PGMMEMBER
  File. . . . . . . . . . . . .  . . . . :  CLOBJECT
    Library . . . . . . . . . . . . . . :    YOURLIBXX

Type choice, press Enter.
Press F12=Cancel to return and not perform the compile operation.

  Delete existing object . . . . . . . . N    Y=Yes, N=No




F12=Cancel
```

After the job is complete, the system issues a message about the result of the compile job. To see if the program has been compiled successfully, you need to look at the system message. At the Work with Members Using PDM screen, type **DSPMSG** (the display messages command) at the command line and press ENTER. This will bring up the Work with Messages screen (Figure 2.36). A message on this screen will state whether the job completed successfully or not.

FIGURE 2.36

```
                          Work with Messages
                                                        System: CHICAGO
 Messages for: INTROxx

 Type options below, then press Enter.
   4=Remove    5=Display details and reply

 Opt  Message
                         Messages needing a reply
    (No messages available)

                         Messages not needing a reply
  _Job 040942/INTROxx/PGMMEMBER completed normally on XX/XX/XX at XX:XX:XX.




                                                                   Bottom
 F1=Help  F3=Exit  F5=Refresh  F6=Display system operator messages
 F16=Remove messages not needing a reply   F17=Top  F24=More keys
```

When a member is compiled, a listing is generated. If errors existed, the listing will contain error messages and a more detailed explanation of the problems.

Running a Program

As mentioned, compiling a program source code member results in a new object being created that contains machine language instructions. It is this version of the program that can be executed. Members contain only the source code version of the program, which cannot be executed by the computer. So to run the newly created program:

- Exit the Work with Members Using PDM screen.

- Access the machine-executable code by going to the Work with Objects Using PDM screen for YOURLIBXX. (Notice that a new object has been created called PGMMEMBER; Figure 2.37).

- Type **16**, the Run option, next to the object name and press ENTER. (To see option 16 as an available option, press F23).

Another way to run the program is to type the command **CALL YOURLIBXX PGMMEMBER** at the command line of any screen and then press ENTER. Using either method will result in the system submitting the newly created program to be run.

The program PGMMEMBER contains the command STRPDM; therefore, when the program is run, the STRPDM command will be executed, and the AS/400 Programming Development Manager (PDM) screen will be displayed.

FIGURE 2.37

```
                    Work with Objects Using PDM

   Library . . . . .    Position to . . . . . . . . _____
                                 Position to type . . . . . _____

   Type options, press Enter.
     2=Change        3=Copy  4=Delete 5=Display    7=Rename
     8=Display description  9=Save    10=Restore   11=Move ...

   Opt Object      Type    Attribute   Text
   __  PGMMEMBER  *PGM    CLP          CL PROGRAM EXAMPLE
   __  CLOBJECT   *FILE   PF-SRC       THIS IS A SOURCE PHYSICAL FILE EXAMPLE




                                                                 Bottom
   Parameters or command
   ===>_____
   F3=Exit       F4=Prompt         F5=Refresh        F6=Create
   F9=Retrieve   F10=Command entry F23=More options  F24=More keys
```

Summary

PDM and SEU provide easy access for programmers to a variety of often used programming functions. Everything from creating objects to hold program source code, to actually compiling and running the programs can be done from screens and functions provided by these two utilities.

Since this is your first exploration of an AS/400 utility, it is hard to fully appreciate all the user-friendly features. For instance, notice the continuity between screens: F6 is always create, whether a library, an object, or a member is being created; F1 is always help; system messages always appear at the same place on the screens; and so on. This consistency makes using the system much easier. On many other systems and application packages, function keys do not have this continuity, and certainly when accessing operating system and other application package functions, this compatibility is lost. The AS/400 has created a seamless user interface regardless of the function being executed.

The programming object structure also provides a means for programmers to clearly and uniformly organize their programs and data. There are still procedures and authorizations that need to be instituted in order to provide an effective and secure programming environment, but the object-oriented nature of the AS/400 provides the basis for this organization.

LAB EXERCISE

In this exercise, you will create a new library and several members that will be used throughout the rest of the chapters. If YOURLIBXX has not been created, create it now:

1. Start PDM from any display screen. Type **STRPDM** at any command line and press ENTER.

2. From the AS/400 Programming Development Manager (PDM) menu, choose option 1, Work with libraries.

3. From the Specify Libraries to Work With screen, leave *ALL in the Library prompt and press ENTER.

4. At the Work with Libraries Using PDM screen, press F6, the Create option.

5. At the Create Library screen, enter **YOURLIBXX** (where your unique two-digit number is substituted for XX) at the Library prompt, enter your name at the Text 'description' prompt, and press ENTER. YOURLIBXX will be created by the system.

6. When the Work with Libraries Using PDM screen is redisplayed, press ESC.

Now create a new source physical file called INVSRC within YOURLIBXX. If the AS/400 Programming Development Manager (PDM) menu is not currently displayed at the workstation, type **STRPDM** at the command line and press ENTER.

1. From the AS/400 Programming Development Manager (PDM) menu, choose option 2, Work with objects.

2. At the Specify Objects to Work With screen, type **YOURLIBXX** at the Library prompt and press ENTER.

3. At the Work with Objects Using PDM screen, press F6, the Create option.

4. From the Create Commands screen, select option 126, Create Source Physical File.

5. At the Create Source Physical File (CRTSRCPF) screen, type **INVSRC** at the File prompt and **YOURLIBXX** at the Library prompt.

6. Press ENTER. File INVSRC will be created.

7. When the Work with Objects Using PDM screen is redisplayed, press ESC.

To create the new members:

1. From the AS/400 Programming Development Manager (PDM) menu, choose option 3, Work with members.

2. At the Specify Members to Work With screen, type **YOURLIBXX** at the Library prompt and **INVSRC** at the File prompt.

3. Press ENTER.

4. At the Work with Members Using PDM screen, press F6 to invoke the Create function.

5. At the `Start Source Entry Utility (STRSEU)` screen, type **ITEM** at the `Source member` prompt and **PF** at the `Source type` prompt.

6. Press ENTER.

7. From the `Edit` screen, press F3 to exit.

8. At the `Exit` screen, type **Y** at the `Change/create member` prompt.

9. Press ENTER. Member ITEM will be created.

10. From the `Work with Members Using PDM` screen, perform steps 4 through 9 to create two more source physical file members with a type of PF called BATCH and CARTON.

REVIEW QUESTIONS

1. What are the three major programming entities on the AS/400?
2. Explain the advantages of setting up separate development, test, and production libraries.
3. How are objects characterized?
4. What type of information do members of source physical files contain?
5. Describe the function provided by PDM.
6. How are member types and program object types related?
7. What are line commands, and how are block line commands performed?
8. How is prompting invoked?
9. What is compiling, and what is created by compiling?
10. What is the CL command to run a program?
11. What is the difference between a file with an attribute of PF-DTA and a file with an attribute of PF-SRC?
12. What is the result of compiling an object?

DISCUSSION QUESTIONS

1. Discuss the path a program travels through the development, test, and production libraries. What events cause the program to be moved between the different libraries?
2. Discuss the user-friendly features encountered so far on the AS/400. List each and explain how it either clarifies a system function(s) or makes the function(s) easier to use.

3. If the members in the following diagram were compiled using PDM, what would be the resulting object and member names, types, and attributes?

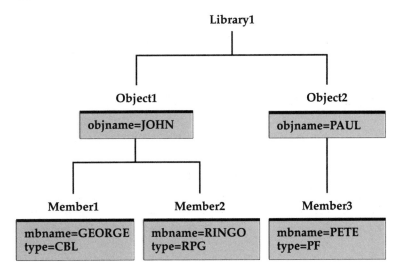

Control Language

3

Overview

Control Language (CL) commands are the means to execute AS/400 operating system functions. Just as DOS or OS/2 allows users to perform operating system commands on a personal computer, CL allows operating system functions such as copying files, starting system utilities, and creating libraries to be performed on the AS/400. In addition, CL allows the user to perform tasks that are needed in a multiuser computer environment (creating userids) and tasks unique to the AS/400 (creating library lists).

This chapter gives the readers an overview of the CL command structure and introduces some common CL commands. In addition, a more complicated CL program will be created, and several CL commands that are used exclusively in CL programs are introduced. How to use on-line help and prompting to find and use the correct CL commands is also covered.

After finishing this chapter, you will understand:

- The general capabilities of CL
- How CL commands are constructed
- The major CL command categories

You also will be able to:

- Use the command screens and prompts to issue CL commands from the command line

- Create, compile, and run a CL program
- Create and manipulate output queues
- Change library lists
- Display messages

CL Commands

In keeping with the AS/400's user-friendly approach, all CL commands try to follow a common naming convention. A noncomputer example of naming conventions is the way people are named in the United States and China. In the United States, people usually have a first, a middle, and a last name, with the last name being the same as their father's. In China, the naming convention is a first and a last name, with the first name being the same as the father's. In other words, in America you would be James Tiberius Kirk, but in China you would be Kirk James.

The CL command naming convention dictates that the maximum CL command size is nine characters. Each command can be broken down into a maximum of three parts, and each part can have a maximum of three characters. The three parts are the command verb, adjective, and object (Figure 3.1).

The verb describes the work or operation that the command performs. For instance, CPY stands for copy, and CHG means change. The command adjective and object describe the object that will be operated on. For instance, SRCPF stands for a source physical file, and USRPRF represents a user profile.

FIGURE 3.1
Three Parts of a Command

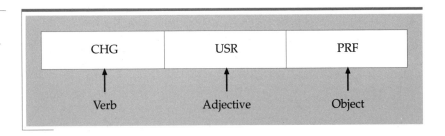

Just as Cher and Madonna are exceptions to the U.S. naming convention, there are also CL commands that are exceptions to the CL naming conventions. For instance, the CL adjective is not always necessary, nor does the adjective or object have to be three characters. Many CL commands simply have a verb and an object, with the object being represented by a single character, such as F, which stands for file.

Once the three (or fewer) character representations of the basic functions and objects are known, the correct command to use can often be guessed.

Groups of CL Commands

There are two major ways to classify all CL commands: by verb and by the object on which they operate. For instance, there is a group of delete commands:

DLTMNU   delete menu
DLTLIB   delete library
DLTUSRPRF   delete user profile
DLTF   delete file

Each of these commands deletes a different object, but they all share the same verb. They all belong to the delete group.

Other common command verbs are:

STR   start
CRT   create
DSP   display

The second way CL commands can be grouped is by the objects they work against. For instance:

CPYF   copy file
SNDF   send file
RCVF   receive file
DLTF   delete file

These commands all process a file; they belong to the file group of commands. Notice that the DLTF command is included in both the file group of commands and the delete group of commands. All commands are classified by the type of processing they perform and the type of object they process.

CL Menus

If the user cannot remember the correct CL command (and has been unsuccessful at guessing), the AS/400 provides a series of menus to help find the desired command. To display the menu of the major CL command groups, type GO MAJOR at the command line of any system screen or move the cursor to the command line of any system screen and press F4. A menu of the major CL command groups (Figure 3.2) will be displayed.

When an option from the Major Command Groups screen is selected, a submenu with a list of more command groups or a screen with a list of commands will be displayed. For instance, choosing option 2, Verb Commands, will result in a menu of verb groups such as Add Commands and Change Commands (Figure 3.3), whereas choosing option 5, File Commands, will result in a list of actual commands, in this case, commands that perform operations against files (Figure 3.4).

FIGURE 3.2

```
MAJOR                    Major Command Groups
                                                    System: CHICAGO
Select one of the following:
     1.  Select Command by Name                     SLTCMD
     2.  Verb Commands                              VERB
     3.  Subject Commands                           SUBJECT
     4.  Object Management Commands                 CMDOBJMGT
     5.  File Commands                              CMDFILE
     6.  Save and Restore Commands                  CMDSAVRST
     7.  Work Management Commands                    CMDWRKMGT
     8.  Data Management Commands                    CMDDTAMGT
     9.  Security Commands                          CMDSEC
    10.  Print Commands                             CMDPRT
    11.  Spooling Commands                          CMDSPL
    12.  System Control Commands                    CMDSYSCTL
    13.  Program Commands                           CMDPGM
                                                        More..

Selection or command
===>
F3=Exit  F4=Prompt  F9=Retrieve  F12=Cancel  F13=User support
F16=AS/400 Main menu
```

FIGURE 3.3

```
VERB                     Verb Commands

Select one of the following:
     1.  Add Commands                               CMDADD
     2.  Allocate Commands                          CMDALC
     3.  Answer Commands                            CMDANS
     4.  Analyze Commands                           CMDANZ
     5.  Apply Commands                             CMDAPY
     6.  Ask Commands                               CMDASK
     7.  Call Commands                              CMDCALL
     8.  Configuration Commands                     CMDCFG
     9.  Change Commands                            CMDCHG
    10.  Check Commands                             CMDCHK
    11.  Close Commands                             CMDCLO
    12.  Cleanup Commands                           CMDCLNUP
    13.  Clear Commands                             CMDCLR
    14.  Compare Commands                           CMDCMP
                                                        More...

Selection or command
===>
F3=Exit  F4=Prompt  F9=Retrieve  F12=Cancel  F16=Major menu
```

FIGURE 3.4

```
CMDFILE                    File Commands

Select one of the following:

  Commands
    1.  Close File                                CLOF
    2.  Copy File                                 CPYF
    3.  Declare File                              DCLF
    4.  Delete File                               DLTF
    5.  Delete Override                           DLTOVR
    6.  Display File Description                  DSPFD
    7.  Display File Field Description            DSPFFD
    8.  Display Override                          DSPOVR
    9.  Receive File                              RCVF
   10.  Restore S/36 File                         RSTS36F
   11.  Save S/36 File                            SAVS36F
   12.  Send File                                 SNDF
   13.  Send/Receive File                         SNDRCVF
                                                     More...
Selection or command
===>_____
F3=Exit   F4=Prompt   F9=Retrieve   F12=Cancel   F16=Major menu
```

Menus can also be invoked by typing the command GO followed by a space and the menu name. Thus, typing GO VERB and pressing ENTER on any system screen would do the same thing as typing 2 and pressing ENTER on the Major Command Groups screen. The question becomes how to tell the difference between menu names and CL commands. The major difference between a CL command and a command menu name is that command menu names usually begin with CMD, whereas CL commands begin with a three-character verb. To every rule, of course, there are exceptions; not all menus begin with CMD (for example, MAJOR and VERB). These exceptions can be picked out as menus, however, because they do not follow the command naming convention of verb, adjective, and object.

There are several ways to execute CL commands from the menus. The easiest is to type the option number at the command line and press ENTER. For instance, typing 4 on the File Commands screen (see Figure 3.4) will result in the DLTF prompt screen being displayed.

Another way to execute a CL command is to type the command at the command line and press ENTER. (Notice on these menus that to the right of each option is a CL command or a menu name.) Issuing CL commands, however, is more complicated than bringing up menus. As mentioned, CL commands can be executed by typing them at any command line and pressing ENTER. The problem with executing CL commands this way is that some commands require more data regarding the work to be done. For instance, just typing DLTF, for delete file, is not enough information for the operating system to work with. The name of the file to be deleted must also be supplied. These command qualifiers, or *parameters*, must be supplied in a certain order and identified by specific keywords. To execute the commands from the command line, the user must know the correct syntax and keywords.

CL Command Syntax

Most CL commands require parameters. For instance, any command that performs an action against an object needs the object name. Sometimes there are also further qualifications regarding the type of work to be done, or there is more than one object involved in the function. For instance, CPYF—copy file—requires the name of the file to be copied and the new file name where the copy will be placed. Rather than making the user remember all the individual command keywords and parameters, the AS/400 provides a CL command *prompt* function. When the prompt function is invoked, one or more screens are displayed, listing all the possible parameters that can be supplied for the command. For each parameter, space is provided to enter a value. After you enter the values, press ENTER. This will submit the command with the correct keywords in the proper order. To invoke the prompt function for a specific CL command, type the CL command on the command line and press F4. As an example, type **CPYF** and press F4. The `Copy File (CPYF)` screen (Figure 3.5) will be displayed.

FIGURE 3.5

```
                          Copy File (CPYF)

 Type choices, press Enter.

 From file . . . . . . . .              Name
   Library . . . . . . . .    *LIBL     Name, *LIBL, *CURLIB
 To file . . . . . . . . .              Name, *PRINT
   Library . . . . . . . .    *LIBL     Name, *LIBL, *CURLIB
 From member . . . . . . .   *FIRST     Name, generic*, *FIRST, *ALL
 To member or label  . . .   *FIRST     Name, *FIRST, *FROMMBR
 Replace or add records  .   *NONE      *NONE, *ADD, *REPLACE
 Create file . . . . . . .   *NO        *NO,*YES
 Print format  . . . . . .   *CHAR      *CHAR, *HEX




                                                            Bottom
 F3=Exit  F4=Prompt  F5=Refresh  F10=Additional parameters  F12=Cancel
 F13=How to use this display      F24=More keys
```

Figure 3.5 shows some of the parameters that can be entered for the copy file command. For instance, there are entry areas to specify the file to be copied—the `From` file, library, and member—and areas that specify where the copied file should go—the To file, library, and member. As mentioned earlier, sometimes further qualification regarding the function can be specified. In the case of CPYF, the system can be instructed to create the To file during the copy function. This saves the programmer from having to execute a whole series of commands to first create and then copy the file. The F10 key provides additional parameters that can be specified for the copy file command. These include parameters to select particular records for copying (by record number or key value) or to limit the number of records to be copied.

When you are unsure of a parameter's purpose, don't forget about the on-line help. For instance, to find out more information about the From file parameter, move the cursor to the parameter field and press F1. Doing this for the From file field would result in the help window in Figure 3.6.

The help window contains several pieces of information. First, there is an explanation of what the parameter signifies. Then there is a list of all the possible values and an explanation of each value. You can enlarge the help window to take up most of the display screen by pressing F20. To retrieve further information about the command and all the parameters, press F2, Extended help. Prompting and field help are invaluable for all AS/400 users and are especially useful to new users.

After all the required parameters have been filled in, press ENTER to execute the CL command. If a required parameter has not been entered or a parameter value has been misspelled, the prompt screen will reappear with an error message and the incorrect field highlighted.

FIGURE 3.6

```
                           Copy File (CPYF)
 Type choices, press Enter.
 From file . . . . . . . . . .          Name
   Library . ...............................................
 To file . . :            From file (FROMFILE) - Help              :
   Library . :                                                      :
 From member : Specifies the name and library of the database file or:
 To member or : device file that contains the records being copied. A :
 Replace or ad: database file can be a physical file or a logical file. A :
 Create file : device file can be a diskette file or a tape file.    :
 Print format :                                                      :
             : The possible library values are:                     :
             :                                                       :
             : *LIBL                                                 :
             :    The library list is used to locate the database file :
             :    or device file.                                    :
             :                                          More...      :
             : F2=Extended help  F10=Move to top  F11=Search index   :
 F3=Exit  F4= : F12=Cancel         F20=Enlarge       F24=More keys    :
 F13=How to us:                                                       :
 Parameter FRO:......................................................:
```

If there is a more complex error—for instance, a `From file` is specified to which the user does not have access authority—the screen from where the prompting was done will be redisplayed. At the command line for that screen will be the syntactically correct CL command, with all the previously specified parameters. There will also be an error message at the bottom of the screen stating the problem.

Rather than reentering the command and all its parameters, the user can edit the command directly on the command line or through the prompt. Pressing F4 will result in the prompt screen being displayed with all the previously specified values carried over. The command can now be changed to specify a file to which the user does have access authority. In this way, the entire command and its parameters do not have to be reentered.

Creating Programming Objects with CL Commands

In Chapter 2, we introduced libraries, source physical files, data physical files, and members. In that chapter, we also covered how to create these objects through PDM. Rather than going through PDM, the user can directly issue CL commands that will create these objects.

To find out which command to use, the user could search the CL create commands menu. However, to save some time, the following instructions briefly explain the most frequently used create commands and the parameters that are required:

To create a library:

- Type **CRTLIB**.

- Press F4 to prompt for the library and type.

- Fill in the library name and library type. (Press F1 for help on the types available.)

- Press **ENTER**.

A message should appear at the bottom of the screen saying that the library was created.

To create a source physical file for source code members:

- Type **CRTSRCPF**.

- Press F4 to prompt for the library and file.

- Fill in the library name and file name.

- Press **ENTER**.

A message should appear at the bottom of the screen saying that the file was created in the library.

To create a source member in a source physical file:

- Type **STRSEU**.

- Press **F4** to prompt for the library, file, member, and type.

- Fill in the library name, file name, new member name, and member type.

- Press **ENTER**.

- The `SEU Edit` screen will be displayed. Source code can be entered, or the user can exit by pressing **F3**.

- When the `SEU Exit` screen appears, a **Y** should always be filled in at the `Create/change member` prompt. (If not, then type a **Y** at the prompt.)

- Press **ENTER**.

A message should appear at the bottom of the screen saying that a member was added to the file and library specified.

To compile a program member:

There are individual commands depending on the type of program member. Here are a few of them:

- To compile a PF member, type **CRTPF**.

- To compile a CLP member, type **CRTCLPGM**.

- To compile a RPG member, type **CRTRPGPGM**.

- Press **F4** to prompt for the library, file, and member to be compiled.

- Press **ENTER** and follow the procedure for displaying messages (see Chapter 2) to check that the compile was successful.

You may have noticed that there are more options on the various compile command prompt screens than were covered in the preceding descriptions of each function. These extra options allow the user to do things such as specify the name of the program object that will be created when the member is compiled or specify the name of the library where the program object will be contained. CL commands generally offer more options and versatility than the system interfaces and utilities. For example, during compiling with PDM, it is assumed that the program object will be in the same library as the source member, and PDM gives the program object the same name as the source member. (For instance, from the earlier example, source code member CURLEY provides the name for the program object CURLEY that is the result of compiling with PDM.) When CL commands are used, there are options to control these parameters.

Generally, as users become more involved and familiar with the AS/400, they find the easy-to-use interfaces and utilities too restrictive. Fortunately, the AS/400 has more explicit—and more complicated—tools such as CL and DDS that allow the user to exert maximum control over system functions.

Creating an Environmentally Sound Programming Environment

Several other objects besides libraries, files, and members are commonly used by programmers. One of these is an *output queue*. Believe it or not, by utilizing output queues you can help protect the environment and save time. To understand how to use an output queue, we first have to learn about another object, called a *spool file*, and how the system uses spool files when dealing with output.

Spool files are temporary files that contain output data. (Spool stands for simultaneous peripheral operations on line.) When the system first creates output, it is written to a spool file. For instance, when a program is compiled, a compilation report is created. The compilation report is initially written to a spool file.

Next, the system must determine where the output should be sent. All output on the AS/400 is sent to a default output device. The compilation report in the spool file is the responsibility of the system processor until the default output device receives it. On the AS/400, the default output device is usually an output queue associated with a printer. Output queues are temporary storage areas on disk, and each printer has a specific disk storage area—an output queue—associated with it. The output queue holds spool files in case information is being sent faster than the printer can print it. (If the default output device was the printer, not the output queue, the system processor would not be able to send the spool file until the printer was ready. Since printers print considerably slower than processors can process, there would be a tremendous degradation in system performance.)

If the default output device is an output queue, the system processor can send the spool file to a location in secondary storage and proceed with other tasks. The printer will read the output queue when it finishes processing its current job.

Output queues do not have to be associated with a printer. There are CL commands that allow users to create output queues and change the default output device for their output. (This is where saving the world's forests comes in.) A user can create an output queue and not associate that queue with a printer but specify it as the default output device. All spool files will now be sent and stored in the new output queue. The user can then access the output queue (again, with CL commands) and decide whether to view, discard, or print the output. For instance, after reading a compilation report, a programmer may decide to discard it. If the report had been sent to an output queue not associated with a printer, it could be read at the workstation and then simply erased from storage. Automatically printing output wastes paper and clogs landfills. (It may seem like only a few sheets of paper, but over a short time and many users, it adds up to a forest's worth.)

As we mentioned, there are CL commands that enable users to create and work with output queues as well as specify an output queue as the default device for all newly created spool files. There are also commands that let users access and view the spool files at their workstations and options that let them manipulate, print, and delete spool files.

To create an output queue:

- Type **CRTOUTQ OUTQ(YOURLIBXX/MYQ)** and press ENTER.

This will create an output queue in YOURLIBXX called MYQ. To verify that the output queue has been created:

- Type **WRKOUTQ YOURLIBXX/MYQ** and press ENTER.

The screen in Figure 3.7 will be displayed. This screen is a list of all the spool files in the output queue. The output queue has no spooled files because it was just created. To place spool files on the output queue, we will define the output queue as the default output device and then generate output. Press F3 to exit this display and return to the AS/400 Main Menu.

FIGURE 3.7

```
                      Work with Output Queue

    Queue: MYQ        Library: YOURLIBXX        Status:RLS

    Type options, press Enter.
      1=Send  2=Change  3=Hold  4=Delete 5=Display 6=Release 7=Messages
      8=Attributes       9=Work with printing status


    Opt  File  User  User Data  Sts  Pages  Copies  Form  Type  Pty

      (No spooled output files)




                                                              Bottom
    Parameters for options 1, 2, 3 or command
    ===>
    F3=Exit  F11=View 2  F12=Cancel  F22=Printers  F24=More keys
```

The output queue can be defined as the default output device through the CHJOB command. Type **CHGJOB** at the command line and prompt for the parameters by pressing F4. Then press F10 for additional parameters. The screen in Figure 3.8 will be displayed.

FIGURE 3.8

```
                    Change Job (CHGJOB)

Type choices, press Enter.

Job name . . . . . . . . . . .   *       Name, *
  User . . . . . . . . . . . .           Name
  Number . . . . . . . . . .             000000-999999
Job priority (on JOBQ) . . . .   *SAME   0-9, *SAME
Output priority (on OUTQ). . .   5       1-9, *SAME
Print device . . . . . . . . .   PRT01   Name, *SAME, *USRPRF...
Output queue . . . . . . . . .   *DEV    Name, *SAME, *USRPRF, *DEV...
  Library . . . . . . . . . .            Name, *LIBL, *CURLIB
Run priority . . . . . . . . .   20      1-99, *SAME

                  Additional Parameters

Job queue  . . . . . . . . .     *SAME   Name, *SAME
  Library  . . . . . . . . .              Name, *LIBL, *CURLIB
Print text . . . . . . . . .     *BLANK
                                                      More...
F3=Exit  F4=Prompt  F5=Refresh  F12=Cancel  F13=How to use this display
F24=More keys
```

In Figure 3.8, *DEV is specified as the default output queue. *DEV is the queue associated with the printer. To change the default output queue, type **MYQ** over *DEV and **YOURLIBXX** at the Library prompt. Press ENTER. This will change the default destination of all the user's spooled files. To check that this is occurring, go back and recompile the CL program that was created in the last chapter. (Doing this will create a compilation report—at last, output!) Issue the **WRKOUTQ** command as before. There will be a spool file listed on the Work with Output Queue screen. You can manipulate the spool file by typing in the appropriate option number next to its name. The spool file can also be deleted or printed from this screen.

There is, however, a problem with defining the default output device with the CHGJOB command from the command line. Any changes made are only for the duration of the session. When the user signs off, the default output device reverts to the printer. The next time the user signs on, the output queue associated with the printer will be the default output queue. This makes it difficult to maintain an output queue as the default; however, there is a way around the problem. Chapter 2 covered how to create CL programs. A CL program could be written to change the output queue, and each time the user signs on, it could be run. As an example, let's create a new program that will set up the output queue as the default and initialize the programming environment in several other time-saving ways.

Create a new physical file member called INITPGM under the object and library created in the last chapter, YOURLIBXX and CLOBJECT. Use either PDM or the appropriate CL command.

(Remember to specify the correct member type for CL source code.) Insert a text description for the new file as follows: **Initial student program - introxx**. For the purpose of this exercise, assume that everyone has a seven-character userid that begins with the characters *intro* and ends with a unique two-digit number. This two-digit number also matches the last two digits of the library name; for example, for the userid INTRO99, the library name is YOURLIB99.

After the member has been created, the SEU Edit screen should be displayed. The member is now ready for code to be entered.

Programming in CL

As discussed in Chapter 2, CL commands can be entered into a file, compiled, and run just like many other programming languages. These CLPs (Control Language Programs) use special "program CL commands" to handle the unique needs of processing CL commands in a program. For instance, when some CL commands are executed, the system sends back a message on the bottom of the screen that may need to be acted on. In a program, there is no person to respond to those messages. So there is a special CL programming command that allows the program to check for system messages and perform certain logic if such a message is received. Some other commonly needed program functions are the ability to define program variables, call other programs from the CL program, send and receive variables to and from these called programs, and perform conditional logic.

CL programs allow users to perform all normal CL functions—create files, delete userids, call system utilities—and they provide a way to control the execution of other programs, even programs written in other programming languages, such as RPG and COBOL. In this way, a CLP can act as a job control manager; it can control the execution of programs based on conditions. For instance, a payroll system may consist of hundreds of programs. Based on the day of the month, different programs may be executed; for example, on the first of the month, all time cards are processed for the previous month, on the fifth, paychecks are printed, and on the seventh, all tax information is accumulated and sent to the IRS. A CLP could be written that checks what day of the month it is and executes the correct series of programs.

CLPs can also check for system error codes that are generated when called programs are executed. The CLP can then take corrective actions based on the specific codes that were returned. This can save time both for the programmer and for the customer, who relies on the successful completion of those programs.

Creating an Initialization Program

So far the initialization program is going to define the previously created output queue, MYQ, as the destination for all spooled files. It will also define the recently created library, YOURLIBXX, as the current library. The current library is the first library searched whenever an object is specified without its associated library. The current library is also used as the default library whenever an object is created. The CL command CHGCURLIB can change the current library value.

Another object, called a *library list*, also affects the programming environment. A library list is a list of all the libraries that a user most commonly uses. If users want to run a particular program, they can just specify the program name. When only the program name is specified, the system goes to the library list and searches each of the libraries in the order that they are listed within the library list. (This is true except when a current library is specified. If a current library is defined, the current library is searched first, and then the remaining user libraries are searched in listed order.) So an object can be identified by its name alone if it is contained in a library that is in the library list.

For instance, say a user's library list contains the libraries shown in Figure 3.9. If program object PAYROLL was contained in library FINANCE, it could be executed by using the CL command CALL and the program name, PAYROLL. When the system saw that no library was specified, it would go to the library list and search each library in the list for a program object called PAYROLL. In this case, it would first search QSYS, then QGPL, and finally find the object in library FINANCE.

FIGURE 3.9
A Library List

Use the CL command DSPLIBL—display library list—to show the contents of the library list. Notice that it currently does not contain YOURLIBXX. To add an entry to the library list, execute the command **ADDLIBLE LIB(YOURLIBXX)**. Redisplaying the list will show that YOURLIBXX has been added. Again, the limitation with using ADDLIBLE from the command line is that the new library is deleted from the library list after the session is over. To permanently add YOURLIBXX to the library list, the ADDLIBLE command will have to be included in the initialization program.

The initialization program will also be written generically, meaning it will be written so that anyone having a userid, as described earlier, will be able to use this program. Rather than creating 99 different programs for userids INTRO01 through INTRO99, we create one program that will work for all of them.

Figure 3.10 is an example of an initialization program that will accomplish everything we have described so far. (Following a short explanation of how the program works will be a line-by-line description and definition of each command in the program.)

Notice the format for the commands. The CL command starts at the first position in each line and is followed by various keywords with values in parentheses. The general syntax for a CL command is:

```
CLcommand keyword(value) keyword(value) ......
```

This program first sets up some program variables using declare (DCL) commands. These variables will be used to store information during the program's execution. The program then reads the userid of the person who submitted the program for execution—the RTVJOBA command on line 7. On line 9, a substring function within the change variable command will strip off the last two digits of the userid; for exmple, if the userid was INTRO99, it would grab the 99. The program variable &NBR is set to 99 with that same command. Next, another program variable, &LIB, is set to the concatenation (see the description of the CHGVAR command that follows for a definition of concatenation) of the character string 'YOURLIB' and the variable &NBR. In our example, this would mean that &LIB is set to YOURLIB99.

FIGURE 3.10

```
          ...+... 1 ...+... 2 ...+... 3 ...+... 4 ...+... 5 ...+... 6 ...+
          ************ Beginning of data ******************************
0001.00 INITPGM:  PGM
0002.00
0003.00 DCL       VAR(&USER) TYPE(*CHAR) LEN(10)   /* defines       */
0004.00 DCL       VAR(&NBR)  TYPE(*CHAR) LEN(2)    /* variables      */
0005.00 DCL       VAR(&LIB)  TYPE(*CHAR) LEN(10)   /* in the program */
0006.00
0007.00 RTVJOBA   USER(&USER)                      /* retrieves the userid */
0008.00
0009.00 CHGVAR    VAR(&NBR)  VALUE(%SST(&USER 6 2))   /* changes pgm */
0010.00 CHGVAR    VAR(&LIB)  VALUE('YOURLIB' *CAT &NBR) /* variables */
0011.00
0012.00 ADDLIBLE  LIB(&LIB)     /* adds a library to the library list */
0013.00 MONMSG     MSGID(CPF0000 CPF9999)    /* monitors for messages */
0014.00
0015.00 CHGCURLIB CURLIB(&LIB)               /* sets the current library */
0016.00 CHGJOB    OUTQ(&LIB/MYQ) /* defines the default output queue */
0017.00 STRPDM                                        /* starts PDM */
0018.00           RETURN
0019.00           ENDPGM
          ************ End of data **********************************
```

The program then issues the ADDLIBLE command, using the program variable &LIB to designate YOURLIB99. Next, the program checks for two possible messages—using the MONMSG command—and allows processing to continue if either of these messages is encountered. On line 15, the program changes the current library to YOURLIB99, again using the variable &LIB to designate YOURLIB99. Finally, the program issues the change job command that sets MYQ to the default output queue and then starts PDM.

Several different CL commands are used in this program. A short description of each CL command and how it functions within the program follows. (For more detailed information, use the on-line help facility or consult the *Control Language Reference* manual.)

- **DCL**. The declare command defines program variables. All CL program variables must begin with &. The type of data (char, numeric, and so on) and its length are then defined by the TYPE and LEN keywords. In the program, a series of variables are defined that will hold the library name (&LIB), userid (&USER), and the unique two-digit number associated with each userid, for example, 99 from userid INTRO99 (&NBR).

- **RTVJOBA**. The retrieve job attributes command gets information from the system regarding the user and certain system variables, for example, the userid that submitted the job, the date the job was submitted, and the current library of the user who submitted the job for execution. In Figure 3.10, on line 7, the userid of the person who submitted the job is retrieved and placed in the variable &USER. Later in the program, the value in the variable &USER is used to determine which library should be defined as the current library and added to the library list. For example, if the value of &USER is INTRO99, YOURLIB99 should be the current library, INTRO77 then YOURLIB77, and so on.

- **CGHVAR**. The change variable command changes the value of a program variable. The VAR keyword is used to define the variable to be changed. The VALUE keyword is used to define the new value of the variable. Within the value keyword, several functions—for both numeric and string variables—are available to manipulate the variable's value:

    %SST. The substring function allows the programmer to identify or pick out certain characters within a character string. In the first CHGVAR command, on line 9, the substring function %SST(&USER 6 2) identifies the character string that will be used. In this case, it is the value contained in the variable &USER. In keeping with our example, the value of &USER would be the characters returned by the system from the RTVJOBA command, that is,

INTRO99. The numbers following &USER specify which character to position at and how many characters to pick. In this case, the 6 and 2 tell the substring function to position itself before the sixth character and then pick the next two characters. Or in other words, pick the sixth and seventh characters of the character string. Because the substring function is within the CHGVAR command keyword VALUE, the characters specified by the substring function are the new value for the variable identified in the VAR keyword. In the program, it means that variable &NBR will be set to the sixth and seventh characters of the userid. For userid INTRO99, the value of &NBR would be changed to 99.

The second CHGVAR command, on line 10, uses a different function within the VALUE keyword:

*CAT. The concatenation function attaches one character string to another. The syntax is:

```
first character string, keyword *CAT, and
second character string
```

On line 10 in the program, the first character string is the constant text YOURLIB. The second character string is the value contained in the variable &NBR. The result of the concatenation is a single character string. In the program, for userid INTRO99, the variable &NBR would contain the character string 99, and the result of the concatenation would be YOURLIB99. Because the concatenation function is used in the CHGVAR command, the result of the concatenation is assigned to the variable &LIB.

Through the use of the concatenation and substring functions, the program is able to isolate the unique number contained in the userid, identify the library that will be defined as the current library, and add that library to the library list. Because of this feature, the program is much more useful. It can be used by any userid that follows the INTROXX format.

At this point in the program, the library to work with has been identified. Remember that this library also contains the output queue to which all spool files will be sent.

- **ADDLIBLE**. The add library list entry command does exactly that—it adds the library specified in the command to the user's library list. As mentioned earlier, a library list is a list of all libraries that will be searched when the user requests an object and does not specify a library. The library list also defines the order of the library search. The system defines a default library list when the userid is first created.

On line 12 of the program, the ADDLIBLE command adds a library to the library list of the user who submitted the program for execution. The library name to add is contained in the variable &LIB. &LIB will always contain the character string YOURLIB, concatenated to the unique two-digit number of the userid that submitted the job. &LIB's value was set in the previous CHGVAR command on line 10.

- **MONMSG**. The monitor messages command specifies actions to take based on specific messages returned by the system. Essentially the MONMSG command is telling the system that the programmer has foreseen the occurrence of this message and will handle the situation within the program. The command's syntax is:

```
MONMSG MSGID(message# message#...) EXEC(CL command)
```

The MSGID keyword allows the programmer to identify the messages to be checked, and the CL command within the EXEC keyword identifies the corrective action to take. In the EXEC clause, the programmer could send control to another section of the program (for example, GOTO program label) or start another program (for example, CALL xyz program). The subroutine or the called program would then perform some function that would, the programmer hopes, rectify the situation that caused the error message.

MONMSG also helps with another aspect of messages. Many messages require an answer. The system will not allow the program to continue executing until a message reply is given. The MONMSG command can be used to tell the system to ignore the message and allow the program to continue processing. (Ignore the message is a valid reply to a system message.) To do this, the programmer can omit the EXEC keyword. In many situations, taking no action and continuing processing is a valid course of action. When a programmer handles a message in this manner, it usually means that the situation causing the error message will not affect any future processing within the program.

For instance, one possible message that could be returned from executing the ADDLIBLE command on line 12 is `Library specified already contained in library list`. This message, when returned to the program, would suspend program execution until a reply was given. This situation (that the library is already in the library list) will not affect any future processing and, therefore, does not require any action. By specifying no EXEC parameter, the reply to the system is ignore the message and continue processing. This is the purpose of the MONMSG command on line 12.

- **CHGCURLIB**. The change current library command changes the current library to the value specified in the CURLIB keyword. The current library is used as a default by the system for object creation; that is, if no library is specified, the system assumes the user wants to create the object in the current library. On Create screens, *CURLIB is automatically filled in at the library prompt when the screen is initially displayed. If the user does not type over *CURLIB, the library defined as the current library will be used.

  In the program, line 15 sets the current library to the library name contained in variable &LIB. In the case of userid INTRO99, the current library would be defined as YOURLIB99. Since YOURLIBXX is where the user will be storing most objects, setting the *CURLIB to YOURLIBXX will save the user from having to specify YOURLIBXX when creating objects.

  Further, the current library is the first user library searched whenever an object is specified without a library. Again, since YOURLIBXX will contain most of the user's objects, the search will be performed faster since YOURLIBXX will be the first user library searched.

- **CHGJOB**. The change job command allows users to change a variety of variables regarding their programming environment. In the program on line 16, the output queue—MYQ, which resides in YOURLIB99—is defined as the destination for all spooled output. Sending output to this queue will cut down on the amount of hardcopy generated. The user will have to go into the output queue and specifically identify output to be printed. This is as opposed to the system default of having all output automatically printed.

- **STRPDM**. The start PDM command will bring up the main PDM screen each time the program executes. Since this command is in the initialization program, the PDM screen will automatically be displayed each time the programming environment is initialized.

Testing the Initial Program

After the program has been entered, saved, and compiled (as covered in Chapter 2), it's ready to be tested. To test the program, first sign off the system. Sign on with the newly created program's name at the Program/procedure prompt and **YOURLIBXX** at the Current library prompt on the initial Sign On screen (Figure 3.11). This tells the system to execute the program INITPGM in YOURLIBXX. Press ENTER, and the PDM menu should appear. Display the library list by typing **DSPLIBL** at the command line and pressing ENTER. The result should look similar to Figure 3.12. Note that the new library is now in the Library list and that YOURLIBXX is listed a second time with Type equal to CUR; this means it is defined as the current library.

FIGURE 3.11

```
                              Sign On

                                    System  . . . . . . :
                                    Subsystem . . . . . : QINTER
                                    Display . . . . . . :

             User . . . . . . . . . .      INTROXX
             Password . . . . . . . .
             Program/procedure  . . . .    INITPGM
             Menu . . . . . . . . . . .
             Current library  . . . . .    YOURLIBXX




                                    (C) COPYRIGHT IBM CORP. 1980, 1991.
```

FIGURE 3.12

```
                          Display Library List
                                                              System:

Type options, press Enter.
  5=Display objects in library
Opt Library      Type    Text
    QSYS         SYS     System Library
    QSYS2        SYS     System Library for CPI's
    QUSRSYS      SYS     *IN USE
    QHLPSYS      SYS
    YOURLIBXX    CUR
    YOURLIBXX    USR




                                                              Bottom
F3=Exit  F12=Cancel  F17=Top  F18=Bottom
(C) COPYRIGHT IBM CORP. 1980, 1991.
```

Summary

CL commands allow users to create and manipulate system resources (like output queues) and programming objects (like libraries). They also provide great control over the systems operations and allow users to customize and optimize their system environment.

Though there are many CL commands, users can find particular ones by executing the GO MAJOR command and choosing options on the resulting menus and screens. Once a command is known, on-line help and the prompt facility will guide users through the process of formatting and executing the command.

CL commands can also be grouped into programs. CL programs can be written to perform system utility functions. As the chapter example showed, by using the special CL programming commands, a generic systemwide initialization utility was created. Rather than requiring users to type in a series of commands each time they signed on the systems, this utility program could be run by each user to quickly initialize his or her programming environment.

CL programs can also manage the execution of other programs. By using program variables, retrieving system information, and monitoring messages, CL programs can control the logical execution of application programs based on conditions external to the individual programs. Used this way, CL becomes a job control language.

LAB EXERCISES

Just as the lab exercise in Chapter 2 created more source physical file members for use in later chapters, so will this exercise. However, this chapter's two new members will be created differently. The first member will be created by CL commands issued directly from the command line. The second member will be created through a CL program. This CL program will also be created in the second exercise.

EXERCISE 1 Create a new member named BATCART with a type of LF within INVSRC and YOURLIBXX as follows:

1. Sign on to the AS/400 specifying INITPGM as the program to initially run. (This assumes INITPGM and MYQ have already been created. If not, create them at this time and run INITPGM.)

2. Type **STRSEU** at any command line and press **F4**.

3. At the appropriate prompts, fill in:

   file name as INVSRC

   library name as YOURLIBXX

   member name as BATCART

   member type as LF

4. Press ENTER.

5. At the SEU Edit screen, press **F3** to exit.

6. At the SEU Exit screen, type **Y** at the Create/change member prompt.

7. Press ENTER, and member BATCART will be created.

EXERCISE 2 This exercise will create a new CL program, CRTMBR. The program will create members in YOURLIBXX and INVSRC, with the user having to specify only the new member's name and type.

1. Perform steps 2 through 4 from the preceding exercise, this time creating a member, CRTMBR, under YOURLIBXX and INVSRC. Define its type as CLP.

2. At the SEU Edit screen, enter the following source code into CRTMBR:

```
         ...+... 1 ...+... 2 ...+... 3 ...+... 4 ...+... 5 ...+... 6 ...+...
         **************** Beginning of data ************************
0001.00 CRTMBR: PGM        PARM(&MEM &MTYP)
0002.00
0003.00 /***********************************************************/
0004.00 /* LINE 1 IDENTIFIES THE VARIABLES FOR WHICH VALUES WILL BE */
0005.00 /* PASSED TO THE PROGRAM FROM THE USER.                    */
0006.00 /***********************************************************/
0007.00
0008.00 DCL     VAR(&MEM)   TYPE(*CHAR)  LEN(8)
0009.00 DCL     VAR(&MTYP)  TYPE(*CHAR)  LEN(3)
0010.00
0011.00 /***********************************************************/
0012.00 /* LINES 8 AND 9 DEFINE THE VARIABLES THAT WILL BE USED IN  */
0013.00 /* THE PROGRAM.                                            */
0014.00 /***********************************************************/
0015.00
0016.00 STRSEU   SRCFILE(YOURLIBXX/INVSRC) SRCMBR(&MEM) TYPE(&MTYP)
0017.00          ENDPGM
         **************** End of data *******************************
```

3. Follow steps 5 through 7 in exercise 1 to save CRTMBR, the new CLP member.

4. To create the new program, the member needs to be compiled. Instead of using PDM to compile, type **CRTCLPGM** (Create CL Program) at any command line and press F4.

5. At the prompt screen, specify the program name to be created as CRTMBR in library YOURLIBXX. Specify the source member to be compiled as CRTMBR in source file INVSRC in library YOURLIBXX.

6. Press ENTER. The member will be submitted for compiling. A message should be displayed that the program CRTMBR was created in YOURLIBXX.

7. Work with objects within library YOURLIBXX and verify that the program object CRTMBR exists in the library.

EXERCISE 3 After the program from exercise 2 has compiled successfully, follow the steps in this exercise to create a second member under YOURLIBXX and INVSRC.

1. From any command line, type **CALL CRTMBR ('ITBATCAR' 'LF')** to execute the CL program created in exercise 2.

2. Follow steps 5 through 7 of exercise 1 to exit and save the new logical file member, ITBATCAR.

REVIEW QUESTIONS

1. What are the three possible components of a CL command?

2. What functions do the following three-character CL verbs represent?

   WRK

   STR

   DSP

   DLT

   CPY

3. What is the purpose of an initialization program?

4. What object controls the search order the system will use to locate a program object?

5. Explain the purpose of a current library.

6. Explain the substring and concatenation functions.

7. Explain the functions of the following CL commands:

   CRTOUTQ

   MONMSG

   ADDLIBLE

   CPYF

   RTVJOBA

   CRTCLPGM

DISCUSSION QUESTIONS

1. What are some of the different types of operating system functions required in a multiuser computing environment? What are the CL commands that enable AS/400 users to perform these functions?

2. Discuss the purpose of spooling and output queues and how they contribute to saving resources and improving system performance.

3. Give several examples of special functions required of a programming language and how CL satisfies those requirements.

4. Discuss the advantages and disadvantages of using PDM versus CL commands to execute system functions.

AS/400 Object Security and Authorization

4

The purpose of this chapter is to introduce the concepts behind system security and the necessity of controls. How the AS/400 provides both data and functional control will be covered. The student will also be introduced to a series of new objects that the AS/400 uses to provide these controls.

After finishing this chapter, you will understand:

- The purpose of profiles
- Different authorities that can be defined for objects and profiles
- Levels of functional and data control and how the AS/400 provides them
- AS/400 system control levels

You also will be able to:

- Manipulate object authority
- Change your user profile
- Create group profiles

What Are Controls?

In any system, whether manual or computer, controls are essential. Checks and balances are built into all procedures to ensure accuracy, integrity, and confidentiality. You are exposed to all sorts of different controls every day of your life. For instance, when buying a ticket to a concert, you believe that the stadium has a control procedure that ensures that the little piece of paper given in exchange for your hard-earned dollars guarantees access to the seat specified. The procedure has worked at all the other concerts you have been to, and you have confidence that it will still be working the next time you purchase a ticket. The stadium owners have created and implemented a very simple access control procedure: Possession of any ticket allows a person to enter the stadium; each ticket further allows the owner access to a specific seat.

An example of another noncomputer control, and a much more stringent control, is the law that requires all publicly owned companies to submit themselves to independent financial audits. For stock to be sold and traded, it is essential that all financial data be accurate and truthful. Having an uninvolved third party come in and audit a company's finances is a control procedure that the government requires to ensure that all the information issued by the company has been verified as accurate. No company can continue to be listed on the stock exchange without submitting the correct forms that confirm that this audit has been done. This is an example of a control that ensures data accuracy and integrity.

Computer Controls

For a computer system to be used, customers must have confidence that controls are in place that ensure authorized access to data and system functions. What would happen to concert attendance if purchasing a ticket did not ensure getting into the stadium? Similarly, if customers cannot count on accurate information, they will not use a computer system. Controls that ensure systemwide data integrity must be in place. If only authorized personnel have access to the data and the functions that can change that data, the chance of errors is greatly decreased. In terms of functions, there are several key times when control should be exercised:

1. When the information is entered into the system. People make mistakes, perhaps press the wrong keys, there are transmission errors, and so on. To catch these types of mistakes, some control is needed to ensure that only authorized people are allowed to enter the data into the system. Also some procedure to check the validity of the data is required.

2. When data is updated. The processing that takes place must be accurate and authorized. Any data manipulation should be done

by authorized personnel, and the updated data should have integrity. For example, individual amount fields when summed should match the total amount field.

3. When data is deleted. Only authorized personnel should be allowed to remove data from the system. If there are mistakes, backup and recovery procedures should be in place to re-create the missing data.

Another key goal of controls is to ensure that data is confidential. This implies several types of control:

- Access control to data as a whole
- Being able to control access to portions of the data
- Control over the functions that can be performed once access is granted

In most computer systems, these access controls are supplied through the operating system, the database management system, and specialized security programs. The AS/400 is no exception. It supplies these controls through its combined database management and operating systems, its journaling functions, and a set of specialized security or authorization utilities.

Control Levels

Access controls specify which data and functions can or cannot be used. However, access to data or a function is not a simple yes or no condition. Controls need to be exercised at many different levels for both data and functions. Someone may have access to a function but can use it on only a small subsection of data. Or someone may have access to an entire file but can perform only a limited set of functions (such as move, copy, and rename but not delete) against that file. The complexity of the control system will depend on how well the data organization matches the business functions and the degree of security required.

Data Levels

Traditionally, data has been controlled at three levels: file, record, and field.

In any large system's application, users need different files or portions of the database to do their jobs. For instance, a manufacturing employee may need to look at inventory location information so that he or she can get raw materials from the stockroom to the manufacturing line. The shipping manager also needs to see the inventory locations in order to ship parts to customers. In addition, before shipping any parts, the customer's payment history must be checked. Therefore, the shipping manager also needs access to the accounts receivable file. This business requires file level control that allows both employees access to the inventory information but only the shipping manager access to the payment data.

Record level security provides a second, finer level of access control. In many instances, people require access to files but do not need everything in the file. For instance, the manufacturing employee works on the razor blade manufacturing line. The inventory location file contains information about stockrooms across the manufacturing site that contain tool kits, batteries, precious metals, hazardous materials, and so on. The razor blade manufacturing line employee has no business need to access any of that information. As a matter of fact, it may lead to temptation if the manufacturing employee knows where the silver and gold are stored. Restricting access to only those inventory parts that he or she uses would solve this problem. Record level control accomplishes this.

Field level control provides further data control within the record. If access to a particular record is granted, control can still be maintained over which fields can be accessed. For instance, our shipping manager also needs to access the employee file. There is record level control such that the shipping manager can access only his or her employee's records. However, even within each employee's file there is medical information that only the company's medical department should see. In this case, field level control is necessary.

AS/400 File Level Security and Functional Control

These three levels of data security (file, record, and field) are all handled by the AS/400. Since files are stored as objects on the AS/400, file level access is controlled by restricting or granting the user access to an object function—view, copy, and so on. As soon as users are granted any object function, they have file level access. Access to object level functions on the AS/400 is grouped into two types of authority, object control and content control. (The AS/400 help screens refer to it as data control.)

Users who are granted object control can manipulate the object as a whole: They can copy it, rename it, and move it. Object control, however, does not provide the capability to go inside the object and change its contents. Content control allows the contents of an object to be changed.

Object and content control can be granted by someone with *object authority*. Object authority is the ability to provide access to object functions—functions that manipulate the object as a whole or modify an object's contents—and change an object's owner. Two users who always have object authority are the owner of the object and the system security officer.

The owner of the object is the user who creates it or someone to whom ownership has been transferred. In the case of an object with an attribute of PFDTA, the person who creates the data object has object authority; the creator automatically gets all object and content control also.

The security officer is someone in the organization who is responsible for all system security. On the AS/400, a special signon id (QSECOFR) is given to that person. QSECOFR has object authority for all objects on the system. (In fact, QSECOFR has access and control over just about everything in the system.)

As an example, say a programmer, Nelson Erd, had created the inventory location data file used by the shipping manager and the manufacturing employee mentioned earlier. As the object creator, Erd was automatically given object authority (and content and object control). He granted George Eek, a systems operator, object control. Part of G. Eek's job is to make sure all data is backed up in case of a disaster. With the object control granted, he can do that. However, he cannot change the contents of the file.

Meanwhile, Joe User needs content control because he receives new parts into the stockroom and must update the amounts in the file. Gina Od, who is security officer for the organization, grants Joe User content control. As security officer, Od also has object authority. When N. Erd gets a new job in another division of the company, it will be G. Od's job to transfer ownership to another user. Transferring object ownership is another function that can be executed by users with object authority.

Working with Object Authorities

The CL command that allows the owner or the QSECOFR to grant object authority, object control, or content control to another user is the GRTOBJAUT (grant object authority) command. The QSECOFR is allowed to use this command for all objects—spool files, program objects, system objects, and so on. The owner is allowed to execute this command for his or her objects only.

Within the GRTOBJAUT command, the owner (or the QSECOFR) can control the functions the new user will be able to perform on the object by specifying up to eight of the following values in the AUT parameter.

For object control functions, the following values can be specified:

- **OBJOPR** (object operational authority). Allows content control authorities to be specified. It also allows viewing of the object's description.
- **OBJMGT** (object management authority). Allows a user to move and rename the object.
- **OBJEXIST** (object existence authority). Allows a user to delete, save, and transfer ownership of an object.

For content control functions (in conjunction with OBJOPR authority), the following can be specified:

- **READ**. Enables the user to look at members in a source file.
- **ADD**. Allows the user to insert new information.
- **UPDATE**. Lets the user modify existing information.
- **DELETE**. Allows the user to erase information.

There are also some other values that provide a combination of content control and object control functions:

- ***EXCLUDE**. Denies all access to the object—it denies file level access.
- ***USE**. Gives OBJOPR control and read-only content control.
- ***CHANGE**. Gives OBJOPR control and all content control functions.
- ***ALL**. Gives object MGT, OPR, and EXIST control and all content control functions.

The syntax for the GRTOBJAUT command is as follows:

```
GRTOBJAUT OBJ(libname objname) OBJTYPE(objtype)
USER(userid) AUT(up to eight of the preceding
values).
```

Executing this command provides the access specified in the AUT parameter to the object specified in the OBJ and OBJTYPE parameters for the signon id specified in the USER parameter. What actually occurs is that the signon id and authority specified in the GRTOBJAUT command are added to the *authorization list* for that object. When an object is created, an authorization list is created for that object. The authorization list identifies the object owner and who has access to the object. Only the owner of the object or the QSECOFR can grant authority or manipulate authorization lists.

Other ways to change the authorization list are:

- Type **GRTOBJAUT**.
- Press **ENTER**.
- Specify the GRTOBJAUT parameter values, as prompted on the screen.

  or

- Choose AS/400 Main Menu option 7, Define or change the system (Figure 4.1).
- From the Define or Change the System screen (Figure 4.2), choose option 3, Security.
- From the Security screen (Figure 4.3), choose option 1, Work with object authority.

FIGURE 4.1

```
MAIN                    AS/400 Main Menu
                                                        System:
Select one of the following:

       1.  User tasks
       2.  Office tasks
       3.  General system tasks
       4.  Files, libraries, and folders
       5.  Programming
       6.  Communications
       7.  Define or change the system
       8.  Problem handling
       9.  Display a menu
      10.  Information Assistant options
      11.  PC Support tasks

      90.  Sign off

Selection or command
===>_____
F3=Exit  F4=Prompt  F9=Retrieve  F12=Cancel  F13=User support
F23=Set initial menu
```

FIGURE 4.2

```
DEFINE            Define or Change the System
                                                        System:
Select one of the following:

       1.  Configuration
       2.  Work with licensed programs
       3.  Security
       4.  Work with support contact information
       5.  System resources
       6.  Program temporary fix
       7.  IBM product information
       8.  Work with system values




Selection or command
===>_____
_____
F3=Exit  F4=Prompt  F9=Retrieve  F12=Cancel  F13=User support
F16=AS/400 Main menu
```

- Type the object name, library, and type at the appropriate prompts on the Work with Objects (WRKOBJ) screen (Figure 4.4).

- Press ENTER.

FIGURE 4.3

```
SECURITY                    Security
                                                        System:
Select one of the following:

        1.  Work with object authority
        2.  Work with authorization lists
        3.  Office security
        4.  Change your password
        5.  Change your user profile
        6.  Work with user profiles
        7.  Work with system values

       70.  Related commands



Selection or command
===>_____
   _____

F3=Exit  F4=Prompt  F9=Retrieve  F12=Cancel  F13=User support
F16=AS/400 Main menu
```

FIGURE 4.4

```
                    Work with Objects (WRKOBJ)

Type choices, press Enter.

Object . . . . . . . . . . .             Name, generic*, *ALL
  Library . . . . . . . . .    *LIBL    Name, *LIBL, *CURLIB...
Object type . . . . . . . .    *ALL     *ALL, *ALRTBL, *AUTL...









                                                        Bottom
F3=Exit F4=Prompt F5=Refresh F12=Cancel F13=How to use this display
F24=More keys
```

FIGURE 4.5

```
                      Work with Objects
Type options, press Enter.
  2=Edit authority      3=Copy 4=Delete 5=Display authority 7=Rename
  8=Display description  13=Change description

Opt   Object     Type    Library   Attribute   Text
      YOURLIBXX   *LIB    QSYS      PROD        student library




                                                        Bottom
Parameters for options 5, 7, 8 and 13 or command
===>
F3=Exit  F4=Prompt  F5=Refresh  F9=Retrieve  F11=Display names and types
F12=Cancel  F16=Repeat position to  F17=Position to
```

- On the Work with Objects screen (Figure 4.5), type **2** (Edit authority) next to the object's name under the Opt header.

- Press ENTER.

- On the Edit Object Authority screen (Figure 4.6), add a new user by pressing F6 or change a user's authority by typing over the current authority.

  or

- Type **EDTOBJAUT**.

- Press ENTER.

- Specify the object name, library, and type (Figure 4.7).

- Press ENTER.

- Add a new user by pressing F6 or change a user's authority by typing over the current authority (see Figure 4.6).

FIGURE 4.6

```
                    Edit Object Authority

Object . . . . . . :   YOURLIBXX   Object type . . . . :   *LIB
   Library. . . . :     QSYS      Owner. . . . . . . . :  BIGSHOT

Type changes to current authorities, press Enter.

   Object secured by authorization list. . . . . . . .    *NONE

               Object
User          Authority
BIGSHOT       *ALL
*PUBLIC       *CHANGE



                                                          Bottom
F3=Exit F5=Refresh  F6=Add new users F10=Grant with reference object
F11=Display detail  F12=Cancel       F17=Top     F18=Bottom
(C) COPYRIGHT IBM CORP. 1980, 1991.
```

FIGURE 4.7

```
               Edit Object Authority (EDTOBJAUT)

Type choices, press Enter.

Object. . . . . . . . . .   YOURLIBXX   Name

   Library . . . . . . . .      *LIBL    Name, *LIBL, *CURLIB
Object type . . . . . . .      *lib      *ALRTBL, *AUTL, *CFGL...








                                                          Bottom
F3=Exit F4=Prompt F5=Refresh F12=Cancel F13=How to use this display
F24=More keys
```

The last two options let the user manipulate the authorization list through the EDTOBJAUT command. Instead of just adding names and authorities to the list, users and their authority can be changed or deleted.

Pressing F11 (display detail) at Figure 4.6 would result in Figure 4.8. Notice that each authority (Change, All) is broken down into its constituent security keywords (Opr, Mgt, Add, and so on). The user can blank out or add Xs for each keyword and create any combination. The system will label the new authority as "user defined."

FIGURE 4.8

```
                    Edit Object Authority

Object. . . . . . . :  YOURLIBXX    Object type . . . . :  *LIB
   Library . . . . . :  QSYS         Owner . . . . . . . :  BIGSHOT

Type changes to current authorities, press Enter.

   Object secured by authorization list . . . . . . .      *NONE


             Object    ____Object____  _____Data_____
User       Authority  Opr  Mgt Exist  Read  Add  Update  Delete
BIGSHOT    *ALL         X    X    X     X     X     X       X
*PUBLIC    *CHANGE      X    _    _     X     X     X       X




                                                       Bottom
F3=Exit F5=Refresh F6=Add new users F10=Grant with reference object
F11=Nondisplay detail    F12=Cancel    F17=Top    F18=Bottom
```

So in our example regarding the shipping manager and the manufacturing line employee, QSECOFR (Gina Od) would execute the GRTOBJAUT command for the inventory location object and specify OBJOPR authority for both users. For the accounts receivable object, she would specify OBJOPR for the shipping manager and *EXCLUDE for the manufacturing employee. The GRTOBJAUT program would check to make sure that QSECOFR has the authority to update the authorization lists for the inventory location and accounts receivable objects. QSECOFR does, so the authorization lists would be updated. The next time the shipping manager tries to access either of these objects (through a menu or a CL command), the authorization list will be checked. If the shipping manager tries to update the object, the request will be rejected. If the manager's actions are within the granted authority—such as reading the data—access will be allowed. The same holds for the manufacturing employee. Any access to the accounts receivable object will be denied, but trying to view the inventory location object will be allowed.

AS/400 Record and Field Level Security

Record and field level control are handled through the AS/400 database management system. There are two types of data objects on the AS/400: *physical files* and *logical files*. Both are created by compiling source physical file members with a type of PF or LF.

Physical files contain data, an access path (a key) to that data, and a definition of the file and field characteristics. Physical files are what most people would simply call keyed files. Logical files offer an alternative view of physical files. Logical files identify physical file fields that will be contained in the logical file. Logical files can also define different keys for the physical file data or set conditions for selecting only certain records from the physical file. However, logical files contain no data. Their access path identifies fields or records from one or more physical files but contain none of the data. Logical files create the illusion of a new physical file containing all or part of many other physical files.

As an example, assume there is a physical file with the following layout:

Employee Name	Employee Address	Date of Birth	Salary	Phone Num	SS Num	Dept Num

This employee file, because it is a physical file, contains all the employees' data and some definition regarding how the file can be accessed—the key is social security number. Any record within this file can be accessed if the social security number is known.

File level security can be maintained by granting object and data authority only to people within the company who need to access this information. For instance, personnel employees would need access to all the data in this file to perform their jobs. Each manager in this company also needs access to this file. If managers needed to contact an employee or if they are planning on giving a raise, they would need to access this file to get an employee's current phone number or salary. However, every manager should not have access to all employees' phone numbers and current salaries. They should have access only to their employees' records. Also, there is no reason for a manager to know the age of an employee, so they should not have access to the date of birth field.

Object and content control cannot help us with this finer level of data control. This is where a logical file can be used. We can create a logical file with a layout that does not include the date of birth field as follows:

Employee Name	Employee Address	Salary	Phone Num	SS Num	Dept Num

To restrict access to only certain records, a selection condition can also be defined for the logical file. Through several specialized DDS (Data Description Specification) commands, the condition will restrict access to only those records that fulfill the condition. For the preceding problem, the selection would be for records whose department number is equal to a certain value. For instance, for Manny Ager, the manager of department 722, a logical file with the preceding layout would be created. In the access path definition, the selection condition would be for only those records that have 722 as their department number. This new logical file does not contain any data. The records for department 722 have not been copied or stored in this logical file. The logical file simply contains the new layout and access path. In this case, our access path is only to records with the value 722 in the department number.

In regard to object control, logical files are treated just like any other object on the AS/400. The creator of the object or the QSECOFR can grant Manny Ager access to the logical file through the GRT-OBJAUT command. Manny could then access the data in the physical file but only the data as defined in the access path of the logical file—his employees' information.

Another characteristic of the relationship between logical files and physical files is the synchronization of updating. Any changes to a physical file will be reflected in all related logical files. If Manny Ager were to update the department number for one of his employees because the employee is transferring out of department 722, he would actually be updating the physical file because that is where the data is stored. However, the change would also be reflected in the logical file. The AS/400 will do this automatically when the physical file is updated. So Manny's data is kept up to date, and we have satisfied the business's need for record and field control through logical files and object authority. (For more information on physical and logical files, see Chapter 5.)

System Function Control

Function level control on the AS/400 begins at the highest level, *system level control*. System level control means prohibiting or allowing access to an entire system. Those of you who have worked mainly on PCs probably have not had much experience with signon procedures. Any large system with multiple users has some auditing procedure to check whether a person is allowed onto the system. When a user attempts to sign on to the system, this procedure validates the user as authorized. Most systems also monitor and track all unauthorized access attempts. The AS/400 is no exception. When the system is initialized, the system access control must be defined as one of the following:

1. **Level 10.** A user can type anything at the signon id prompt, and the system will grant the user access.

2. **Level 20.** Requires a signon id and a password be created and entered whenever access to the AS/400 is desired. Once access to the system is allowed, all functions and data on the AS/400 may be used.

3. **Level 30.** Requires a signon id and a password for system level access and provides further security by object—object authority, object control, and content control.

4.　　**Level 40**. Provides all security present at level 30 and adds security regarding access to Machine Interface (MI) objects: programs that make up the lowest level of software in the operating system and communicate directly with the computer hardware. At level 30, user-defined programs can issue MI commands and possibly access objects to which they are not authorized. Level 40 will prevent this.

To further clarify, let's extend the concert example from the beginning of the chapter. A signon is comparable to a ticket, and the seats in the stadium are the system objects. Running a level 10 concert would mean no tickets would be required to get into the stadium and anyone could access any seat. It would be a 1960s-style "free concert," where there is no control over who gets in and where they go. This sounds as if it could lead to problems, but some people would say it is a much freer and friendlier environment.

A level 20 concert would require a ticket to get into the show, but seating is open—anyone can sit anywhere. (A level 20 system requires a signon to get into the system, and once inside, the user can access all objects.)

A level 30 show requires a ticket for access to the stadium, and what is written on the ticket will determine what seats can be used. The ticket acts as an authorization list for the seats and provides general access to the stadium.

A level 40 concert would also have special authority for people to get backstage. Concerts (and systems) are very complicated and require a lot of behind-the-scenes work. For some shows, lighting, acoustic, and electrical work (hardware interfacing) may be needed. If so, only certain people should be allowed to get to those areas and perform the work required. A normal ticket allows a person to view the show. A backstage ticket allows the person to go behind the scenes and change the show.

Profiles

Every signon id has a whole series of system information associated with it—its password, the initial menu to be displayed, the initial program to be called, and so on (Figure 4.9). This signon-related data is called a *profile*.

The AS/400 also provides further functional control by controlling the system functions that a userid can perform. Each userid is assigned access to predefined groups of AS/400 system functions. These groupings fall along system function lines (for example, one group contains all the security functions) or according to a user's job type (for example, another group contains all the system functions a programmer would need to perform his or her job). The system function groups are assigned through a userid's *special authorities* parameter, and the job groups are assigned through the *user class* parameter. A series of special authorities and class types can be specified in the special authority and user class parameters.

FIGURE 4.9

```
                    Create User Profile (CRTUSRPRF)

 Type choices, press Enter.

 User profile . . . . . . . .   JOEUSER    Name
 User password  . . . . . .     RAITT      Name, *USRPRF, *NONE
 Set password to expired. . .   *YES       *NO, *YES
 Status . . . . . . . . . .     *ENABLED   *ENABLED, *DISABLED
 User class . . . . . . . .     *USER      *USER, *SYSOPR, *PGMR...
 Assistance level . . . . .     *SYSVAL    *SYSVAL, *BASIC, *INTERMED...
 Current library  . . . . .     *CRTDFT    Name, *CRTDFT
 Initial program to call  . .   *NONE      Name, *NONE
   Library  . . . . . . . .     _____    Name, *LIBL, *CURLIB
 Initial menu . . . . . . .     MAIN       Name, *SIGNOFF
   Library  . . . . . . . .     *LIBL      Name, *LIBL, *CURLIB
 Limit capabilities . . . . .   *NO        *NO, *PARTIAL, *YES
 Text 'description' . . . . .   *BLANK    _____

 _____                                                         Bottom
 F3=Exit F4=Prompt F5=Refresh F10=Additional parameters F12=Cancel
 F13=How to use this display  F24=More keys
 Parameter USRPRF required.
```

Special Authorities

As mentioned, groups of system functions can be specified in the Special authority parameter of the signon id's profile (Figure 4.10). The functional authority granted through these values is more closely in line with system functions than with user functions. Some examples are:

- ***JOBCTL**. Allows an id to hold, release, cancel, or clear all jobs.

- ***SPLCTL**. Grants access to all spooling functions.

- ***SECADM**. Allows access to all security functions.

- ***SAVSYS**. Lets a user save and restore all objects on the system.

Special authorities allow the userid to perform groups of functionally related CL commands. If system functions are to be assigned according to the user's job, the value *USRCLS needs to be entered in the Special authority parameter, and one of the following user *class types* must be specified in the user class parameter (Figure 4.11).

Class Types

One of the security officer's functions is to create signon ids for users and to define the associated profile parameters. As we mentioned earlier, a special signon id, QSECOFR, has this capability. The ability to perform security functions comes from the class type defined for the QSECOFR id. The QSECOFR id's class type is *SECOFR. Having a class of *SECOFR allows the id to perform all the special authorities previously mentioned and more. For instance, some CL commands covered by the *SECOFR special authority are CRTUSRPRF (create user profile) and CHGUSRPRF (change user profile). Userids with *SECOFR authority can issue these commands for any userid.

FIGURE 4.10

```
                    Change User Profile (CHGUSRPRF)

Type choices, press Enter.
                       Additional Parameters

Special authority . . . . . .    *ALLOBJ    *SAME, *USRCLS, *NONE...
                                 *JOBCTL
                                 *SAVSYS
                                 *SECADM
                                 *SERVICE
                                 *SPLCTL
Special environment . . . . .    *SYSVAL    *SAME, *SYSVAL, *NONE, *S36
Display sign-on information .    *SYSVAL    *SAME, *NO, *YES, *SYSVAL
Password expiration interval.    *SYSVAL    1-366, *SAME, *SYSVAL, *NOMAX
Limit device sessions . . . .    *SYSVAL    *SAME, *NO, *YES, *SYSVAL
Keyboard buffering  . . . . .    *SYSVAL    *SAME, *SYSVAL, *NO...
Maximum allowed storage . . .    *NOMAX     Kilobytes, *SAME, *NOMAX
Highest schedule priority . .    3          0-9, *SAME

                                                              More...
F3=Exit F4=Prompt F5=Refresh F12=Cancel F13=How to use this display
F24=More keys
```

FIGURE 4.11

```
                    Change User Profile (CHGUSRPRF)

Type choices, press Enter.

User profile . . . . . . . > BIGSHOT     Name
User password . . . . . .     *SAME      Name, *SAME, *NONE
Set password to expired .     *NO        *SAME, *NO, *YES
Status . . . . . . . . . .    *ENABLED   *SAME, *ENABLED, *DISABLED
User class . . . . . . . .     *SECOFR    *SAME, *USER, *SYSOPR...
Assistance level . . . . .    *SYSVAL    *SAME, *SYSVAL, *BASIC...
Current library  . . . . .    *CRTDFT    Name, *SAME, *CRTDFT
Initial program to call. .    INITPGM    Name, *SAME, *NONE
  Library. . . . . . . . .    QGPL       Name, *LIBL, *CURLIB
Initial menu . . . . . . .    MAIN       Name, *SAME, *SIGNOFF
  Library. . . . . . . . .    *LIBL      Name, *LIBL, *CURLIB
Limit capabilities . . . .    *NO        *SAME, *NO, *PARTIAL, *YES
Text 'description' . . . .    'Security Administrator'


                                                              More...
F3=Exit F4=Prompt F5=Refresh F12=Cancel F13=How to use this display
F24=More keys
```

This is as opposed to the CHGPRF (change profile) command. Everyone can use the CHGPRF command because everyone needs to be able to change his or her own profile. Prove this by using the CHG-PRF command to change the initial program parameter in your profile. Change the initial program parameter to INITPGM, the program created in Chapter 3. Changes to a profile are put into effect only after the session ends and the user signs on again. So, after changing the initial program parameter, sign off the system. When you sign back on, PDM should be immediately started. Check that the current library has been changed as specified in INITPGM. Do this by choosing the

`Work with libraries` option from the PDM menu and see what library name is filled in at the prompt. If the profile was updated correctly, it should be the library defined in INITPGM.

QSECOFR can perform the same functions and more on all profiles. This is accomplished through object control. Each profile is an object. All signon ids are given access to their profile object. QSECOFR, however, by having a class type of *SECOFR, can access *all* objects, including every user's profile on the system.

*SECADM (security administrator) is another class type. An id that has *SECADM as its class can access the systems security functions—create and change profiles, change authorization lists, change passwords, and so on. By creating other ids with a class of *SECADM, the security officer does not have to perform all security tasks. These *SECADM ids enable the QSECOFR to distribute some of the system security work.

*USER class provides no special authorities. An id defined with a class of *USER can access and edit objects for which it has ownership.

*PGMR and *SYSOPR provide access to system functions regarding saving objects and job control. For instance, these classes allow a user to compile and run programs or cancel programs that are running. In general, the AS/400 developers created these class types to make it easier to grant authority to the system functions that are most likely to be used by programmers and system operators.

If the USER classes had not been created, the alternative would be adding each new programmer's and system operator's userid to each system program's authorization list. To issue the GRTOBJAUT or CHGUSRPRF commands for all the system functions needed would be very time consuming. However, knowledge of CL programming could simplify the procedure. A CL program could be created that contained all the security commands needed. The security officers could be granted authority to this special program, and when a new programmer or system operator id was created, the CL program would be run by the security administrator to authorize the user to the needed functions.

Through CL programs, the same control could be achieved that class type provides. CL programs could be created that grant authority to specific system functions. The functions allowed could match the needs of jobs that are unique to the work environment. In other words, users are not limited to just the class types that are predefined on the system. CL programs can be created to tailor a userid's profile to unique business needs.

The AS/400 also provides another way to tailor ids—*group* profiles.

Group Profiles

A group profile is created just like a user profile. It is granted access to certain objects and functions and then linked with user profiles. A new user profile can be associated with a group profile through the group profile parameter on either the `Create User Profile` or

Change User Profile screen. If the CL command CRTUSRPRF or CHGUSRPRF is used, the group profile name is specified in the parameter GRPPRF. With either command, the user profile is tied to the group profile. If the user tries to access an object where his or her signon id is not specified on the object's authorization list but the group id is, the user gets the authority granted to the group.

The group profile is an easy way to provide access to sets of data and program objects that are needed for a specific business function or job. Through the create user profile function, users can easily create the group profile and assign it to individual signon ids.

Controlling User-Defined Functions

User programs are usually created to ensure the integrity of the data on the system. For instance, whenever our shipping manager ships a part, the following steps need to be performed:

- Decrease the inventory quantity in the inventory file.
- Write a shipping record to the shipping file.
- Update the customer order status as SHIPPED in the customer order file.

The SEU or DFU system utilities could be used to manipulate the different files. With proper authority, this method would be possible but not very fast or safe. The shipping manager will, once in a while, type in the wrong information (make a subtraction error when entering the new inventory quantity or transpose numbers when filling in the date of shipment). Because of the need for data integrity and efficiency, a specialized program should be written to perform this function. The shipping manager will only have to invoke this function and enter the customer order number being shipped. This solution does not eliminate all chances of human error (the customer order number could still be wrong); however, it does cut down on the number of opportunities for entering incorrect information.

There is still a security problem with creating this new function. An unscrupulous employee could invoke the program, type in a customer's order number, and keep the goods. Some access control to this program is needed. Object security, which we covered earlier, can provide control over user-created functions such as the shipping program.

User programs are objects on the AS/400. Access can be granted or restricted to these functions through the object's authorization list. In this way, only select people are allowed to perform these functions. (This assumes that the programs are created in line with people's jobs.)

With logical files, the data could be even further secured by granting each shipping clerk access to only a subsection of the inventory file.

The manager could have several shipping clerks performing the shipping function and cut down on the chance of abuse by controlling which part's information each clerk could update with the program.

Summary

Controls are required for all systems whether they are manual or computer systems. These controls can range from the checks and balances defined in the United States Constitution for the different government branches to automatic spell checkers included in word processing applications.

The AS/400 provides extensive functional and data level control capabilities. Through its object-oriented approach, it is able to provide access control to multiple levels of data, system functions, and user applications. Though most systems provide this, the AS/400's object-oriented architecture—treating all data and programs as objects—allows control through the same command set and utilities. Normally, there are separate commands, functions, and systems for data versus program control. For instance, most systems require a separate database management system if record or field level control is needed.

The AS/400 architecture also provides several methods to easily grant systems functions. Through the use of a profile, a userid can be granted access to groups of functions. These can be groups that the AS/400 has predefined (user classes and special authorities), or they can be user defined (group profiles).

There is also systemwide access control provided through control levels. These control levels define the level of object control that will be in force throughout the system. As with all controls, they are effective only if used. If the correct control level is not defined, no object or data control will be active.

As with most commands and functions, the security and authorization functions are supported with prompts, screens, and on-line help to facilitate their use and understanding. All security functions can be accessed through either the associated CL commands or the extensive menu system.

LAB EXERCISE

In this exercise, you will change the authorization list for the source physical file you created earlier, INVSRC in YOURLIBXX.

1. Grant authority to another user by typing the following at any command line and pressing ENTER. (Substitute someone else's userid for INTROXX in the USER keyword.)

    ```
    GRTOBJAUT OBJ(YOURLIBXX/INVSRC) OBJTYPE(*FILE)
    USER(INTROXX) AUT(*USE)
    ```

2. Type EDTOBJAUT at the command line and press F4.

3.   At the `Edit Object Authority (EDTOBJAUT)` screen, enter **YOURLIBXX**, **INVSRC**, and ***FILE** at the appropriate prompts.

4.   At the `Edit Object Authority` screen, notice that the userid specified in the GRTOBJAUT command is in the authorization list.

5.   Press F11 for more detail on each userid's authority. For instance, notice that the *USE authority just granted comprises OBJOPR and READ authority.

6.   Delete the userid (just entered through the GRTOBJAUT command) by blanking it out with the spacebar.

7.   Change the *PUBLIC authority by blanking out all the Xs under the various authority headings and press ENTER.

8.   Notice that by not granting OBJOPR, OBJMGT, and OBJEXIST you have defined the special authority of *EXCLUDE. Other users cannot access your INVSRC file.

REVIEW QUESTIONS

1.   What is the purpose of data processing controls?

2.   Who has object authority?

3.   What is an authorization list?

4.   Explain how logical files help with data control.

5.   What are the levels of system control available on the AS/400? Explain the controls provided at each level.

6.   When is a user profile created, and what is its purpose?

7.   Explain the differences and similarities between special authorities and a user class.

8.   How are user-written applications and functions controlled on the AS/400?

9.   Describe the scope of authority granted to the QSECOFR userid.

10. What object does the EDTOBJAUT command allow a user to modify?

DISCUSSION QUESTIONS

1.   Explain the different levels of data control and give reasons why each level would be needed.

2.   Discuss the role of a group profile on the AS/400 and how a group profile differs from a regular profile.

3.   Why are controls important in a computer system?

4.   You are opening up a computer dating service. All your customers are very concerned with the confidentiality of the information they are supplying. Allay their fears by explaining how the AS/400 controls access to data and how access can be granted only to people they authorize.

AS/400 Database Management

5

Overview

Data management is an essential component of all computer systems. How data is stored and accessed on a computer will affect every program and user. This chapter covers some data management theory regarding the efficiency, flexibility, and security of data management systems and explains several different database models. How the AS/400's database tackles these issues and how to define AS/400 data files are also demonstrated.

After finishing this chapter, you will understand:

- The major features of database systems
- The three primary data models and their differences
- Data definition languages
- The difference between logical, physical, and source data files
- The capabilities of DDS and IDDU
- What a record format is

You also will be able to:

- Define files and record formats
- Specify field definitions
- Specify field edits and audits

Information as an Asset

There has been a gradual change of opinion on the value of information. Before modern business practices were introduced, "keeping track" was not done in an organized manner. For instance, a stockroom attendant in a 1700s barrel-making shop would simply walk through a stockroom's aisles to find an item. As industry grew, a smart barrel maker finally realized that if the locations of all of the inventory were written down, the item could be found faster. He also discovered that not so many stockroom attendants would be needed to manage his inventory. Now that the items could be found immediately, less time was wasted wandering the aisles, and fewer people were needed. This decreased the cost of doing business and increased profits. Thus was born paperwork.

Over time, keeping track of essential business information became necessary to conduct business. Information became vital to the health of a business; what's more, it grew in volume and complexity. In some cases, the data regarding an item or event became as important as the item itself. For instance, a large grocery chain maintains a record of where all their products are stored within their warehouse (just like the old barrel maker). Every time new products are received, a record is made of the date and time received as well as where they are placed. Just like the barrel maker, the grocery chain needs to know where each item is located to function efficiently. However, to see why information is vital, imagine what happens if the location information is lost. The warehouse for the grocery chain is the size of ten football fields and has shelves 20 feet high. If a stockroom attendant puts 15 crates of fresh grapes on a shelf and records the wrong location—instead of aisle 753 and shelf 41, the attendant records aisle 75 and shelf 41—how easy would it be to find those grapes? The grapes are as good as lost. Losing the location data is just as bad as losing the grapes themselves. Even if they could be found within several days, they would be spoiled. Not only are assets ruined because of a lack of information but customers are lost because their orders could not be filled.

This example indicates that the information about a business's assets has become as important as the assets themselves. And just as businesses protect their physical assets, businesses came to realize that they needed to protect their information, both from loss and from inaccuracy. Quick and reliable access to the information also became a necessity. Having the data but not being able to access it was just as bad as not having the data, or the asset, at all. Not having information meant business could not be carried on. So maintaining and protecting data were needed to avoid this disaster. Gathering and maintaining information were no longer regarded simply as costs of doing business; they became viewed as necessary to survive.

Recently, the perception of information has changed again. Information still provides efficiencies and enables the company to function, but information can actually add value beyond the scope of a company's primary business function. To maintain the item's inventory quantity, the grocery chain also records each of its customers' purchases. For instance, it knows that the Joneses purchased ten jars of baby food from one of its stores last week. One day, a marketing executive had the bright idea to customize advertising. When a sales flyer was sent to the Joneses, it included information about many other baby items—baby oil, disposable diapers, and the like—rather than information on sport socks or leisure-time items. (The theory being that the Joneses are probably too busy with the baby to be playing racquetball or "enjoying" bungee jumping.) The Joneses were prime customers for these baby items, and by bringing these products to their attention, the store would probably sell more of them. As a matter of fact, the store discovers that by customizing advertising it realizes a 20 percent increase in sales. The store makes more money because of what it knows. It has not offered the goods cheaper or provided them more conveniently; it has made more money from information. Information has become a resource that can be used to increase this company's sales and beat out the competition. In fact, a local children's daycare center would be willing to pay the grocery chain for its list of customers who buy baby products. Information suddenly has value itself over and above what it tells about the business or its assets.

A *database management system* (DBMS) is a collection of programs that allows users to create, store, and access data in a database. A database is made up of groups of related data. A DBMS provides utilities that allow users to define individual data elements, group the related data elements, and build relationships between data groups. A user-friendly DBMS will also provide functions to easily enter, change, and retrieve the stored data.

Another key feature of a DBMS is that it protects data. There are programs in the DBMS that back up data (that is, store duplicate copies) and, in the case of processing errors, that can reverse incorrect updates. A DBMS also provides efficient access to data and ensures the accuracy and integrity of all data contained within the database.

Database Models

As mentioned earlier, databases are groups of related data. The three major database types are hierarchical, network, and relational. Each of these provides a different approach toward grouping data and creating and maintaining data relationships.

As an example, imagine a dairy that needs to store three major groups of information.

Item information is data about each product produced at the dairy. For instance, each item has a name (skim milk, 1% lowfat milk, egg nog, and so on) and an item number.

Batch information is stored regarding each "processing group" of product. The expiration date of milk depends on the day it is received at the dairy. All milk received on the same day is stored and processed together and identified with a batch number. Therefore, the batch has an expiration date. The government requires that extensive information be kept on the processing of all food products. Since each batch is processed individually, processing data (like the temperature at which the batch was stored) and expiration date are unique to each batch and, therefore, stored together on a batch record.

Carton information is stored for each container of product sold. Each container is identified by a unique serial number and information about the container. This information includes data such as container amount (pint, quart, gallon, and so on) and the store to which it was sent.

The three groups of data can be seen in Figure 5.1. Each group would also contain individual data records. Figures 5.2, 5.3, and 5.4 are examples of the data each group contains.

There are also relationships between these groups of data. Relationships between groups of data records can be described in two ways. The first way is to describe the number of relationships a record has with records from another group. For instance, there are many batches of skim milk. Therefore, each item record can have many batch records associated with it. This type of relationship is described as a one-to-many relationship. It is also possible to have a one-to-one or a many-to-many relationship.

FIGURE 5.1
Three Groups of Data

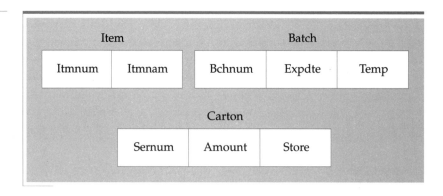

The second way to describe a relationship concerns the direction of access. For example, say a dairy worker needs to find all the batch records for a particular item. The worker would need a unidirectional relationship between items and batches. The access between the item and batch groups needs to go in only one direction, from item to batch. The other option is bidirectional access. If the user needs to find each batch for an item and, for each batch record, needs to be able to find the item record, then the relationship between these two groups is said to be bidirectional.

ITEM	
Itmnum	Itmnam
111111	Whole milk
888888	Skim milk
666666	1% lowfat milk
444444	Chocolate milk
⋮	⋮
222222	2% lowfat milk

	BATCH	
Bchnum	Expdte	Temp
1234	10/23/92	45
2345	09/30/93	38
5678	05/18/90	42
3456	08/03/92	44
⋮	⋮	⋮
6789	01/23/89	40

FIGURE 5.4
Carton Data

| CARTON | | |
Sernum	Amount	Store
A36SS234	Half gallon	8612745
J836H527	Pint	9370397
F838938D	Quart	8937626
5GDQ3752	Gallon	2894628
M7462650	Quart	8458532
FY86DY83	Half pint	2894628
⋮	⋮	⋮
87Q83J93	Gallon	1274007

Each of the database models supports these types of relationships in a different manner and with different costs and efficiencies.

Hierarchical Databases

A *hierarchical database* allows a user to define a parent–child relationship. A parent–child relationship is a one-to-many, unidirectional relationship. An example of this type of relationship is the dairy worker who wants to find all batches of skim milk—the worker wants to access batches by the item with which they are associated. The relationship and access desired between items and batches would be shown as follows:

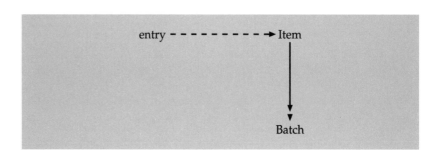

The connecting arrow—between item and batch—pointing in one direction means the relationship is unidirectional. The double arrowhead means that each item can have many batches. The word *entry* denotes that the user must go through the item group to get to the batch information. In parent–child terminology, someone would say that item is the parent of batch or that batch is a child of item. Each item record can have many child batch records, but each batch record has only one parent item record. A hierarchical DBMS would allow a user to define item, batch, and carton segments and create parent–child relationships between them.

Another condition of hierarchical databases is that entry to the database must be through one segment only. That segment is called the root segment and has no parent.

In our dairy example, batch records and carton records also share a parent–child relationship. Each batch has many cartons associated with it, and in turn, each carton comes from one batch. The relationship would be depicted as follows:

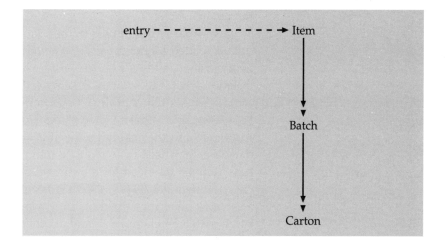

In this hierarchical database, item is the root segment. It has no 106parent. Any time data is needed from the database, access has to be through the item segment. For instance, if the dairy worker wanted to know the expiration date for batch number 1234, he or she would have to know the item number of that batch.

Another "rule" of hierarchical databases is that access to a child segment must be through its parent. So access to data about a particular carton would require:

- The carton serial number (the "key" of the carton record)
- The batch number of its parent batch record

and, to get the batch record,

- The item number of the batch record's parent item record

As you can see, this can quickly become complicated and cumbersome. To get a particular child record, all its parent keys must be specified. The user must keep track of a large amount of data and specify it whenever the data is requested. A single point of entry to the database and the need to specify all parent record keys is one of the drawbacks to the hierarchical model.

Somewhat offsetting this drawback is that the hierarchical model permanently stores and maintains the relationships between records. Another way to think of it is that the DBMS keeps track of each record's location. When the particular record is specified—by specifying its parent, grandparent, great-grandparent, and so on—the DBMS simply looks up the location and very quickly retrieves the record.

However, the downside to storing the relationships is that when the data is updated, the relationships must also be maintained. This means that updating data will take a little longer because the relationships between records also need to be updated. Also, extra space, beyond what is needed to store the data, is required to store the relationships.

Another shortcoming of the hierarchical model is that not all data is related hierarchically. Some data does not relate in a one-to-many fashion, and users often wish to access data bidirectionally. For instance, what if the dairy workers need to find out what type of milk a particular batch contains? Let's hope they can tell the difference between whole milk and chocolate milk, but what if they have a batch in storage and they cannot tell if it is 1% or 2% milk? In terms of the database, they need to access item information by batch number. They have defined the need for a bidirectional relationship between batch data and item data. They also now need to enter the database through a segment other than the root. They want to access the database sometimes with the item number and at other times with the batch number. In database terminology, the users require multiple entry points into the database.

Network Databases

Network databases, like hierarchical databases, also maintain permanent relationships between data records. Networks, however, allow multiple entry points into the database and support more complex relationships. For instance, the bidirectional, multiple-entry-point requirements just described can be supported in a network database. Figure 5.5 depicts the bidirectional relationship between item and batch by having a relationship arrow between item and batch pointing in both directions. This means a user knowing the item number can get all the batches, and if the batch number is known, the item record can be accessed. The multiple entry points are shown with a broken arrow and the word *entry*.

FIGURE 5.5

A Bidirectional, Multiple-Entry-Point Database

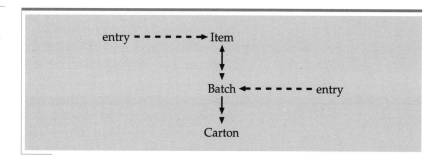

Network databases can also support a many-to-many relationship between groups of data. The relationship between item and batch became more complex, in terms of access, when the dairy workers realized that they needed bidirectional access. However, the relationship remained one to many. For each item record, there were many batch records, but each batch record still had only a single item record associated with it. A batch of milk could not be associated with both the skim and the 1% milk item records. The batch was either skim or 1% milk. There was still a parent–child relationship between the two types of data.

Networks can handle more than the simple parent–child relationship; they can also support many-to-many relationships. As an example of a many-to-many relationship, imagine that the dairy comes up with a new method of pasteurizing milk. There has been a breakthrough in low-level radiation technology, and by exposing milk to a small dosage of radiation, the milk is safer for human consumption. However, public concern over the use of radiation in food products is high, so a law is passed that states that no carton may contain more than 40 percent radiated milk. To comply with the law, the dairy begins blending milk from different batches into cartons. The relationship between cartons and batches is no longer one to many. A carton can now be associated with multiple batches. Of course, the old relationship of a batch having many cartons still holds. Our new model would now look like Figure 5.6.

FIGURE 5.6

A Bidirectional, Many-to-Many Relationship

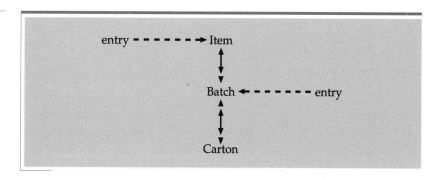

Carton and batch now share a many-to-many relationship. Fortunately for the dairy, network databases can support this type of relationship.

For all the advantages and flexibility of network databases, there are some drawbacks. Just like the hierarchical database, the network database must update the stored relationships whenever the data is changed. Since networks support more complex relationships, the time required to maintain the relationships is greater. Moreover, because of the complexity of the network model, the DBMS packages tend to be very complicated and require specialized personnel or training to set them up and use them. This, of course, means that more time and money are required to store and maintain the data.

Relational Databases

Relational databases are the easiest of the three models to understand. In general, the associated relational DBMSs are also the most user friendly and easiest to learn. You'll be pleased to know that in keeping with its goal of user friendliness, the AS/400 employs a relational database to store all data.

The two major characteristics of the relational model are that permanent relationships between data are not stored and that all groups of data are viewed as tables.

Compared to the complex organization and access rules of network and hierarchical data models, the relational model is simple. Data elements are grouped into tables (also called relations). Each row in a table is comparable to a record, and each column is a field. The tables can have a key, and each row can be referenced by the value contained in the key field.

So in a relational database, each group of our dairy database would be considered a table. If carton information was needed, the parent record's key value would not be needed—as in a hierarchical database—nor would a new entry point into the database for carton need to be set up—as in a network database. With a relational database, carton is simply created as a table and accessed by the defined key.

To relate information between different tables, the relational model uses duplicate data fields. For instance, if the dairy worker wanted to retrieve the expiration date and storage temperature for a particular carton, the carton and batch tables would have to share a common field. One way this could be done is to define a batch number field in the carton table (Figure 5.7). When data from the two tables is required, a JOIN using the shared field BCHNUM from both tables would be specified. The relational DBMS would search through the carton and batch records and join the rows that have the same batch number. The results of the join can be saved, but the relationship between each of the records in the two groups cannot.

FIGURE 5.7
A Relational Database Implementation

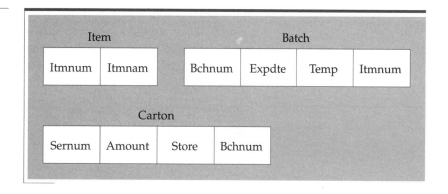

This approach has its advantages and disadvantages. Certainly the concept of tables with shared fields is easier to understand than the ideas of database entry points, parent–child relationships, and multi-directional access paths. Therefore, most users of relational databases do not need any extensive data processing background. This saves on training and personnel costs. Moreover, most relational DBMSs provide a menu-driven user-friendly interface and extensive help.

One of the disadvantages of the relational model is the required data redundancy. Implementing many-to-many relationships or joining multiple tables requires extensive duplication of data. Besides the cost associated with the required extra space, coordinating the maintenance of data that is stored multiple times becomes a complex and time-consuming task. This work is usually handled by user-developed programs outside the DBMS. This means extra time and money to develop the programs and extra processing time when the data is updated.

Another disadvantage of the relational model is that by not using predefined relationships, retrieval performance suffers. Since the relationship must be created each time the data is accessed, retrievals are slower in the relational model than in the other two models. However, because table changes do not require updating any stored relationships, relational databases provide faster updating of nonredundant data.

Database Management System Features

All database management systems offer some capability to define data structures and manipulate the data contained in those structures. Generally, these features are called the *data definition language* (DDL) and the *data manipulation language* (DML). Depending on the individual software purchased, these functions can take many forms; they do not necessarily have to take the form of traditional commands. Data could be managed through screens, menus, or even a graphical interface. The AS/400 provides several different ways to define, modify, and view data.

In terms of DDL functions, the AS/400 provides two ways to

define data. Data can be defined internally or externally. Internally defined data is defined within application programs using a programming language's data definition commands or SQL (Structured Query Language) commands. On the AS/400, a file could be defined using RPG, COBOL, or any of the other supported programming languages.

Externally defined files are defined outside application programs using a DDL. On the AS/400, files can be defined externally using SQL, IDDU (Interactive Data Definition Utility), or DDS (Data Description Specifications).

SQL commands can define data both externally—through a feature called interactive SQL—and, as mentioned earlier, internally—by embedding the commands in an application program. SQL also has data manipulation capability. In addition to commands that define data structures, there are commands to load, view, and modify data.

IDDU is a menu-driven data definition utility. Through a series of menus and screens, IDDU provides data definition options and prompts the user for information necessary to define data on the AS/400. After the information has been gathered, IDDU generates and compiles DDS source code for the file.

DDS is strictly a definition language. It contains commands that allow a user to define:

File structures

Individual field characteristics

Field edits and audits

Though IDDU generates DDS code, it is limited in the DDS commands it offers. Furthermore, because IDDU is menu driven, it does not offer the flexibility of PDM and SEU in terms of updating. For these reasons, this chapter will confine itself to discussing DDS for file definition on the AS/400. And since manipulating data on the AS/400—another feature of most DBMSs—is handled by utilities separate from DDS, we cover the AS/400 data manipulation options in the next chapter.

Physical and Logical Data Files

A DBMS will also usually offer three ways to view a database. There is a physical view, a logical view, and the capability to build multiple user views of the data. What is traditionally called the physical view of data is mostly hidden from the AS/400 user because of the AS/400's single-level approach to storage. The user does not know the disk, track, or sector on which the data is being stored. In addition, any indices or specific location addresses are used internally by the DBMS and are not readily available to the user. However, DDS does provide a global view of all the data as files and allows construction of individual views. This is achieved through physical and logical files.

As mentioned in Chapter 4, "AS/400 Object Security and Authorization," physical files contain the definition of individual tables and files. In addition to a file definition, physical files include an access path to the data (a key) and the data itself. If a file is defined without a key, the records are said to be in *arrival sequence* or the file is said to have an *arrival sequence access path*. This means that records are stored in the file in the order in which they arrived (or were input) into the file. In some other computer systems, this type of file is called a sequential file. If a key is defined, the file is said to be in *keyed sequence* or to have a *keyed sequence access path*. Defining a key for a file results in an index being built for that file. An index contains each record's key value and the location of the record in the file. Therefore, a keyed file's records can be accessed according to the value in the key field.

If a file does not have an index, its records are accessed by starting at the first record and proceeding one by one through the file to the last record entered in the file. With an index, the file can be accessed sequentially in a different order. The DBMS can start with the record with the smallest key value and progress through all the records to the record with the largest key value. The key offers an alternative path through the data.

The index can also be used to retrieve specific records faster. When used this way, the file index works just like an index to a book. Rather than searching through each page of a book for a particular topic, a reader can go to a book's index. The index has an entry for each topic and a page number where that topic is covered. After searching the index, the reader goes directly to the correct page.

The same holds for a file's index. For each specific key value, the index contains a storage location. The storage location contains the record for that specific key value. A particular record can be found by first searching the index for the record's location. The DBMS then goes directly to that location and reads the data record. If the file had been nonkeyed, each record would have had to be read, in arrival sequence order (like searching through each page of a book), and each record's data checked to see if it contained the value being searched for.

Logical files also contain file definitions. However, logical files contain only field names and an access path; they contain no data. Because logical files contain no data, they can reference only fields that have already been defined in a physical file. However, a logical file can reference fields from many physical files. Through logical files, unique combinations of the data seem to exist without duplicating any data. There is no data in a logical file—just a different definition of how to access physical file data.

Physical and logical files are created by compiling source physical file members. These members contain the DDS statements that define the file's fields and record formats. (Several other types of nondata definitions can also be held in source physical file members, for instance, screen definitions.) Source physical file members can be defined with a type of LF or PF (logical file or physical file). This member type determines the file type (physical or logical) that will be created when the member is compiled.

For instance, from our dairy example, each group of data—item, batch, and carton—would be defined by DDS statements contained in a source physical file member. The data fields for each file would be as shown in Figure 5.7, and the library, file, and members that contain the DDS can be seen in Figure 5.8. Compiling these members would result in three new physical files being created, each having an empty member with no type (Figure 5.9). The new physical files contain the compiled file definitions, and the empty members will eventually hold the data.

FIGURE 5.8

AS/400 Source Member Organization

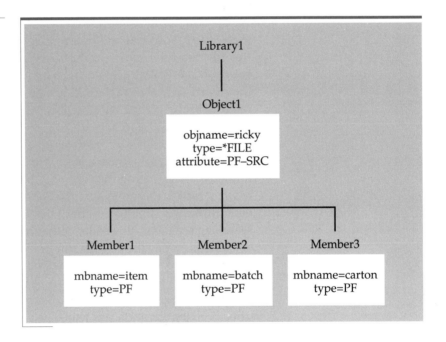

The organization of fields in physical files is usually done to maximize storage efficiencies (minimize the amount of storage space used, decrease data redundancy, and so on). However, there may be business reasons that require users to "see" the data differently from how it is stored. For instance, if a dairy customer (a store) wanted the expiration date of a particular carton, there is no single source for that information. The store employee would be forced to search both the CARTON and the BATCH files. That is, the store employee would have to access the CARTON file and search for the particular carton's batch number. The BATCH file would then have to be searched for the particular record that contains the expiration date. This approach is cumbersome and not necessarily the best option for both the dairy and the store. Not only does the store employee have to wade through

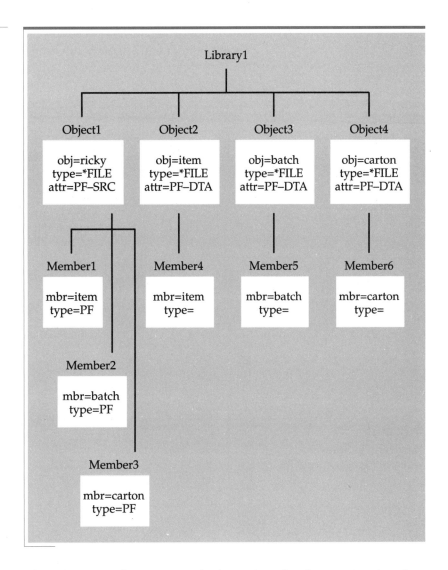

FIGURE 5.9

Source Member and File Organization After Compiling

a large amount of nonpertinent information, thereby wasting time, but the dairy may not want each store to have access to the dairy's production information regarding every batch.

To solve this problem, a new logical file could be defined—BATCART—that contains fields from both the BATCH and CARTON files. DDS statements would specify that BATCH and CARTON records that share the same batch number are to be joined. The DDS could also specify the fields that are to be joined from each file. In this case, the logical file fields would be limited to expiration date (from BATCH) and carton number, batch number, and store (from CARTON). The DDS would be stored in a source physical file member with a type of LF called BATCART (Figure 5.10). When this member is compiled, a new file is created with an attribute of LF (Figure 5.11). Remember that logical files contain no data; therefore, a logical file has no members. Logical files simply "point" to the physical files that contain the data and specify how the data should be accessed. The DDS also specifies how the fields will be sequenced within the logical file record.

FIGURE 5.10

Logical File Source Member

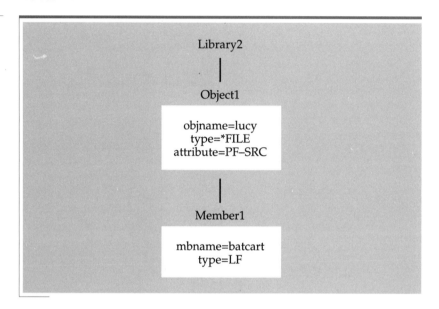

FIGURE 5.11

Logical File Source Member and Logical File

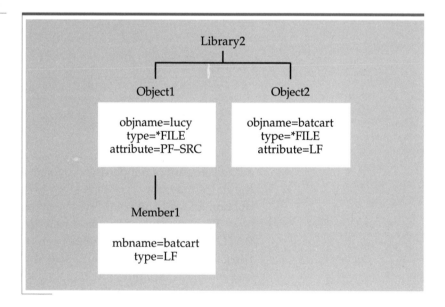

Creating a Physical File

Creating a physical or logical file starts with creating a source physical file member to hold the DDS definition. PDM can be used to create a library, a source physical file, and a member with a type of PF or LF. (See Chapter 2 for instructions on creating these objects using PDM or Chapter 3 for creating them with CL commands.) For this chapter's purposes, you need a source physical file called INVSRC in library YOURLIBXX. Within INVSRC, create a member called INVDATA with a type of PF. Once the member has been created, SEU can be used to enter the DDS code to define the physical file.

A few words about DDS before we cover individual commands and syntax. DDS is a semipositional language, meaning that many commands and values must be placed in certain column positions on the line. Unlike a free format language, DDS is strict about where on the line, for instance, the name of a field is defined. Other optional specifications, such as edits and audits (an example of an audit is verifying that all quantities entered are greater than zero), are not as strictly governed.

When defining either a physical or a logical file, certain rules also must be followed. For instance, a physical file can have only one record format (a layout and definitions of individual fields) defined, and the record format must contain at least one field definition.

For our example, we are going to define a file that holds information about a grocer's inventory and suppliers. The fields that make up the file will be as follows:

Field Name	Field Description
ITMNUM	Item Number
ITMNME	Item Name
EOQ	Economic Order Quantity
QTYNST	Quantity in Stock
REORDP	Reorder Point
UNTPRC	Unit Price
SUPPL	Supplier Name
SUPADD	Supplier Address
SUPCTY	Supplier City
SUPST	Supplier State
SUPZP	Supplier Zip Code

EOQ and REORDP are fields needed to determine when and how much product to order. REORDP is the quantity of product in stock that, when reached, signifies that more product should be ordered. Based on factors such as time required for delivery and item consumption rate, each item's reorder point is calculated and assigned by the grocer.

EOQ is the optimal amount of an item that should be reordered. This is usually based on consumption rate, shelf life, and order quantity discounts offered by the supplier. Again, for each item, the grocer will calculate and assign the value.

DDS

By using DDS, a programmer gets several advantages inherent to an externally described file. If a file is described internally, each program that accesses that file must also include a definition of the format or view of the data that will be used. With DDS, that format can be defined once, outside the program, and any program can use that definition. This saves the programmer from having to reenter the definition for each program. Further, any changes to the file structure are made in the DDS definition. Nothing in the programs is affected. Rather than going into multiple programs and changing each internally defined format, the DDS definition provides one stored copy of the definition that can be accessed and updated. This greatly speeds up and simplifies the updating process and reduces the chance of mistakes.

DDS file specifications are entered into a source physical file member and can span one or more lines. Each line is broken up into several different areas. All positional entries are specified between columns 1 and 44. Columns 45 through 80 are considered the function area.

The three levels of definition for a physical file are file, record, and field. Respectively, these levels determine whether the keywords specified affect the entire file, a record, or an individual field.

An example of a file level specification would be whether records with duplicate keys are allowed in the file. If duplicate keys are allowed, then another file level specification needs to be made regarding the order that duplicate records will be processed; that is, is the first duplicated record written to the file the first record that is printed out, or is the last entered duplicated record the first printed? File level specifications such as these are designated by entering the proper keywords in the function area (columns 45–80) of a line that precedes all record or field level specifications.

Figure 5.12, line 3, is an example of a file level specification. By having a keyword in column 45 as the first specification statement and not associating it with an individual record or field, the keyword applies to the entire file. In this example, the keyword UNIQUE specifies that each record in the file must have a unique key value.

Line 4 shows a record level specification. An R in column 17 signifies that the specification is for a record, and the name of the record format is entered in columns 19 through 28. In the function area, the keyword TEXT is specified. TEXT allows the user to specify descriptive information about the record format. When the record format is used in a program, the text will be included in the program as documentation. The syntax of the TEXT command requires enclosing the description with single quotes and parentheses. The TEXT keyword can also be used for field level specifications.

The remaining entries in Figure 5.12 are all examples of field level specifications. The field name is specified in the same column positions as the record name. Field specifications, however, require a length. Positions 30 through 34 are reserved for length entries. Column 35 is reserved for the data type. A blank indicates a character field, and several values (P, S, B, F, H) can be specified for numeric fields. These values each designate unique ways to store numeric information. For this example, all numeric fields are specified with a P, meaning packed. (Packed is one of the more efficient ways to store numeric data.) If decimal places are needed, the number of places required is entered in positions 36 and 37.

While typing in the DDS specifications, positioning the cursor at the correct column and entering the data can become a nuisance. SEU supplies a DDS input prompt that will easily position entries in the correct columns. Pressing F4 tells the system to display the input prompt. The type of member determines what prompt will be displayed. Because this is a physical file member, the DDS prompt will be displayed in the bottom portion of the screen (Figure 5.13). On the second half of the screen, notice a prompt field called Functions. This is where function keywords, such as UNIQUE or TEXT, would be entered. Press ENTER, and SEU will place the keyword in column 45.

FIGURE 5.12
INVDATA DDS Definition

```
Columns . . . :  1   71              Edit              YOURLIBXX/INVSRC
SEU==> _____ INVDATA
FMT A* .....A*. 1 ...+... 2 ...+... 3 ...+... 4 ...+... 5 ...+... 6 ...+... 7
       *************** Beginning of data ****************************************
0001.00     *      THIS PHYSICAL FILE IS FOR INTRO TO AS/400
0002.00     *
0003.00                                   UNIQUE
0004.00           R INVFMT                TEXT('INVENTORY FORMAT')
0005.00             ITMNUM      6P 0      COLHDG('ITEM' 'NUMBER')
0006.00                                   TEXT('ITEM NUMBER')
0007.00                                   CHECK(ME)
0008.00             ITMNME     15         COLHDG('ITEM' 'NAME')
0009.00                                   TEXT('ITEM NAME')
0010.00             EOQ         2P 0      COLHDG('EOQ' 'AMOUNT')
0011.00                                   TEXT('EOQ AMOUNT')
0012.00                                   COMP(GT 0)
0013.00                                   CHECK(ME)
0014.00             QTYNST      2P 0      COLHDG('QUANTITY' 'IN STOCK')
0015.00                                   TEXT('QUANTITY IN STOCK')
0016.00                                   COMP(GE 0)
0017.00                                   CHECK(ME)
0018.00             REORDP      2P 0      COLHDG('REORDER' 'POINT')
0019.00                                   TEXT('REORDER POINT')
0020.00                                   CHECK(ME)
0021.00             UNTPRC      4P 2      COLHDG('UNIT' 'PRICE')
0022.00                                   TEXT('UNIT PRICE')
0023.00                                   CHECK(ME)
0024.00             SUPPL      20         COLHDG('SUPPLIER' 'NAME')
0025.00                                   TEXT('SUPPLIER NAME')
0026.00                                   CHECK(ME)
0027.00             SUPPADD    20         COLHDG('SUPPLIER' 'ADDRESS')
0028.00                                   TEXT('SUPPLIER ADDRESS')
0029.00                                   CHECK(ME)
0030.00             SUPCTY     15         COLHDG('SUPPLIER' 'CITY')
0031.00                                   TEXT('SUPPLIER CITY')
0032.00                                   CHECK(ME)
0033.00             SUPST       2         COLHDG('STATE')
0034.00                                   TEXT('STATE')
0035.00                                   CHECK(ME)
0036.00             SUPZP       5P 0      COLHDG('ZIPCODE')
0037.00                                   TEXT('ZIP CODE')
0038.00                                   CHECK(MF)
0039.00           K ITMNUM
       ****************** End of data ****************************************
```

FIGURE 5.13

DDS Prompt Example

```
 Columns . . . : 1 71              Edit              YOURLIBXX/INVSRC
 SEU==> _____ INVDATA
 FMT A* ....A*. 1 ...+... 2 ...+... 3 ...+... 4 ...+... 5 ...+... 6 ...+... 7
        ************* Beginning of data ****************************
 0001.00    *       THIS PHYSICAL FILE IS FOR INTRO TO AS/400
 0002.00    *
 0003.00                               UNIQUE
 0004.00            R INVFMT                TEXT('INVENTORY FORMAT')
 0005.00              ITMNUM      6P 0      COLHDG('ITEM' 'NUMBER')
 0006.00                               TEXT('ITEM NUMBER')
 0007.00                               CHECK(ME)
 0008.00              ITMNME      15        COLHDG('ITEM' 'NAME')
 0009.00                               TEXT('ITEM NAME')
  Prompt type . . . PF   Sequence number . . .  0003.00

  Name                          Data    Decimal
  Type      Name    Ref  Length  Type    Positions       Use
  _         _____     ____    _       __              _
 Functions
 Unique _____

 F3=Exit  F4=Prompt  F5=Refresh       F11=Previous record
 F12=Cancel          F23=Select prompt F24=More keys
```

Several other keywords can also be specified for field level edits. Lines 5 through 7 contain the ITMNUM field definition. The 6 in column 39 signifies that the field is six positions in length, and the non-blank entry in column 40 defines the field as numeric. (A blank in column 36 signifies that no decimal places are required.) Several new keywords appear in columns 45 through 80. The COLHDG keyword defines the text that will appear as a column heading for the field on any data entry or data display screens. Fields defined by DDS can be placed on screens. When a data field is specified to appear on a screen, the AS/400 screen definition utilities (SDA, DFU) use the text defined in the COLHDG keyword as the column heading to appear with the field. In the case of ITMNUM, the text ITEM NUMBER will be the default text for any screen that uses the field.

The TEXT keyword on line 6 is an example of a DDS keyword that is used at multiple data levels. On line 4, the TEXT keyword describes the entire record. On line 6, it is used to describe a single field, in this case, the ITMNUM field. As mentioned before, this text will be included as program documentation. In this case, any program that uses the ITMNUM field will contain the text.

On line 7, the CHECK keyword appears for the first time. CHECK further defines what type and amount of data a field can accept. An explanation of the valid options will clarify the purpose of CHECK.

Specifying AB (allow blank) in parentheses following the CHECK keyword means that no data entry is necessary for this field. (Blanks are allowed.) If no data is entered, blanks and zeros will be substituted for character and numeric fields, respectively. ME (mandatory entry) says that at least one character or number must be entered in the field.

A single blank or zero is a valid entry. MF (mandatory fill) specifies that all field positions must be filled. (Line 38 shows an example of mandatory fill—zip code. All zip codes must fill the entire length of the field. There are no three- or four-digit zip codes.)

Line 8 is the ITMNME field definition. Its length is defined as 15, and it has text defined for a column heading and program documentation. Notice that it has no CHECK keyword specified. AB will be used as the default.

The definition of EOQ beginning on line 10 shows the next new keyword, COMP. COMP specifies that a comparison is to be performed when data is being entered. Only data entered that results in the comparison being true will be allowed in the file. The example on line 12 of Figure 5.12 ensures that any number entered in the EOQ field is greater than zero. Other valid operators include:

EQ   equal

NE   not equal

LT   less than

LE   less than or equal

GT   greater than

GE   greater than or equal

Many other keywords can be specified. The following three are used most frequently:

- **RANGE**. This keyword specifies to check that a number being entered is within a range of values specified by the keyword. For instance, a date field could be made up of separate month, day, and year fields. A range could be specified for the month field as RANGE(1 12). Any number that is entered in the month field will be checked, and if the value entered is not between 1 and 12, inclusive, it will not be allowed in the database.

- **VALUES**. This keyword specifies that an edit should be performed against a specific group of values. Using the month example again, month could also be defined as a character field. This field should contain only the discrete values of 'January,' 'February,' and so on. To specify this edit, use the VALUES keyword as follows:

  VALUES('January' 'February' 'March' 'April' 'May' 'June' 'July' 'August' 'September' 'October' 'November' 'December')

- **EDTCDE**. This keyword allows the user to control the appearance of numeric and date fields. Various single character and number codes control whether there should be a thousands separator, leading zeros should be suppressed, a positive or negative sign should be displayed, and the like. The various alphanumeric codes and their functions can be found in the *DDS Reference* manual.

Figure 5.12, line 39, also demonstrates a different type of field specification. The K in column 17 defines the statement as a key specification. The field name specified in columns 19 through 28 will be the key field for the file. Users can process the file in key field sequence or retrieve individual records based on the value contained in ITMNUM.

Once the source DDS has been entered, press F3 to exit and save the member (as described in Chapter 2). Compiling the DDS member will create the physical file and member that will hold the data.

Logical Files

A logical file provides a different access path to physical file records and fields. Logical files appear to contain a rearrangement of physical file fields, a subset of fields from a single physical file, or information from multiple files. In reality, however, they do not contain any data. Logical files are usually built to correspond to an individual user's (or group of users') view of the data.

The keywords and procedures to create and define a logical file are much the same as for a physical file. There are, however, some special requirements on referencing fields in the physical files as well as rules on combining multiple physical files.

As a simple logical file example, we will define a logical file, INVACCT, for the INVDATA file. This logical file will correspond to an accountant's view of inventory data.

Accountants are concerned with the value of inventory. They are not concerned with who supplies the item or what the reorder quantity is. Accountants need to see an item's number, name, and unit price as well as the quantity in stock. From this information, they can calculate the total dollar value of the current inventory in stock.

To create a logical file, the user must first create a physical file member in which to store the logical file definition. For the INVACCT example, the user would create a physical file member within INVSRC called INVACCT with a type of LF. The DDS shown in Figure 5.14 would then be entered. (Use the browse and copy functions to retrieve the INVDATA definition. Then modify the INVDATA definition to match Figure 5.14.)

Notice that the logical file also has file, record, and field level specifications. As mentioned, a logical file definition contains many of the same keywords as a physical file. In Figure 5.14, the TEXT keyword defines the new logical file's format text. Using field level keywords in the logical file will override any physical file field definition. For instance, column headings could be redefined for each of the logical file fields using the COLHDG keyword. If no COLHDG keyword is specified, the value defined in the physical file is used.

There are, however, some important differences between logical

FIGURE 5.14

```
Columns . . . : 1 71              Edit              YOURLIBXX/INVSRC
SEU==>_____          INVACCT
FMT A* .....A*. 1 ...+... 2 ...+... 3 ...+... 4 ...+... 5 ...+... 6 ...+... 7
        ************* Beginning of data *************************
0001.00     *    THIS IS THE LOGICAL FILE THAT DEFINES THE
0002.00     *    ACCOUNTING VIEW OF INVENTORY DATA
0003.00                                 UNIQUE
0004.00          R ACCFMT               PFILE(YOURLIBXX/INVDATA)
0005.00                                 TEXT('ACCOUNTING FORMAT')
0006.00            ITMNUM
0007.00            ITMNME
0008.00            QTYNST
0009.00            UNTPRC
0010.00          K ITMNUM
0011.00          O QTYNST               COMP(LE 0)
****************** End of data ********************************


F3=Exit  F4=Prompt  F5=Refresh  F9=Retrieve  F10=Cursor
F16=Repeat find      F17=Repeat change        F24=More keys
```

and physical file definitions. For instance, the record level keyword PFILE is required in a logical file (line 4 in Figure 5.14). Since a logical file provides a different view of a physical file(s), the physical file(s) must be specified. In the case of a single physical file, this is done through the PFILE keyword.

A new field level specification is also shown in Figure 5.14. Line 11 demonstrates an *omit specification*. The keyword COMP was used earlier as a validity checker. In a logical file, however, it can also be used to select or omit physical file records from the logical file. Entering the letter O in position 17 will define the field level specification as an omit. Line 11 omits any physical file records that have a quantity of zero or less. This was done because accountants are concerned with the value of inventory. If an item has no inventory (its quantity in stock is zero), there can be no dollar value for that item's inventory.

Screening out the zero value records could also have been accomplished with a selection. To define a field level specification as a select, enter an S in position 17. If the same function were to be accomplished with a select specification, the COMP condition would be changed to QTYNST GT 0.

All the COMP operands listed for physical files are valid for logical files.

To create the logical file, exit the SEU Edit screen and save and compile the member. The accountants would be told that their inventory information is stored in the INVACCT file. They would not even have to know that INVDATA exists. Whenever the logical file

INVACCT is requested, the AS/400 database will retrieve data from the associated physical file defined in the PFILE keyword, INVDATA.

Joining Files

A more complicated logical file is a *join logical file*. A join logical file can contain information from multiple physical files. There are many different types of relational joins. (See Chapter 7 for a detailed explanation of join types.) Essentially, DDS provides the capability to select and join individual fields from different physical files into one logical file. To demonstrate this capability, the BATCH and CARTON files that we discussed earlier need to be created. Assuming that the two physical file members called BATCH and CARTON have already been created, DDS in Figure 5.15 and Figure 5.16 would be entered into the two members. Then BATCH and CARTON would be saved and compiled.

Assuming that the logical file member called BATCART in INVSRC and YOURLIBXX already exists, enter the DDS in Figure 5.17.

Notice that several new keywords are needed to define a logical join file. For instance, the JFILE keyword (line 4 in Figure 5.17) identifies the files to be joined. Up to 32 files can be specified. (Warn the local power company before you try to join 32 files! Well, calling the power company isn't really necessary; however, you might want to think twice before doing a join of that size. The resources needed to perform that large a join could be considerable, and overall system performance might be affected.)

The logical file must also have a *join specification*. The join specification must follow the record specification and is indicated by placing a J in column 17 (line 7 in Figure 5.17). This identifies which files are to be joined and the basis for the join. The keyword JOIN (entered in the function area of the join specification) is used to identify the files to be joined. The JOIN keyword is not required if only two files are specified in the JFILE keyword, since they are the only possible files that can be joined. Further, library and file names do not have to be used to identify join files. When files are specified in the JFILE keyword, they are assigned a relative file number. The first file is 1, the next is 2, the file specified after the second is 3, and so on. Whenever the file needs to be identified, the relative file number can be used instead of the longer file and library names. The join specification on line 7 uses the relative record numbers.

The JFLD keyword identifies the field(s) that will be used to join the records. In this case, line 8 specifies that records in the CARTON and BATCH files that share the same value in their batch number fields will be joined. More than one field can be defined as the join condition. This might be necessary if more than one field is needed to uniquely identify a record. For instance, the only way to absolutely distinguish each record in a file may be to check the last name, first name, and phone number fields. If this were the case, any records being joined from two different files should have matching data in all these fields. This could be done by using three JFLD keywords.

FIGURE 5.15

```
         ******* Beginning of data ******************************
0001.00    * THIS PHYSICAL FILE IS THE BATCH FILE DDS DEFINITION
0002.00    *
0003.00                              UNIQUE
0004.00            R BCHFMT          TEXT('BATCH FORMAT')
0005.00              BCHNUM      4   COLHDG('BATCH' 'NUMBER')
0006.00                              TEXT('BATCH NUMBER')
0007.00                              CHECK(ME)
0008.00              EXPDTE      6   COLHDG('EXPIRATION' 'DATE')
0009.00                              TEXT('EXPIRATION DATE')
0010.00                              CHECK(ME)
0011.00              TEMP        2   COLHDG('TEMP')
0012.00                              TEXT('TEMPERATURE')
0013.00                              CHECK(ME)
0014.00              ITMNUM      6   COLHDG('ITEM' 'NUMBER')
0015.00                              TEXT('ITEM NUMBER')
0016.00                              CHECK(ME)
0017.00            K BCHNUM
         ************ End of data ******************************
```

FIGURE 5.16

```
         ******* Beginning of data ******************************
0001.00    * THIS PHYSICAL FILE IS THE CARTON FILE DDS DEFINITION
0002.00    *
0003.00                              UNIQUE
0004.00            R CRTFMT          TEXT('CARTON FORMAT')
0005.00              CRTNUM      8   COLHDG('CARTON' 'NUMBER')
0006.00                              TEXT('CARTON NUMBER')
0007.00                              CHECK(ME)
0008.00              AMOUNT     12   COLHDG('CARTON' 'SIZE')
0009.00                              TEXT('CARTON SIZE')
0010.00                              CHECK(ME)
0011.00              STORE       7   COLHDG('STORE' 'CODE')
0012.00                              TEXT('STORE CODE')
0013.00                              CHECK(ME)
0014.00              BCHNUM      4   COLHDG('BATCH' 'NUMBER')
0015.00                              TEXT('BATCH NUMBER')
0016.00                              CHECK(ME)
0017.00            K CRTNUM
         ************ End of data ******************************
```

The last new keyword is JREF. The JREF keyword is required for any field whose name is specified in more than one file. In the example, BCHNUM is in both the CARTON and BATCH files. It is required to specify from which file the field value is to come. In this example, there is no difference since both fields contain the same value. If, however, two files had a field called DATE—one date field containing the employees' date of hire and another containing the date of last salary increase—specifying would make a difference in the value.

To create the BATCART logical file, save and compile member BATCART.

FIGURE 5.17

```
       ****** Beginning of data *****************************
0001.00  * THIS LOGICAL FILE FOR THE JOIN OF THE BATCH AND CARTON FILES
0002.00  *
0003.00                             UNIQUE
0004.00        R BATCARTFMT         JFILE(YOURLIBXX/CARTON +
0005.00                             YOURLIBXX/BATCH)
0006.00                             TEXT('BATCH FORMAT')
0007.00        J                    JOIN(1 2)
0008.00                             JFLD(BCHNUM BCHNUM)
0009.00          CRTNUM
0010.00          BCHNUM             JREF(1)
0011.00          EXPDTE
0012.00          AMOUNT
0013.00        K CRTNUM
       ************** End of data ****************************
```

Summary

Data is a cornerstone of modern business. The complexity and the amount of data stored by businesses have grown in proportion to the importance of the data. To store and protect data, database management systems have been widely adopted. These collections of programs enable users to define different types of relationships between their data and access the data in a fast and efficient manner.

There are three different database models: hierarchical, network, and relational. Each has its own advantages and disadvantages regarding performance and ease of use. Hierarchical and network databases maintain predefined relationships that provide faster access but relatively slower updating. Network databases also support a wider variety of relationships than hierarchical but pay for that versatility with slower performance and greater complexity. The relational database model establishes relationships as requested by the user. It does this through shared data fields. This means slower retrieval but faster updating of nonredundant data. In keeping with the AS/400's overall goal of ease of use, the AS/400's DBMS uses a relational database model—the simplest and clearest of the three data models.

The AS/400 provides a variety of tools to perform both data definition and data manipulation. The primary data definition tool is DDS. By using PDM to create the source physical file member (process 1 in Figure 5.18) and SEU to enter DDS source code specifications into the member (process 2 in Figure 5.18), a user can compile the member and create an AS/400 file and data member (process 3 in Figure 5.18). The AS/400 also provides ease-of-use features such as prompts and on-line help.

Further control over data is provided through logical files. Different views can be built to match individual users' data needs. Rather than accessing and retrieving data from multiple physical files, a single logical file can be created that appears to combine all the needed data into one file. In actuality, no data is duplicated, but access to the data is made easier. Logical files can also be used to exert record and field level control over data.

FIGURE 5.18

The Processes Required to Create an AS/400 File and Data Member

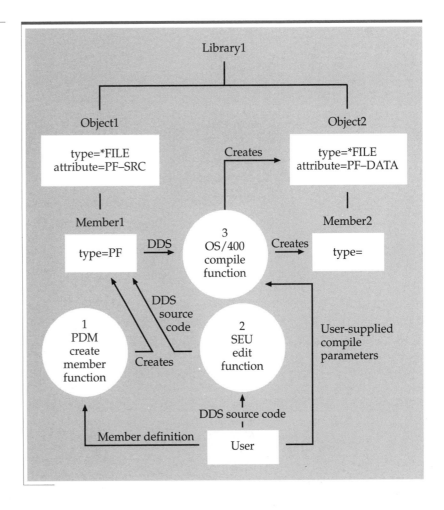

LAB EXERCISE

This database lab exercise will create a joined logical file of three physical files. The three files will be the BATCH, CARTON, and ITEM files defined in the chapter. The logical file will contain each carton's number, store it was sent to, date of expiration, and type of milk.

1. If the BATCH and CARTON files have not been created, create the members in YOURLIBXX within INVSRC, enter the DDS source (see Figures 5.15 and 5.16 for the DDS source), and compile the members.

2. If the members ITEM and ITBATCAR in YOURLIBXX within INVSRC have not been created, create them now. (Use CRTMBR, the CL program created in the second lab exercise in Chapter 3 to create these new members.)

3. Enter the following DDS into member ITEM:

```
************** Beginning of data ***************************
0001.00    *     THIS PHYSICAL FILE IS THE ITEM FILE DDS DEFINITION
0002.00    *
0003.00                                UNIQUE
0004.00          R ITMFMT              TEXT('ITEM FORMAT')
0005.00            ITMNUM    6         COLHDG('ITEM' 'NUMBER')
0006.00                                TEXT('ITEM NUMBER')
0007.00                                CHECK(ME)
0008.00            ITMNAM   15         COLHDG('ITEM' 'NAME')
0009.00                                TEXT('ITEM NAME')
0010.00          K ITMNUM
************** End of data ****************************
```

4. Press **F3** to exit the SEU Edit screen and from the Exit screen, save the DDS.

5. Go to the Work with Members screen and compile ITEM.

6. Enter the following DDS into ITBATCAR:

```
************** Beginning of data ***************************
0001.00    *    THIS IS THE LOGICAL FILE FOR THE JOIN OF THE BATCH, CARTON,
0002.00    *    AND ITEM FILES
0003.00                                UNIQUE
0004.00          R ITBATCARFT          JFILE(YOURLIBXX/CARTON +
0005.00                                      YOURLIBXX/BATCH +
0006.00                                      YOURLIBXX/ITEM)
0007.00                                TEXT('LOGICAL CARTON')
0008.00          J                     JOIN(1 2)
0009.00                                JFLD(BCHNUM BCHNUM)
0010.00          J                     JOIN(2 3)
0011.00                                JFLD(ITMNUM ITMNUM)
0012.00            CRTNUM
0013.00            ITMNAM
0014.00            EXPDTE
0015.00            STORE
0016.00          K CRTNUM
************** End of data ****************************
```

7. Save and compile the member. A new logical file, ITBATCAR, will be created that contains the carton number and store number from CARTON, the type of milk in the carton from ITEM, and the carton's expiration date from BATCH.

Notice the two join specifications and JFLD keywords that were required to join the three files. The CARTON and BATCH files were linked by their shared field of BCHNUM, and then the correct ITEM record was linked through ITMNUM (the field ITEM shares with BATCH). Also notice that the join fields do not have to have field level specifications. Even though the join fields are used to create the logical file, they are not included in the file definition. The join fields are just used to build the access path to the data. No information contained in the join fields can be accessed through the logical file because the join fields do not have a field level specification.

REVIEW QUESTIONS

1. Why is DDS the primary data definition tool on the AS/400?
2. What are the three database models?
3. Describe a parent–child data relationship.
4. Which database model organizes data into tables?
5. What is a DDL? A DML?
6. Explain the relationship between logical and physical files.
7. Explain the relationship between logical files, source physical file members with a type of LF, and physical file members with no type.
8. What is the difference between file, record, and field specifications? Give a keyword function example that is available at each level.
9. What advantages are there to including edits and audits in the file definition rather than the application programs?
10. What is the user view of data, and how does the AS/400 support it?

DISCUSSION QUESTIONS

1. What are the advantages and disadvantages of the three database models? Evaluate them in terms of speed of retrieval and updating, ease of use, storage efficiency, and complexity of relationships supported.

2. What other situations can you think of where information about an item could be as important as the item itself? For instance, which is more valuable, the money that each customer owes a company or the company file that keeps track of how much each customer owes? What would happen if a company's accounts receivable information was lost?

3. Discuss the advantages of externally described files over internally described files.

Data File Utility

6

This chapter deals with creating programs to load and modify data using the system-provided Data File Utility (DFU). A brief discussion of data manipulation on the AS/400 starts the chapter and is followed with a DFU example that walks through the DFU program definition screens, explaining the options available at each screen. The result of the example is a program that allows data to be entered into the INVDATA file (created in the previous chapter).

After finishing the chapter, you will understand:

- The capabilities of a Data Manipulation Language (DML)
- How DFU performs typical DML functions
- The advantages and disadvantages of DFU

You also will be able to:

- Create and define permanent and temporary DFU programs
- Load data by running a DFU program
- Save, retrieve, and modify DFU programs

Data Manipulation Languages

Data Manipulation Languages (DMLs) allow a user to change, add, delete, and, to a limited extent, display data. These languages have unique commands and syntax to easily perform these functions. The AS/400 does not have a stand-alone DML. Rather, standard DML functions can be performed using any of the AS/400-supported programming languages or either of two AS/400 utilities.

- **Applications**. Application programs can be written to perform data manipulation. To perform complex calculations or follow complex logic, it is best to use a programming language and develop individual update programs. Though SQL (Structured Query Language) and DFU can perform many database functions, no DML or utility can provide the control of a programming language. To use a medical example, a DML is like a surgeon's scalpel. It can perform many delicate operations. However, for complex or very precise work, a laser may be needed. A programming language is like a laser. It can provide greater precision and control. However, just as with a laser, a programming language is much more complicated and time consuming to use. The time and effort to develop, debug, and execute an application program can be considerably longer than updating with a DML. For simple updating tasks, it is usually easier to use DFU or SQL; however, for complex operations, an application program will be required.

- **SQL/400**. SQL/400 is the AS/400's version of SQL. SQL is a relational database language that allows users to manipulate and define data. It combines the functions of DDS (Data Description Specification), DFU, Query/400, and the data retrieval capability of a high-level programming language. SQL has specific commands that allow the user to perform data manipulation functions such as adding, updating, and deleting.

- **DFU**. DFU provides an even easier, simpler way to enter and change data. Rather than writing a data update program in a programming language, DFU writes the program for you. Through a series of menus and screens, DFU prompts for information regarding the data to work with, the program functions to be included, and the screen format. It then creates an update screen and program that can enter, change, or delete data in a file. The user also has the option to save or discard this system-created update program. Essentially, DFU provides the user with a "quick and dirty" way to create update programs for files that were defined with DDS, IDDU (Interactive Data Definition Utility), or RPG.

Invoking DFU

To start DFU, type in the CL command **STRDFU** at any command line and press ENTER. This will result in the AS/400 Data File Utility (DFU) screen (Figure 6.1). This display allows users to create permanent

FIGURE 6.1

```
                        AS/400 Data File Utility (DFU)

Select one of the following:

         1.  Run a DFU program
         2.  Create a DFU program
         3.  Change a DFU program
         4.  Delete a DFU program
         5.  Update data using temporary program








Selection or command
===>_____
                                                              _
F3=Exit        F4=Prompt        F9=Retrieve       F12=Cancel
```

or temporary programs to manipulate data in the database. If a permanent DFU program already exists, this screen enables the user to change or delete it.

To choose an option from the AS/400 Data File Utility (DFU) screen, type the option number at the command line and press ENTER.

Entering and Saving Data Using Temporary DFU Programs

As an example, let's create a temporary program to add data to the inventory file we defined in the last chapter. Choose option 5 and press ENTER. The Update Data Using Temporary Program screen will be displayed (Figure 6.2). At this screen, identify the data file created in the previous chapter by entering the correct library, file, and member names. Press ENTER. DFU will begin creating a program that allows a user to change or enter data to the file. After the program has been created, DFU will automatically execute it, and an update screen will be displayed (Figure 6.3).

Since the data member from the last chapter is empty, the program defaults to *entry mode*. Entry mode allows a user to append records to the end of the file. The update screen will have input areas for each field defined by the file's DDS. The input area is designated by underscores to the right of the field name, and the size of the area is defined by the DDS. To add a record to the file, fill in the fields as shown in Figure 6.4 and press F9. This will bring up another blank entry screen, where another record can be inserted.

To exit and save the new data, press F3. This will bring up the End Data Entry screen (Figure 6.5), which displays information on

FIGURE 6.2

```
                    Update Data Using Temporary Program
      Type choices, press Enter.

      Data file . . . . . . .      invdata    Name, F4 for list
        Library . . . . . . .                 yourlibXX Name, *LIBL, *CURLIB
      Member. . . . . . . . .      invdata    Name, *FIRST, F4 for list

      F3=Exit        F4=Prompt         F12=Cancel
```

FIGURE 6.3

```
      WORK WITH DATA IN A FILE              Mode . . . . : ENTRY
      Format . . . . :    INVFMT            File . . . . : INVDATA

      ITEM NUMBER:          ____
      ITEM NAME:            _____
      EOQ AMOUNT:           ___
      QUANTITY IN STOCK:    ___
      REORDER POINT:        ___
      UNIT PRICE:           _____
      SUPPLIER NAME:        _____
      SUPPLIER ADDRESS:     _____
      CITY:                 _____
      STATE:                __
      ZIPCODE:              _____

      F3=Exit       F5=Refresh      F6=Select format
      F9=Insert     F10=Entry       F11=Change
```

the changes, additions, and deletions that were made by the DFU program. Enter Y at the End data entry prompt and press enter. At this point, DFU will create an audit report that contains the changed data and other audit report information (Figure 6.6).

Changing Data Using DFU

To change existing information, invoke DFU again. Because the file now contains data, the DFU program will default to change mode. The change screen will contain only the key field(s) (Figure 6.7).

FIGURE 6.4

```
WORK WITH DATA IN A FILE                 Mode . . . . . : ENTRY
Format . . . . :      INVFMT             File . . . . . : INVDATA

ITEM NUMBER:          1
ITEM NAME:            turnip
EOQ AMOUNT:           25
QUANTITY IN STOCK:    43
REORDER POINT:        50
UNIT PRICE:           22
SUPPLIER NAME:        American Turnip Corp
SUPPLIER ADDRESS:     101 Vegetable Lane
CITY:                 Bangor
STATE:                ME
ZIPCODE:              11111




F3=Exit        F5=Refresh      F6=Select format
F9=Insert      F10=Entry       F11=Change
```

FIGURE 6.5

```
                        End Data Entry

Number of records processed

   Added . . . . . :       1
   Changed . . . . :       0
   Deleted . . . . :       0




Type choice, press Enter.

   End data entry . . . . . . . Y      Y=Yes, N=No





F3=Exit        F12=Cancel
```

The user would enter the key value for the particular record to be changed. To change the turnip record, type **1** in the ITEM NUMBER input area and press **F11**, the Change option. The turnip record would appear with all the previously defined field values displayed. To change any of the data, move the cursor to the field to be changed and type over the current value. For instance, say two turnips were sold this week (probably the biggest non-Thanksgiving run on turnips all year). This means the quantity in stock has decreased to 41. Move the cursor to the QUANTITY IN STOCK field and type the new stock quantity, **41**. The new data is

FIGURE 6.6

```
5738SS1   V2R1M0 910524   AUDIT LOG              9/23/92 13:37:56  PAGE 1


Library/File . . . . .    YOURLIBXX/INVDATA
Member . . . . . . . .    INVDATA
Job Title . . . . . .     WORK WITH DATA IN A FILE


           ITEM      ITEM      EOQ       QUANTITY    REORDER   UNIT
           NUMBER    NAME      AMOUNT    IN STOCK    POINT     PRICE
Added      1         turnip    25        43          50        .22


           SUPPLIER            SUPPLIER            CITY     STATE ZIPCODE
           NAME                ADDRESS

American Turnip Corp  101 Vegetable Lane  Bangor    ME    11111

              1 Records Added
              0 Records Changed
              0 Records Deleted
        * * * * E N D   O F   D F U   A U D I T   R E P O R T * * * * * * * *
```

FIGURE 6.7

```
WORK WITH DATA IN A FILE           Mode . . . . . : CHANGE
Format . . . . : INVFMT            File . . . . . : INVDATA

ITEM NUMBER:          ____












F3=Exit        F5=Refresh      F6=Select format
F9=Insert      F10=Entry       F11=Change
```

not inserted into the file when the old value is typed over. To make the change to the file, press F11. A blank change screen will reappear (Figure 6.7). This means that the data has been inserted into the file. To verify that the change was made, type item number 1 again and press ENTER. The turnip record will appear with the new value, 41, in the QUANTITY IN STOCK field.

Several other functions can be performed from the change screen by pressing the appropriate function key.

To *delete* a record, enter the key value for the record to be deleted and then press F23. The data fields and the values for the record specified will appear. Pressing F23 a second time will confirm that this is the record to be deleted, and the record will be deleted.

To *insert* data into the file, press F9. A blank screen with all the file's fields will be displayed. Enter field values for the new record and press F9. The new record would be appended to the file and the index updated accordingly. If the file has no key, insert mode would be the same as entry mode—the record would simply be appended to the end of the file. The user can switch between insert, entry, and change modes by pressing F9, F10, and F11, respectively.

For files with multiple formats, the format being used can be changed. Pressing F6 (select format) will result in a list of valid formats for the file being displayed. Select the format by typing 1 next to the format name and pressing ENTER.

As an exercise, enter the records in Figure 6.8 into the file using a temporary DFU program.

FIGURE 6.8
Sample Records

ITEM NUMBER:	2	3	51
ITEM NAME:	cantaloupe	radish	onion
EOQ AMOUNT:	15	75	50
QTY. IN STOCK:	15	0	20
REORDER PT.:	10	50	40
UNIT PRICE:	72	6	350
SUPPLIER NAME:	Amalgamated Fruits	Radishes 'R Us	Stinky's
SUPPLIER ADDRESS:	1 Cherry Blossom Ct	1 Dirt St	Pea-Yew Dr
CITY:	Walla Walla	Larchmont	Vadalia
STATE:	WA	TX	GA
ZIPCODE:	99999	44444	33333

Permanent DFU Programs

The problem with temporary programs is that they must be redefined each time an update is desired. To avoid having to do this, DFU allows users to define and permanently save update programs. More options are available regarding the function and appearance of permanent update programs than are available regarding temporary programs. For instance, permanent programs provide more control over the appearance of the update screen. When a permanent DFU program is created, a permanent screen definition file is also created. This definition can be recalled and changed through several DFU options. The user also has the option to save the screen definition source code. If the source code is saved, it can be edited directly with Source Entry Utility (SEU) or Screen Design Aid (SDA) rather than using the DFU screens. (However, editing the definition directly requires a good understanding of DDS. Further,Chapter 6 on tailoring DFU-created display files in the *DFU Users Guide and Reference Manual* should be studied first.)

Just like temporary programs, permanent programs enable users to enter, insert, change, and display file information. When a permanent program is run, the user selects the mode in which to work. (Temporary programs default to a mode depending on whether the file is empty.) Permanent programs allow the user to select between change mode and display mode. Change mode allows the user to toggle between insert mode and entry mode by using function keys. Display mode does not allow switching to other modes. Display mode provides a very limited viewing function; a user can display only one record at a time by specifying the key value. (For more sophisticated display capabilities, see Chapter 7.)

Creating Permanent Programs

To create a permanent program, select option 2 from the `AS/400 Data File Utility (DFU)` screen (see Figure 6.1). The `Create a DFU Program` screen will be displayed (Figure 6.9). This screen prompts for the library and file name of the data to be updated; this is the same prompt that was used when creating a temporary program. Also on this screen, the library and object that will contain the permanent DFU program need to be specified. The object specified will eventually contain the compiled version of the program.

After the information is entered, press ENTER. This will bring up the `Define General Information/Indexed File` screen (Figure 6.10).

Defining Screen Format and Program Function

The `Define General Information/Indexed File` screen has a series of yes/no prompts that will define what the program does and how the data fields will be displayed on the update screen. For instance, the `Display format` prompt specifies how the fields should be arranged on the update display. The format options are:

- `Single`. Single column is the style used in temporary programs (option 1).
- `Multiple`. Depending on the number of fields, DFU will use two, three, or four columns to fit all the data fields on one screen (option 2).
- `Maximum`. DFU will not "line up" all the entry fields in columns as it did on the temporary program screen. Instead, it will fit as many fields as possible on the screen (option 3).

FIGURE 6.9

```
                         Create a DFU Program

         Type choices, press Enter.

            Program . . . . .   INVDFU        Name, F4 for list
              Library . . . .     YOURLIBXX   Name, *CURLIB

            Data file . . . .   INVDATA       Name, F4 for list
              Library . . . .     YOURLIBXX   Name, *LIBL, *CURLIB







         F3=Exit      F4=Prompt      F12=Cancel
```

FIGURE 6.10

```
                Define General Information/Indexed File

         Type choices, press Enter.

            Job title . . . . . . . . . .     INVDFU
            Display format . . . . . . .      4      1=Single,  2=Multiple
                                                     3=Maximum, 4=Row oriented

            Audit report  . . . . . . . .     Y      Y=Yes, N=No
            S/36 style  . . . . . . . . .     N      Y=Yes, N=No
            Suppress errors . . . . . . .     N      Y=Yes, N=No
            Edit numerics . . . . . . . .     N      Y=Yes, N=No
            Allow updates on roll . . . .     Y      Y=Yes, N=No
            Keys:
              Generate  . . . . . . . . .     N      Y=Yes, N=No
              Changes allowed . . . . . .     Y      Y=Yes, N=No




         F3=Exit      F12=Cancel       F14=Display definition
```

- Row oriented. DFU will display the fields horizontally rather
  than in vertical columns (option 4).

Some examples of options that control the function of the
program are:

- `Allow updates on roll`. This option specifies whether updating should occur when **PAGE UP** or **PAGE DOWN** is pressed. A value of No means **ENTER** must be pressed to save changes. Yes means rolling, as well as pressing **ENTER**, will force updates.

- `Audit report`. This option determines whether an audit report of the changes is generated at the end of the program's execution. Specifying **Y** for this prompt will cause the `Define Audit Control` screen to be displayed (Figure 6.11). This screen allows a user to define the format of the audit report. The information to appear on the audit report can also be specified: just changes, changes and deletions, just additions, and so on.

Once the program, screen, and audit report characteristics have been defined, the fields to be updated must be selected and sequenced. After the audit report specifications have been entered, DFU will prompt for the record format to be used (Figure 6.12). Once the record format is specified, a list of the file's fields is displayed on the `Select and Sequence Fields` screen (Figure 6.13).

To the left of each field name is an underscored area. This is where the field's relative screen position is specified. By typing in numbers—with 1 designating the field that is to appear first—the user can select which fields will appear on the screen and control the order of their appearance. (Typing in a sequence number means the field is also being selected for display.)

FIGURE 6.11

```
                         Define Audit Control

Type choices, press Enter.

     Print additions . . . . . . . .   Y        Y=Yes, N=No
     Print changes . . . . . . . .     Y        Y=Yes, N=No
     Print deletions . . . . . . .     Y        Y=Yes, N=No
     Printer:
        Line width  . . . . . . . .    132      60-198
        Column spacing. . . . . . .    1        0-9




     F3=Exit      F12=Cancel      F14=Display definition
```

FIGURE 6.12

```
                        Work with Record Formats
File . . . . : INVDATA                    Library . . . . : YOURLIBXX

Type options, press Enter. Press F21 to select all.
  2=Specify    4=Delete


                   Multiple
Opt   Format      Records     Defined    Description
 2    INVFMT         N           N       INVENTORY FORMAT












                                                              Bottom
F3=Exit                        F5=Refresh        F12=Cancel
F14=Display definition         F21=Select all
```

FIGURE 6.13

```
                      Select and Sequence Fields
File  . . . . . . . : INVDATA              Library . . : YOURLIBXX
Record format . . . : INVFMT

Select fields and their sequence or press F21 to select all; press Enter.

Sequence  Field     Attr     Length   Type      Description
1         ITMNUM    KEY         6,0    PACK      ITEM NUMBER
2         ITMNME                 15    CHAR      ITEM NAME
11        EOQ                   2,0    PACK      EOQ AMOUNT
8         QTYNST                2,0    PACK      QUANTITY IN STOCK
9         REORDP                2,0    PACK      REORDER POINT
10        UNTPRC                4,2    PACK      UNIT PRICE
3         SUPPL                  20    CHAR      SUPPLIER NAME
4         SUPADD                 20    CHAR      SUPPLIER ADDRESS
5         SUPCTY                 15    CHAR      CITY FOR SUPPLIER
6         SUPST                  °2    CHAR      STATE
7         SUPZP                 5,0    PACK      ZIP CODE
                                                            Bottom
F3=Exit        F5=Refresh    F12=Cancel   F14=Display definition
F20=Renumber   F21=Select all
```

After typing in the sequence numbers, press ENTER. The fields will be rearranged on the screen according to the specified sequence numbers. Pressing ENTER a second time will confirm and record the sequence choice.

(For more information on all the options available and a detailed explanation of each, see Chapter 8 of the *DFU Users Guide and Reference Manual*.)

Defining Field Format

After the field sequence information is entered, the `Work with Fields` screen will be displayed (Figure 6.14). This screen allows the user to specify each field's header and gives the option to define a field's display characteristics.

The headers are initialized to the first word that is specified in the COLHDG keyword of the DDS file definition. If no header values were specified in the DDS, the heading fields will be blank. The user can change the headers by simply typing over the default values.

To specify extended field display information, type **2** in the option field to the left of the field name. This will bring up the `Specify Extended Field Definition` screen (Figure 6.15). Go to the second screen of options by pressing PAGE DOWN (Figure 6.16). Some options that can be specified are:

- `Heading location`. This option defines the header's location relative to the field value—above or before the field.

- `Initial value`. This option allows the user to specify a default value for a field. The default value will be placed in the input area when a new record is being entered.

- `Output only`. This option allows the user to prohibit a value from being entered for this field while in entry mode. The field will be shown only while the program is in display mode.

FIGURE 6.14

```
                        Work with Fields

      File  . . . . . . . :  INVDATA          Library . . :  YOURLIBXX
      Record format . . . :  INVFMT

      Type options, press Enter. Press F21 to select all.
        2=Specify extended definition
        4=Delete extended definition

                        Extended
      Opt Field       Definition          Heading
       2  ITMNUM          N               ITEM
          ITMNME          N               ITEM
          SUPPL           N               SUPPLIER
          SUPADD          N               SUPPLIER
          SUPCTY          N               CITY
          SUPST           N               STATE
          SUPZP           N               ZIPCODE
          QTYNST          N               QUANTITY
                                                            More...

      F3=Exit                      F5=Refresh      F12=Cancel
      F14=Display definition       F21=Select all
```

FIGURE 6.15

```
                    Specify Extended Field Definition

 Field . . . . . . . . :  ITMNUM          Record format . . . :  INVFMT

 Type choices, press Enter.

    Auto-duplicate . . . . . . . .     N            Y=Yes, N=No
    Accumulate . . . . . . . . .       N            Y=Yes, N=No
    Extended field
      heading. . . . . . . . . .       ITEM
                                       NUMBER

    Heading location . . . . . . .     *ABOVE       *ABOVE, *BEFORE
    Initial value . . . . . . . .
    Auto-increment . . . . . . .
    Validity checks. . . . . . .                    2=Change, 4=Delete



                                                                  More...

 F3=Exit        F12=Cancel        F14=Display definition
```

FIGURE 6.16

```
                    Specify Extended Field Definition

 Field . . . . . . . . :  ITMNUM          Record format . . . :  INVFMT

 Type choices, press Enter.

    Begin on new line . . . . . .     N        Y=Yes, N=No
    Field exit required . . . . .     Y        Y=Yes, N=No
    Output only . . . . . . . . .     N        Y=Yes, N=No
    Non-display . . . . . . . . .     N        Y=Yes, N=No
    Default spacing . . . . . . .     Y        Y=Yes, N=No
      For choice N=No:
        Number of spaces . . . . .    01       0-40
    Edit code . . . . . . . . . .     L        Blank, 1-4, A-D, J-M,...
    Edit word . . . . . . . . . .



                                                               Bottom

 F3=Exit        F12=Cancel        F14=Display definition
```

For a further explanation of each option, move the cursor to the option field and press F1. This will activate field help.

After the extended field definitions have been entered, press ENTER. This will bring back the Work with Fields screen. Pressing ENTER at this screen will bring up the Exit DFU Program Definition screen (Figure 6.17). This screen, which is similar to the Exit SEU screen, provides several options regarding saving the DFU program:

FIGURE 6.17

```
                    Exit DFU Program Definition

Type choices, press Enter.

    Save program . . . . . . .   Y          Y=Yes, N=No
    Run program  . . . . . . .   N          Y=Yes, N=No
       For choice Y=Yes:
          Type of run  . . . . .  1          1=Change, 2=Display
    Modify program . . . . . .   N          Y=Yes, N=No
    Save DDS source  . . . . .   Y          Y=Yes, N=No

    For Save program Y=Yes:
       Program . . . . . . . .   INVDFU      Name
          Library . . . . . . .     YOURLIBXX   Name, *CURLIB,. . .
       Authority . . . . . . .    *CHANGE     Name, *LIBCRTAUT, . . .
       Text  . . . . . . . . .   INVDFU

    For Save DDS source Y=Yes:
       Source file . . . . . .   INVSRC Name
          Library . . . . . . .     YOURLIBXX   Name, *CURLIB, . . .
       Source member . . . . .   INVDFUDDS   Name

F3=Exit   F14=Display definition   F17=Fast path
```

- Save program. This option saves the compiled version of the program as an object within a library. The object and library where the program will be stored are specified in the For Save program Y=Yes section.

- Run program. Specifying **Y** will result in the update program being run after the screen is exited. When choosing to run the program, the mode to run in—Change or Display—must also be specified.

- Authority. This option specifies the access others will have to the DFU-generated update program. *CHANGE will give operational authority and all data rights, thereby allowing users to run and change the update program.

- Save DDS source. This option allows users to save the DDS source code that defines the update program's display screen. At the bottom of the screen the library, file, and member names to store it under would also need to be specified. Saving the DDS source code gives the user the option to modify the screen by editing the DDS source code directly rather than working through the DFU screens.

After specifying the program options, press ENTER. In the example shown in Figure 6.17, it was specified not to run the program. Pressing ENTER will cause the Create a DFU Program screen (see Figure 6.9) to be redisplayed with a message saying that the DFU program was successfully saved.

Running a DFU Program

To run a saved program, choose option 1 from the AS/400 Data File Utility (DFU) screen (see Figure 6.1). Choosing this option will bring up two screens where the program to be run, the mode, and the data file to be used are specified. Permanent programs can be run against data files different from the one specified during program definition. The only restriction is that the new file's characteristics—field names, lengths, and so on—match the original file's. For the example, it is assumed that change mode was selected and that the original file was specified.

The DFU display screen will prompt for the key of the record to be changed. Typing in 1 at the ITEM NUMBER prompt and pressing F11 will result in Figure 6.18.

Notice that fields are displayed horizontally, just as we specified in the Display format option on the Define General Information/Indexed File screen (see Figure 6.10). Data is entered and saved with a permanent DFU program the same way as with a temporary program. Also notice that F9, F10, and F11 allow the user to switch between modes.

FIGURE 6.18

```
INVDFU                                  Mode . . . . :    CHANGE
Format . . . . :   INVFMT               File . . . . :    INVDATA

  ITEM      ITEM      SUPPLIER               SUPPLIER
 NUMBER     NAME      NAME                   ADDRESS
   1        turnip    American Turnip Corp   101 Vegetable Lane

CITY      STATE   ZIPCODE    QUANTITY     REORDER    UNIT      EOQ
                             IN STOCK     POINT      PRICE     AMOUNT
Bangor    ME      11111         41          50         22       25




F3=Exit        F5=Refresh      F6=Select format
F9=Insert      F10=Entry       F11=Change
```

Changing DFU Programs

To change the function or screen layout of a permanent DFU program, select option 3 from the AS/400 Data File Utility (DFU) screen (see Figure 6.1). This option leads through all the definition screens covered in the Creating Permanent Programs section. On each screen, the values that were defined when the program was created will be displayed. At that time, the user has the option to change the values and save them.

Deleting DFU Programs

Selecting option 4 from the AS/400 Data File Utility (DFU) screen (see Figure 6.1) will allow the user to delete a permanent program. The Delete a DFU Program screen (Figure 6.19) will be displayed. To delete a program, specify the program name and library and then press ENTER. A confirmation screen will be displayed. Pressing ENTER at the confirmation screen will delete the program.

FIGURE 6.19

```
                        Delete a DFU Program

   Type choices, press Enter.

       Program . . . . . . . .   INVDFU       Name,   F4 for list
       Library . . . . . . .     YOURLIBXX    Name,   *LIBL, *CURLIB

















   F3=Exit        F4=Prompt        F12=Cancel
```

Summary

DFU provides a quick and easy way to add and update data to AS/400 files. AS/400 files (and their source definition members) are created by using PDM and SEU. These data files, in turn, can be updated by DFU-generated temporary and permanent programs (process 1 in Figure 6.20). Data files are not updated by DFU. Rather, DFU creates programs (process 2 in Figure 6.20), based on user specifications, that access and update data members (Figure 6.20). These temporary or permanent programs display data to and receive data from the user (process 1 in Figure 6.20). The data is then updated according to the mode in which the program is running. DFU acts as an application program generator.

For the definition of permanent programs, a wider variety of program function options are provided that allow the user to tailor the update function. For instance, programs and screens can be defined for selected portions of files, thereby providing field-level security for updating the data.

Though DFU is a quick way to generate update programs, any significant amount of data would be burdensome to load through a

DFU-generated program. Moreover, any coordination of updating between files or calculations to generate information are beyond DFU's capabilities. In either of these cases, a "home grown" or purchased application program would probably be a more cost-efficient and effective solution.

FIGURE 6.20

Creating and Using DFU-Generated Update Programs

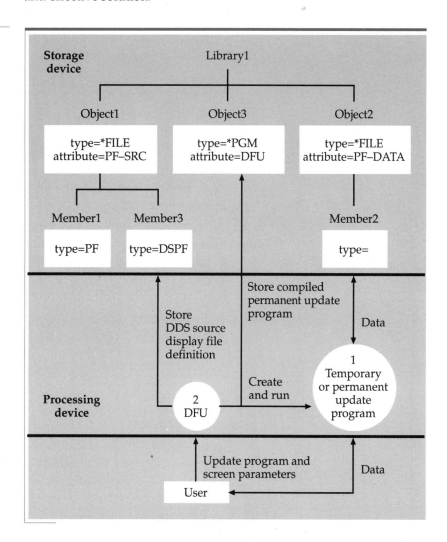

LAB EXERCISE

This exercise will load data into the previously defined physical files ITEM, BATCH, and CARTON using programs created through DFU.

1. Invoke DFU by typing the **STRDFU** command at the command line and pressing ENTER.

2. Enter option 2 at the command line of the AS/400 Data File Utility (DFU) screen and press ENTER.

3. At the `Create a DFU Program` screen, enter **ITEMDFU** at the `Program` prompt, **YOURLIBXX** at the `Library` prompt, **ITEM** at the `Data file` prompt, and **YOURLIBXX** at the `Data file Library` prompt. Press **ENTER**.

4. At the `Define General Information/Indexed File` screen, specify **4** at the `Display format` option and press **ENTER**.

5. At the `Define Audit Control` screen, make sure **Y** is specified for all print options. Press **ENTER**.

6. At the `Work with Record Formats` screen, type **2** next to the only format option available, `ITMFMT`.

7. At the `Select and Sequence Fields` screen, have item name appear before item number by typing **2** next to `ITMNUM` and **1** next to `ITMNME`. Press **ENTER** twice.

8. At the `Work with Fields` screen, type **2** next to `ITMNUM` and press **ENTER** to further define how the fields will appear on the update screen.

9. At the `Specify Extended Field Definition` screen, press **PAGE DOWN** to display the `Default spacing` prompt. Enter **N** at the prompt and specify **15** at the `Number of spaces` prompt. Press **ENTER** twice. (This will force 15 spaces between the item number and item name fields on the update screen.)

10. At the `Exit DFU Program Definition` screen, make sure **Y** is specified at the `Save program`, `Run program`, and `Save DDS source` prompts. Press **ENTER**.

11. At the `For Save DDS source Y=yes` prompt, specify **INVSRC** as the `Source file`, **YOURLIBXX** as the `Library`, and **ITEMD-FUDDS** as the `Source member`.

12. Press **ENTER**. This will save the update program in an object called ITEMDFU, the update screen's DDS definition in a member called ITEMDFUDDS, compile the screen definition member, and save the compiled screen defintion in YOURLIBXX. The update program will also be invoked.

13. At the `Change a Data File` screen, press **ENTER**.

14. At the entry screen, load the following data into the ITEM file.

ITEM NAME	ITEM NUMBER
WHOLE MILK	111111
SKIM MILK	888888
1% LOWFAT MILK	666666
CHOCOLATE MILK	444444
2% LOWFAT MILK	222222

15. After the 2% lowfat milk data has been entered, press **F3** to exit.

16. At the `End Data Entry` screen, make sure a **Y** is specified at the `End data entry` prompt and press ENTER.

17. At the command line, type **WRKSPLF** to view a list of all spool files. (This assumes that the INITPGM was created and defined in the user profile as the initial program to call and is directing all spooled output to a queue.)

18. Look at the audit report generated by the update program by typing **5** next to the last spool file listed.

19. Compare the audit report data to the data specified in step 14. If there are any differences, rerun the ITEMDFU update program in change mode and enter the correct data.

20. Issue the WRKOBJ command to look at the objects currently in YOURLIBXX. Do this by typing **WRKOBJ** at the command line and pressing ENTER.

21. Specify **YOURLIBXX** at the `Library` prompt and ***ALL** for the other prompts. Press ENTER.

22. Notice that there are two new objects in the library: ITEMDFU with a type of *PGM and ITEMDFU with a type of *DSPF. There is also one new member in file INVSRC—ITEMDFUDDS with a type of PF. These were created and stored in YOURLIBXX in step 12. Exit by pressing F3.

23. At the command line, type **DSPPFM** for the display physical file member command. (This command will display the contents of the physical file; however, any numeric fields that were defined as packed will not be readable.)

24. Press F4. At the prompts, specify **ITEM** and **YOURLIBXX** and press ENTER. Notice that the information is stored in arrival sequence even though a key was defined for that file. Also notice that the item number is stored first (as defined in the DDS) rather than how it was entered on the update screen.

25. Exit the `Display Physical File Member` screen by pressing F3.

26. At the `AS/400 Data File Utility (DFU)` screen, choose option 5, `Update data using temporary program`.

27. Use a temporary program to enter the following data into the BATCH and CARTON files.

    For the BATCH file:

BATCH NUMBER	EXPIRATION DATE	TEMP	ITEM NUMBER
1234	102392	45	666666
2345	093093	38	111111
5678	051890	42	888888
3456	080392	44	111111
6789	012389	40	222222

For the CARTON file:

CARTON NUMBER	CARTON SIZE	STORE CODE	BATCH NUMBER
A36SS234	HALF GALLON	8612745	3456
J836H527	PINT	9370397	6789
F838938D	QUART	8937626	1234
5GDQ3752	GALLON	2894628	6789
M7462650	QUART	8458532	2345
FY86DY83	HALF PINT	2894628	3456
87Q83J93	GALLON	1274007	6789

28. Access the audit reports (as in steps 17 and 18) and verify that the data was entered correctly for BATCH and CARTON.

REVIEW QUESTIONS

1. What two types of update programs can be generated through DFU?
2. What is the other major data manipulation utility (besides DFU) available on the AS/400?
3. Explain the modes in which a DFU-generated update program can work.
4. What is an audit report, and to what extent can the user control the report's data content and format?
5. To what extent does DFU allow the user to modify already existing update programs?
6. How can a user control access to DFU-generated update programs?
7. What are the guidelines regarding running update programs against files other than the file originally defined?
8. What are the disadvantages of using DFU-generated update programs for large quantities of data?

DISCUSSION QUESTIONS

1. What are the advantages and disadvantages to using DFU versus a user-written application program to update files on the AS/400?
2. Discuss the functions and user control available when creating temporary versus permanent programs.

Query

7

The AS/400 offers many utilities to access and manipulate stored data. The easiest and most user friendly is Query/400. Through a series of easy-to-use screens and menus, Query/400 enables the user to select and view data. Query/400 also provides an extensive set of options to control and format the appearance of the output. This chapter covers how to invoke and use Query/400 to access data and how to define, save, and change often used queries. In addition, we walk through the screens and options to define the format of a query report.

After finishing this chapter, you will understand:

- The basic functions of a query tool
- How Query/400 implements these functions

You also will be able to:

- Define, save, recall, and modify a query using Query/400
- Understand and specify the reporting options available

Query Languages

As was discussed in Chapter 5, defining and storing information are of vital interest to computer users. However, the best database systems are worthless if access to the data is not provided. It would be like designing the safest vault in the world that allowed people only to put money in, not take it out. Query languages are a method to gain access to the very valuable data that the last two chapters have shown how to define and load.

A query language is generally defined as a nonprocedural language for database information retrieval. The term *nonprocedural language* usually means a menu-driven system where the user is not required to know any commands or syntax. The user is given options and prompted for a response. The options chosen describe the output or functions to be performed, and the query utility handles the actual retrieval. This is as opposed to many report writers that are command-driven languages. A user must know the commands and their related syntax to get a report. Generally, command languages are geared to hardcopy output.

Query languages, on the other hand, are geared to interactive processing and usually default to sending their output to the display screen. In addition, they offer the options of having the output printed or sent to a file on disk. Most query languages also allow users to store frequently used queries and retrieve them at a later date for execution.

Query/400 allows users to perform all these query functions and provides a great deal of control over the output format. Common report writer features such as report breaks, subtotaling, and summary reporting are also available.

Query/400

Query/400 provides access to information contained in AS/400 data files. Just like the other AS/400 utilities (DFU, PDM, and so on), Query/400 has an easy-to-use menu and screen interface. For instance, rather than typing in file or field names, a user can choose files and fields from lists provided by Query/400.

As discussed in Chapter 5, one method to specify groups of fields is through data formats. Query allows users to specify predefined formats as a way of identifying particular data fields for output. Further, the appearance of each field and its location on the output report can be controlled by selecting options from a Query/400 display screen.

Getting Started

To start Query/400, type in the CL command **STRQRY**. This brings up the Query Utilities screen (Figure 7.1). From this screen, users can select options to work, run, or delete a query using Query/400. The work option is the most flexible. Not only does it allow users to create a query but it also allows users to modify, run, or delete existing queries. There are also several options regarding managing queries.

FIGURE 7.1

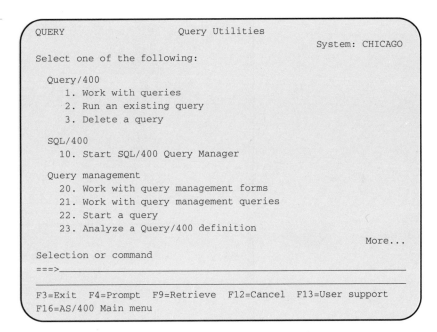

```
QUERY                    Query Utilities
                                              System: CHICAGO
Select one of the following:

  Query/400
     1. Work with queries
     2. Run an existing query
     3. Delete a query

  SQL/400
    10. Start SQL/400 Query Manager

  Query management
    20. Work with query management forms
    21. Work with query management queries
    22. Start a query
    23. Analyze a Query/400 definition
                                                  More...
Selection or command
===>_____

F3=Exit  F4=Prompt  F9=Retrieve  F12=Cancel  F13=User support
F16=AS/400 Main menu
```

To begin creating a query, choose option 1, Work with queries, or type in the CL command **WRKQRY** at the command line and press ENTER. Either of these methods will bring up the Work with Queries screen (Figure 7.2).

Defining a Query

On the Work with Queries screen, specify the library where the query definition is to be stored. At the Query prompt, supply a name for the query definition.

As our example, we are going to build a query that will use the file that was loaded with data in the previous chapter, INV-DATA. So, call the query INVQRY and specify YOURLIBXX as the library in which to store it. To begin creating the query, choose option 1, Create, and press ENTER. This will bring up the Define the Query screen (Figure 7.3), which allows users to choose options that will define the function of the query and the format of the output.

FIGURE 7.2

```
                        Work with Queries

Type choices, press Enter.

  Option . . . . . . _           1=Create, 2=Change,3=Copy,4=Delete
                                 5=Display, 6=Print definition
                                 8=Run in batch, 9=Run
  Query . . . . . . _____   Name, F4 for list
    Library. . . . . YOURLIBXX_  Name, *LIBL, F4 for list
```

```
F3=Exit      F4=Prompt       F5=Refresh       F12=Cancel
```

FIGURE 7.3

```
                        Define the Query
Query . . . . . . :              Option . . . . . : CREATE
  Library . . . . : YOURLIBXX

Type options, press Enter. Press F21 to select all.
  1=Select

Opt   Query Definition Option

 1    Specify file selections
 _    Define result fields
 _    Select and sequence fields
 _    Select records
 _    Select sort fields
 _    Select collating sequence
 _    Specify report column formatting
 _    Select report summary functions
 _    Define report breaks
 _    Select output type and output form
 _    Specify processing options

F3=Exit          F5=Report        F12=Cancel
F13=Layout       F18=Files        F21=Select all
```

Some functional options available on the Define the Query screen are:

- File, record format, and field specifications
- Record selection criteria
- Type of summary information to be created
- Definition of calculated fields
- Decimal rounding

Output format options include:

- Sorting sequences
- Column format
- Report breaks
- Output media

Selecting Files

At the `Define the Query` screen, a 1 will already be in the `Specify file selections` option field. Press ENTER. This will result in the `Specify File Selections` screen being displayed (Figure 7.4). On this screen, the user specifies the library, file, member, and record format to be queried.

FIGURE 7.4

```
                       Specify File Selections

  Type choices, press Enter. Press F9 to specify an additional
    file selection.

  File . . . . . . . . . .     _____    Name, F4 for list
     Library. . . . . . . .    YOURLIBXX_ Name, *LIBL, F4 for list
  Member . . . . . . . .       *FIRST____   Name, *FIRST, F4 for list
  Format . . . . . . . .       *FIRST____   Name, *FIRST, F4 for list




  F3=Exit            F4=Prompt       F5=Report     F9=Add file
  F12=Cancel         F13=Layout      F24=More keys
```

This screen also allows the user to specify more than one file. To identify more than one file, press F9. A new field, `File ID`, will be added to the file definition (Figure 7.5). The file id is an abbreviated way to identify each field's library and file for the rest of the query definition process. Each file and library identified will be assigned a file id. The file id can be up to three alphanumeric characters. If no file id is specified, the system will use T01 and increment the digit for each additional file (that is, the second file would have an id of T02). File id is required for multifile queries because of some added complications regarding identifying fields. The AS/400 allows different files to have fields with the same name; therefore, when a field is specified (in a multifile query), the field name alone is not enough to identify it. The file and library name of the field must also be specified.

FIGURE 7.5

```
                      Specify File Selections

     Type choices, press Enter. Press F9 to specify an additional
       file selection.

       File  . . . . . . . . .   _____   Name, F4 for list
          Library . . . . . . .   YOURLIBXX_   Name, *LIBL, F4 for list
       Member  . . . . . . . .   *FIRST____   Name, *FIRST, F4 for list
       Format  . . . . . . . .   *FIRST____   Name, *FIRST, F4 for list
       File ID . . . . . . . .   *ID          A-Z99, *ID




                                                             Bottom
       F3=Exit              F4=Prompt          F5=Report     F9=Add file
       F12=Cancel           F13=Layout         F24=More keys
```

For instance, say a bank has three files. One file—the customer file—contains the names, addresses, and total assets of all the customers of the bank. The other two files contain savings and checking account information. The savings file has each customer's savings account number, name, amount in savings, and interest paid to date. The checking file has each customer's checking account number, name, amount in the checking account, and date of the last transaction that took place in the checking account. See Figure 7.6 for the file structures and field names.

FIGURE 7.6
Three Bank Files

Customer

Name	Address	Totamt

Savings

Acct#	Name	Totamt	Intamt

Checking

Acct#	Name	Totamt	Dolt

As you'll soon see, when you are specifying the fields to use as output or the fields to use in calculations, it quickly becomes tedious to have to type in the library and file name for each field. This is where the file id field comes in handy. If the customer file was given an id of A, the savings file B, and the checking file C, these single-character ids could be substituted for the library and file names of the fields. In other words, to reference the customer file's TOTAMT field, simply enter A.TOTAMT rather than YOURLIBXX/INVSRC.TOTAMT. The file id is an "annoyance alleviator."

After the files have been identified for a multifile query, press **ENTER**. The `Specify Type of Join` screen will be displayed (Figure 7.7). At this screen and the follow-on screen, the *join criteria* are specified. As mentioned in Chapter 5, several types of relational joins can be performed. At the `Specify Type of Join` screen, the three Query/400 join options are displayed. An explanation of each follows:

- `Matched records`. Selects and displays records that have matching records in all the files (option 1). If several files shared a common field (item number) and a matched record join was specified, only items that had records in all the files would be displayed, and the records from each of the files would be displayed.

FIGURE 7.7

```
                        Specify Type of Join

  Type choice, press Enter.

  Type of join . . . . . .  1    1=Matched records
                                 2=Matched records with primary file
                                 3=Unmatched records with primary file














  F3=Exit            F5=Report          F10=Process/previous
  F12=Cancel         F13=Layout         F18=Files
```

- `Matched records with primary file`. For all records in the primary file (the first file that was specified), displays the primary record and any secondary records that match the join field (option 2). In this case, a printout of every record in the first file plus any matching records from any of the other files would be produced. So a primary record that had a match in all files would be displayed, as well as primary records that had a match in any of the other files. All secondary matching records would also be displayed.

- Unmatched records with primary file. For each record in the primary file that does not have a match in a secondary file, displays the primary record and any matches from the secondary files (option 3). For the multifile example, if a record in the primary file did not have a match in one of the other files, the primary record and the matching records from all the other files would be displayed.

To clarify the difference between the joins, assume that there are four items. Item 1 has a record in each of files A, B, C, D, and E. Item 2 has a record in files A, B, D, and E. Item 3 has a record in file A. And item 4 has a record in files C and D. (See Figure 7.8. An X indicates a record is present in the file for the item number.)

FIGURE 7.8

Record Presence Across Files

Item #	File A	File B	File C	File D	File E
1	X	X	X	X	X
2	X	X		X	X
3	X				
4			X	X	

A matched join using item number as the join field would display information on only item 1. This is because item 1 is the only item that has a record in all five files. The information displayed would be records from each of the five files (Figure 7.9).

FIGURE 7.9

Result of a Matched Records Join

Item1 record A + record B + record C + record D + record E

A matched join with primary file using item number as the join field and file A as the primary file would display information on items 1, 2, and 3, because each of these items has a record in the primary file. This type of join displays all records from the primary file and any matching records from the nonprimary files. The specific records displayed are shown in Figure 7.10.

FIGURE 7.10

Result of a Matched Records with Primary File

Item1 record A + record B + record C + record D + record E

Item2 record A + record B + record D + record E

Item3 record A

An unmatched join with primary file using item number as the join field and file A as the primary file would display information on items 2 and 3. An unmatched join stipulates that items that have a record in the primary file but that are missing a record in any of the nonprimary files should have their information displayed. The information will consist of records from all the files that contain information on that item. Figure 7.11 shows the results for the unmatched join with primary file.

FIGURE 7.11

Result of an Unmatched Records with Primary File Join

Item2 record A + record B + record D + record E

Item3 record A

An unmatched join is often used to check a database's integrity. For instance, if an item was supposed to have a record in each file, an unmatched join would help locate some of the problem items. Notice how the choice of the primary file will affect which items are displayed. In the example, items 2 and 3 were displayed because they had records in file A. Notice that item 4 also is missing records from some of the files. Using A as the primary file will not catch item 4. In fact, file C or D must be specified as the primary file to highlight item 4 as a problem. To do a thorough search for items with missing records, an unmatched join using each of the five files as the primary file must be done.

If there is still some confusion, another way to think of the three joins is that the data produced by a `Matched records with primary file` join is equal to the data produced by the `Matched records` join and the `Unmatched records with primary file` join combined. (If that was even more confusing, forget I mentioned it.)

Once the type of join has been selected (which for the bank query example would be option 1), the `Specify How to Join Files` screen would be displayed (Figure 7.12). At this screen, specify the common field(s) that the files share and the argument to determine the records chosen. For the bank example, all three files share the customer's name. The customer's name would be the shared field used to join each of the three files' records, and EQ (equal) would be the argument (that is, each record that shares the same value for the field will be joined).

For our exercise in this chapter, we will not be querying multiple files. We will build a query to access the file that was loaded in Chapter 6 (INVDATA) and display items that need to be reordered. The query will also calculate the cost for each order and an overall total cost for all orders. So, identify INVDATA in library YOURLIBXX as the file to be selected (see Figure 7.4) and press ENTER. This will select INVDATA as the file to be queried, and the `Define the Query` screen will be redisplayed.

FIGURE 7.12

```
                    Specify How to Join Files

Type comparisons to show how file selections are related, press Enter.
   Tests: EQ, NE, LE, GE, LT, GT

Field                 Test       Field
_____      _____      _____
_____      _____      _____
_____      _____      _____
_____      _____      _____



                                                            Bottom
                                                           More...
F3=Exit        F5=Report    F10=Process/previous  F11=Display text only
F12=Cancel  F13=Layout  F18=Files              F24=More keys
```

Defining Result Fields

Select the Define result fields option from the Define the Query screen. The Define Result Fields screen will be displayed (Figure 7.13). At this screen, new fields to be calculated can be defined and selected for display by the query. These new fields can use any data selected in the previous options.

Several pieces of information are required whenever a new field is defined. Of course, Query/400 prompts for this information and provides all the available options on the Define Result Fields screen. The required information and the data areas to specify them are as follows:

- Field. Specifies the name of the new field to be calculated.

- Expression. Shows how to calculate the new field. Both numeric and string operators are available for defining the new field. The basic numeric operations—addition, subtraction, multiplication, and division—are performed with the +, -, *, and / symbols. The string functions of substring and concatenation are expressed by SUBSTR and | |. The string operators can be used on character fields or constants.

    At the bottom of the screen, Query/400 conveniently provides a list of all the fields in the file(s) that have been specified for this query. This saves the user from leaving the query definition and looking up the names or the correct spelling of the fields.

- Column Heading. Allows text to be defined that will appear as a column heading on the query report.

FIGURE 7.13

```
                        Define Result Fields
   Type definitions using field names or constants and operators,press Enter.
     Operators: +, -, *, /, SUBSTR, | |

   Field              Expression                Column Heading    Len   Dec
   ORDCST_____      UNTPRC*EOQ_____        Order_____    _6    _2
                      _____         Cost_____
                      _____         _____
   _____          _____         _____         __    __
                      _____         _____
                      _____         _____
                                                                         Bottom
   Field              Field            Field
   ITMNUM             REORDP           SUPCTY
   ITMNME             UNTPRC           SUPST
   EOQ                SUPPL            SUPZP
   QTYNST             SUPADD
                                                                         Bottom
   F3=Exit      F5=Report     F9=Insert        F11=Display text only
   F12=Cancel   F13=Layout    F20=Reorganize   F24=More keys
```

- Len and Dec. Len defines the length of the field, and for numeric fields, Dec defines the number of positions within the length that should be devoted to decimals.

For our example, we are going to calculate a new field called ORDCST (order cost). This field is the cost, in dollars, of ordering items for inventory. It is calculated by multiplying each item's economic order quantity (EOQ) by its unit price (UNTPRC). Since it is a dollar figure, we will need two digits for decimals and a maximum of six digits overall. Let's have Order Cost appear as the header.

To define the new field, type the information as shown in Figure 7.13 and press ENTER. The Define the Query screen will be redisplayed.

Selecting and Sequencing Fields

The Select and sequence fields option from the Define the Query screen allows the user to select specific fields to appear on the query output and designate the order in which they will be displayed. Up to this point, there have been only options that allow the user to specify groups of data, such as files, for the query report. This option begins the process of fine-tuning the query to retrieve the exact data needed.

After the option has been selected, the Select and Sequence Fields screen will be displayed (Figure 7.14). All the fields from the files selected and any result fields that were defined will appear on this screen. To specify which fields should appear on the output, type a number (up to four digits) in the sequence field to the left of the field name. This sequence number both selects the field for display and

FIGURE 7.14

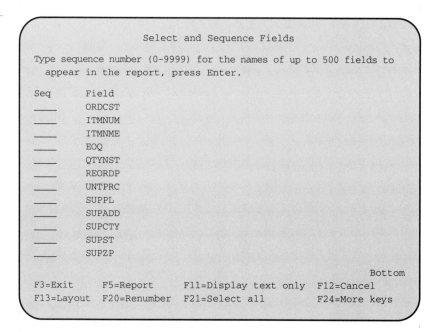

```
                    Select and Sequence Fields
  Type sequence number (0-9999) for the names of up to 500 fields to
    appear in the report, press Enter.

  Seq        Field
  _____      ORDCST
  _____      ITMNUM
  _____      ITMNME
  _____      EOQ
  _____      QTYNST
  _____      REORDP
  _____      UNTPRC
  _____      SUPPL
  _____      SUPADD
  _____      SUPCTY
  _____      SUPST
  _____      SUPZP

                                                             Bottom
  F3=Exit      F5=Report      F11=Display text only   F12=Cancel
  F13=Layout   F20=Renumber   F21=Select all          F24=More keys
```

indicates the field's relative "left to right" position in regard to the other selected fields. For instance, a field with sequence number 100 would be to the right of a field with sequence number 90 and to the left of a field with sequence number 110. However, if there were no fields with a sequence number from 1 to 99, the field with sequence number 100 would be the leftmost field on the query output.

For our example, select the following fields and have them displayed in the shown order:

ITMNUM

SUPPL

SUPADD

SUPCTY

SUPST

SUPZP

ITMNME

ORDQTY

ORDCST

After entering the data, press ENTER twice. The first time will sequence the fields in the order of the sequence numbers specified. The second time confirms the field's order and makes it a permanent part of the query definition.

Selecting Records

Query/400 also allows specific records to be selected. Records can be chosen based on their field values and according to tests specified by the query creator. For instance, from the bank example earlier, the query could be defined to display only account records for people with assets over $100. This means selecting records based on the value of the TOTAMT field in the customer file, and the criterion or test is "Is TOTAMT greater than $100" (TOTAMT GT 100). Choosing the `Select records` option on the `Define the Query` screen will result in the `Select Records` screen being displayed (Figure 7.15).

At this screen, the user would specify the field(s) to be tested in the field area and the test in the test area. The test options are displayed at the top of the screen. The most common operands are equal to, not equal to, less than, and greater than. Also on this screen is an area to specify the value to be used in the test. This can take the form of a number, a character string, or the value contained in another field. In the bank example, it would be the number 100.

Another area on the `Select Records` screen has a header of `AND/OR`. This field allows the user to create a compound argument for the test. Records could be selected based on more than one value for a field or more than one field's value. For instance, if a list of all customers with balances less than $100 and all customers with $1000 or more was needed, the TOTAMT field would be specified twice with two different tests. The first test would check for TOTAMT less than $100 (TOTAMT LT 100), and the second test would be for TOTAMT greater than or equal to $1000 (TOTAMT GE 1000). These two tests would be connected by the operand OR. This means that if either test is true (the amount of the record is less than $100 OR greater than or equal to $1000), the record will be displayed by the query. An AND connector can also be used. The AND operand says that both tests must be true in order to select the record. If the tests had been connected with an AND, no records would be chosen because no amount can be both less than $100 and greater than or equal to $1000.

The same field does not have to be used in each test. The first test could be specified for the TOTAMT field and the second one against the name field—TOTAMT GT 100 AND NAME EQ 'John Q. Public'. This query would select records only for anyone with the name John Q. Public and total assets greater than $100.

For the inventory example, we want to choose all items in the INVDAT file whose stock quantity has fallen below the reorder point. To build that argument, type in the information as seen in Figure 7.16 and press ENTER.

FIGURE 7.15

```
                              Select Records
Type comparisons, press Enter. Specify OR to start each new group.
  Tests: EQ, NE, LE, GE, LT, GT, RANGE, LIST, LIKE

AND/OR  Field              Test    Value (Field, Number, or 'Characters')
        _____       ____    _____
 ____   _____       ____    _____
 ____   _____       ____    _____
 ____   _____       ____    _____
 ____   _____       ____    _____
                                                                  Bottom
Field              Field              Field
ITMNUM             SUPZP              REORDP
SUPPL              ITMNME             UNTPRC
SUPADD             ORDQTY
SUPCTY             ORDCST
SUPST              QTYNST

                                                                 More...
F3=Exit    F5=Report    F9=Insert       F11=Display text only
F12=Cancel F13=Layout   F20=Reorganize  F24=More keys
```

If multiple files had been chosen for this query, this would have been one of the screens where the file id would have come in handy. Without the file id, a library and file name would be necessary for each field referenced in a test. With the file ids, the customer file's and checking file's fields could be easily specified as A.TOTAMT for the total amount file in the customer file or C.DOLT for the date of last transaction field in the checking file.

Also notice how Query/400 displays a list of all the fields that can be used by the query. This includes all fields in the file(s) selected, not just the display fields selected in the previous option.

FIGURE 7.16

```
                              Select Records
Type comparisons, press Enter. Specify OR to start each new group.
  Tests: EQ, NE, LE, GE, LT, GT, RANGE, LIST, LIKE

AND/OR  Field              Test    Value (Field, Number, or 'Characters')
        QTYNST_____     LT___   REORDP_____
 ____   _____       ____    _____
 ____   _____       ____    _____
 ____   _____       ____    _____
 ____   _____       ____    _____
                                                                  Bottom
Field              Field              Field
ITMNUM             SUPZP              REORDP
SUPPL              ITMNME             UNTPRC
SUPADD             ORDQTY
SUPCTY             ORDCST
SUPST              QTYNST

                                                                 More...
F3=Exit    F5=Report    F9=Insert       F11=Display text only
F12=Cancel F13=Layout   F20=Reorganize  F24=More keys
```

Sorting

After the fields and records for display have been specified, the output's appearance can begin to be defined. One of the first options is selecting sort fields. Choosing this option will result in the `Select Sort Fields` screen being displayed (Figure 7.17). All the fields specified on the `Select and Sequence Fields` screen will be listed and can be selected as sort fields.

To choose a field, type a number in the sort priority field to the far left of the field name. This will select the field as a sort field. The number given to the field will determine its relative importance. The smaller the number, the higher the sort priority. The field with the smallest sort priority number is the primary sort field. All other sort fields are secondary sorts, and their order of precedence is according to increasing priority number.

For instance, if SUPST was selected with number 50, SUPZP was selected with number 51, and the sort was in ascending order, the list of records would be in alphabetical order by supplier's state (Alabama first, Alaska second, and so on), and records from the same state would be sorted in zip code order.

FIGURE 7.17

```
                          Select Sort Fields

   Type sort priority (0-999) and A (Ascending) or D (Descending) for
     the names of up to 32 fields, press Enter.

   Sort
   Prty     A/D        Field
   ____      _         ITMNUM
   ____      _         SUPPL
   ____      _         SUPADD
   ____      _         SUPCTY
   ____      _         SUPST
   ____      _         SUPZP
   ____      _         ITMNME   .
   ____      _         EOQ
   ____      _         ORDCST

                                                             Bottom
   F3=Exit      F5=Report   F11=Display text only   F12=Cancel
   F13=Layout   F18=Files   F20=Renumber            F24=More keys
```

Another option to specify for each sort field is the order of the sort—ascending or descending. One field can be sorted in ascending order and another field in descending order. For instance, the sort based on SUPZP could be in descending order by typing **D** in the A/D field next to the field name. In this case, the list of records would still be displayed in ascending alphabetical order by the supplier's state, but records with the same state value would progress from the largest zip code for that state to the smallest zip code. If A or D is not specified, ascending is assumed.

Another option in the Define the Query screen, Select collating sequence, can also affect sorting. This option gets very particular about character sorts. Character data can be treated in several different ways. For instance, how should uppercase and lowercase letters be sorted—uppercase first or lowercase first? Further, a different order may be required to get foreign language words into alphabetical order. The Select Collating Sequence screen gives the option to define a sort order for each character. (Users who are unsure of the significance of the collating sequence can read the section on the subject in the *Query/400 Users Guide* or simply accept the default.)

For the inventory query example, select the supplier's name as the primary sort field, choose ascending for the sort order, and press ENTER twice.

Specifying Report Characteristics

Three more options on the Define the Query screen allow further specification regarding the content and appearance of the query output. The options following Select collating sequence control the format of the report columns, the summarization processing the query is to perform, and the location of report breaks.

Selecting Specify report column formatting will bring up the Specify Report Column Formatting screen (Figure 7.18). This screen allows the user to:

1. Specify the spacing between columns. The number entered is the number of spaces to be skipped before the column begins.

2. Specify the wording of the column headings. Initially, any column heading defined in the DDS for each field is used as the default. For a query, this can be changed by simply typing over what is displayed in the column heading field for each field.

3. Specify the size of the fields for each column. Again, the default size is the DDS definition for that field. However, for reporting purposes, a user may decide to change the size of the display field. For instance, unit price is defined in the DDS as four digits with two decimal places. If a query were created to display unit prices, but only for items that were under a dollar, you would want to redefine the value of the unit price field to two digits with two decimal places.

   The length parameter can also be used to suppress a field. By specifying a length of 0, a field will not be displayed on a query report. For instance, specifying a 0 in the quantity in stock (QTYNST) field length would stop any value from being printed for that column. (However, why someone would want to suppress a field explicitly chosen for display is not totally clear to this author.)

FIGURE 7.18

```
                Specify Report Column Formatting

Type information, press Enter.
  Column headings: *NONE, aligned text lines

                  Column
  Field           Spacing     Column Heading        Len  Dec Edit

  ITMNUM             0         ITEM_____      6      0
                              NUMBER_____
                              _____

  SUPPL              2         SUPPLIER_____    20      __
                              NAME_____
                              _____

  SUPADD             2         SUPPLIER_____    20      __
                              ADDRESS_____
                              _____
                                                            More...

  F3=Exit       F5=Report    F10=Process/previous  F12=Cancel
  F13=Layout    F16=Edit     F18=Files             F23=Long comment
```

4. Specify formats for numeric fields. The edit field at the far right of each field can be accessed for numeric fields only. Pressing **F16** will bring up a screen where the type of numeric editing to be performed is defined. Initially, the user specifies whether the field is a date, time, or regular number field. Based on this answer, further options are available regarding how each type of field could be displayed. For nondate and nontime fields, display options cover whether the number should be displayed with a dollar sign, whether leading zeros should be shown or replaced with blanks, whether a comma should be used to indicate thousands, and so on. An example of a date field option is the ability to specify the order of day, month, and year fields.

For our example we will accept all the default values.

The `Select Report Summary Functions` screen (Figure 7.19) allows the user to specify the type of summarization functions to be performed by the query. The options available are:

- Calculate the sum or average
- Find the minimum or maximum value
- Provide a count of the number of values for a field

These functions are similar to the @sum, @max, @min, @count, and @avg functions in Lotus 1-2-3® and most other spreadsheet programs. At the end of the report, the selected summary fields will be displayed for the specified columns. For our example, let's have the query calculate a total amount for order cost (ORDCST).

Up to this point in the query definition, the query is selecting all inventory items to be reordered and calculating the cost of ordering each item. By specifying a summary function for the ORDCST field, a total cost amount of all the items needed by our business will be generated. This is useful information. For instance, we might want to make sure enough money is in the checking and savings accounts to cover this total. Enter the data as seen in Figure 7.19 and press ENTER.

FIGURE 7.19

```
                    Select Report Summary Functions

     Type options, press Enter.
       1=Total  2=Average  3=Minimum  4=Maximum  5=Count

     ---Options---              Field
      _  _  _  _  _             ITMNUM
      _  _  _  _  _             SUPPL
      _  _  _  _  _             SUPADD
      _  _  _  _  _             SUPCTY
      _  _  _  _  _             SUPST
      _  _  _  _  _             SUPZP
      _  _  _  _  _             ITMNME
      _  _  _  _  _             EOQ
      1  _  _  _  _             ORDCST



                                                            Bottom
     F3=Exit      F5=Report    F10=Process/previous  F11=Display text only
     F12=Cancel   F13=Layout   F18=Files             F23=Long comment
```

Report breaks group records on the query report. They also, in conjunction with the summarization options, create subtotals for each group of records specified. However, the effectiveness of report breaks heavily depends on the order of the records.

For instance, if the orders are sorted by supplier's name and if a report break is specified by supplier name, the output records will be grouped by supplier. Because an order cost field has been defined, a subtotal of order cost for each supplier will be generated at the break between each group of supplier records.

If, however, SUPST (supplier state) was specified as the break field, each time a new state was encountered, a subtotal for all the records for that new state would be generated. Since the records are not in state order, the subtotal amount would not include all the orders from that state. In fact, the number would have no meaning.

To clarify, say there were five order records as follows:

Supplier	State	Amount
Jones	Maryland	66.00
Jones	Maryland	100.00
Lane	Maryland	99.00
Smith	Arkansas	50.00
West	Maryland	200.00

If the query was defined to sort these records by supplier name, they would appear as shown in the order of Jones, Lane, Smith, and West. The break field, however, has been set to supplier state. When the query is ready to display the results, the first break will occur after the Lane record. Lane is from Maryland, and Smith is from Arkansas; therefore, since report breaks are by state, and Arkansas is different from Maryland, a report break will be inserted after Lane. A subtotal field for total cost, which includes the first three records, will also be printed.

Next, the Smith record will be printed, and another report break will be inserted because the next record, West's, has a value of Maryland for the state, and this is different from Smith's. Again, a subtotal field will be printed. Then, West's record will be printed, followed by a subtotal field with only West's total cost. Finally, a total summary field for all the records will be included. The output would appear as follows:

Supplier	State	Amount
Jones	Maryland	66.00
Jones		100.00
Lane		99.00
	subtotal	265.00
Smith	Arkansas	50.00
	subtotal	50.00
West	Maryland	200.00
	subtotal	200.00
	total	515.00

Because the order of the sort is by supplier name but the breaks are occurring at each new occurrence of state, the subtotals have no meaning. They do not represent each supplier's order amount nor do they show each state's subtotal. Care should be taken to coordinate sort and break fields.

A nice feature of report breaks is the suppression of repeated values within the record group. For all records within a record group, the value of the break field will be the same (for example, each record in the Maryland group is from Maryland). Therefore, Query/400 will display the value only once, in the first record of the group. A query that has state as the break field would display only the state value for the first record within each report group. The state name would not be repeated in each succeeding record within that group.

Query allows users to define report breaks (Figure 7.20) and also provides report-breaking options to suppress summary data, skip to a new page at each break, or specify text to be printed at each break.

For our example, set up a report break by supplier and press ENTER twice. Another screen will be displayed with the above-mentioned options. Select no for these options and press ENTER again.

FIGURE 7.20

```
                        Define Report Breaks

Type break level (1-6) for up to 9 field names, press Enter.
  (Use as many fields as needed for each break level.)

Break          Sort
Level          Prty          Field
  _                          ITMNUM
  _             10           SUPPL
  _                          SUPADD
  _                          SUPCTY
  _                          SUPST
  _                          SUPZP
  _                          ITMNME
  _                          EOQ
  _                          ORDCST

                                                        Bottom
F3=Exit      F5=Report    F10=Process/previous   F11=Display text only
F12=Cancel   F13=Layout   F18=Files                    F23=Long comment
```

Selecting Output Type and Form

At the Select Output Type and Output Form screen (Figure 7.21), the medium to be used for output is specified. The choices are sending the data to a display, printer, or file.

If option 3, Database file, is specified as the medium, the library, file, and member name where the data is to be sent must be specified. Choosing Database file and pressing ENTER will result in the Define Database File Output screen being displayed (Figure 7.22). This screen allows the user to specify the "send to" library, file, and member. Query/400 also provides the capability to create the file or member to which the query output is to be sent. If this option is chosen, the public authority—that is, the level of object control that the public will have—must also be assigned. The easiest way to do this is to accept the library's authority, *LIBCRTAUT. If the default is not wanted, a list of valid authorities can be displayed by pressing F4.

Another feature of choosing file as the medium is that all column formatting is ignored. The format specifications are saved in case the user wants Query/400 to print the output at a later date; however, the appearance of the output in the file will not follow the column formatting specifications. Choosing option 2, Printer, as the output type will require the user to specify a particular printer, accept the default printer, or spool the file to an output queue. Of course, Query/400 has a screen to enable the user to do this.

FIGURE 7.21

```
┌─────────────────────────────────────────────────────────────┐
│            Select Output Type and Output Form                 │
│ Type choices, press Enter.                                    │
│                                                               │
│    Output type . . . . . . . . . .   1         1=Display      │
│                                                2=Printer       │
│                                                3=Database file │
│                                                               │
│    Form of output . . . . . . . . .  1         1=Detail       │
│                                                2=Summary only  │
│                                                               │
│    Line wrapping . . . . . . . . . .  N         Y=Yes, N=No    │
│       Wrapping width . . . . . . . .  ___       Blank, 1-378   │
│       Record on one page . . . . . .  N         Y=Yes, N=No    │
│                                                               │
│                                                               │
│                                                               │
│                                                               │
│ F3=Exit        F5=Report       F10=Process/previous           │
│ F12=Cancel     F13=Layout      F18=Files                      │
└─────────────────────────────────────────────────────────────┘
```

FIGURE 7.22

```
┌─────────────────────────────────────────────────────────────┐
│               Define Database File Output                     │
│ Type choices, press Enter.                                    │
│  (The printed definition shows the output file record layout.)│
│                                                               │
│    File . . . . . . . . QQRYOUT____   Name, F4 for list        │
│       Library. . . . .    YOURLIBXX__ Name, F4 for list        │
│    Member . . . . . . . *FILE_____   Name, *FIRST, *FILE, F4 for list │
│                                                               │
│    Data in file . . . . 1             1=New file, 2=Replace file │
│                                       3=New member, 4=Replace member │
│                                       5=Add to member         │
│    For a new file:                                            │
│       Authority . . . . *LIBCRTAUT  *LIBCRTAUT, *CHANGE, *ALL, │
│                                     *EXCLUDE, *USE,            │
│                                     authorization list name   │
│       Text . . . . . . . _____  │
│    Print definition . . N           Y=Yes, N=No               │
│                                                               │
│ F3=Exit       F4=Prompt    F5=Report   F10=Process/previous   │
│ F12=Cancel    F13=Layout   F18=Files                          │
└─────────────────────────────────────────────────────────────┘
```

Also on the Select Output Type and Output Form screen, just a summary report can be requested. By specifying Summary only, all detail records will be suppressed and only the totals specified earlier will be sent. If Detail is selected, both detail and summary records are sent. For our example, choose output type 1, Display, and accept the default values for all the other options.

The last option from the `Define the Query` screen is `Specify processing options`. This option allows the user to control decimal formatting and the overall appearance of numeric fields.

Exiting and Saving the Query

At this point, the query has been defined. To exit the query definition function, press **F3**. The `Exit this Query` screen will be displayed (Figure 7.23). The query can be saved or run from this screen. To save the query definition, enter a **Y** at the `Save definition` prompt. The query name and library where it is to be stored must also be specified at the appropriate prompts. The query name specified will be the name of the object that will hold the definition. Normal AS/400 naming conventions are in force: Names must begin with an alphabetical character or the symbol $, #, or @, and the following characters (up to nine) can be alphanumeric or the symbols $, #, @, ., or _. For our example, save the query as INVQRY in YOURLIBXX (as was specified earlier).

FIGURE 7.23

```
                        Exit this Query

 Type choices, press Enter.

    Save definition . . .      Y            Y=Yes, N=No

    Run option  . . . . .      3            1=Run interactively
                                            2=Run in batch
                                            3=Do not run

 For a saved definition:
    Query . . . . . . .  INVQRY____         Name
       Library . . . . .     YOURLIBXX _    Name, F4 for list

    Text  . . . . . . .  _____

    Authority . . . . .  *LIBCRTAUT         *LIBCRTAUT, *CHANGE, *ALL,
                                            *EXCLUDE, *USE,
                                            authorization list name

 F4=Prompt        F5=Report      F12=Cancel          F13=Layout
 F14=Define the query
```

When the query definition is saved, an object with the query name specified will be created. Its object type will be equal to

*QRYDFN (query definition). At this screen's Authority prompt, the public's authorization to this new object must also be specified. Press F1 for an explanation of the options available.

There are several ways to run a query:

1. From the Exit this Query screen (see Figure 7.23), enter the run option number at the Run option prompt and press ENTER.

2. From the Work with Queries screen (see Figure 7.2), type in the name of the saved query and the run option number and press ENTER.

3. From the command line, type **RUNQRY** and press F4 to prompt for the query name and other command parameters.

For our example, run the query in any of the three ways. The output should appear as in Figure 7.24. To see the rest of the report, press F20. This will move the screen to the right (Figure 7.25).

FIGURE 7.24

```
                        Display Report
Query . . . : YOURLIBXX/INVQRY        Report width . . . . . : 133
Position to line . . . . _____      Shift to column . . . . . ____
Line ....+....1....+....2....+....3....+....4....+....5....+....6....+....7..
        ITEM   SUPPLIER            SUPPLIER          CITY       S
        NUMBER NAME                ADDRESS
000001      1 AMERICAN TURNIP CORP 101 VEGETABLE LANE BANGOR
000002      3 RADISHES 'R US       1 DIRT ST          LARCHMONT
000003     51 STINKY'S             PEA-YEW DR         VADALIA
000004
000005
000006
****** ********* End of report *********
```

FIGURE 7.25

```
                           Display Report
Query . . . : YOURLIBXX/INVQRY      Report width . . . . . : 133
Position to line . . . . ____        Shift to column . . . . ____
Line...+....7....+....8....+....9....+...10....+...11....+...12....+...13...
              STATE  ZIPCODE  ITEM           EOQ    UNIT        ORDER
                              NAME        AMOUNT   PRICE         COST
000001        ME     11,111   TURNIP         25     .22          5.50
000002NT      TX     44,444   RADISH         75     .06          4.50
000003        GA     33,333   ONION          50    3.50        175.00
000004
000005                                           FINAL TOTALS
000006                                              TOTAL      185.00
************** End of report ********
```

Changing Saved Queries

Notice from Figure 7.25 that there seems to be a problem with the way that zip codes are being displayed: Commas are being inserted to denote thousands. To avoid this, select option 2, Change, from the Work with Queries screen. This option will allow the user to go through all the query definition screens for any saved query. After specifying the saved query to be changed, each screen will display the values previously specified for that query. To change the values, simply type over any of the existing values and exit the screen. When you exit the query definition, there is an option to save the changes.

For our example, access the Specify Report Column Formatting screen (see Figure 7.18). At this screen, page down so that the screen appears as in Figure 7.26. Move the cursor to the zip code field and press F16. The Define Numeric Field Editing screen will appear. This screen provides options to edit different types of numeric fields (date fields, time fields, and so on). For the zip code field, choose option 1, Numeric editing choices and press ENTER. The Describe Numeric Field Editing screen will be displayed (Figure 7.27). Notice the option to specify the thousands separator. The zip code field should not have a separator, so select option 5, None, and press ENTER twice to return to the Define the Query screen.

FIGURE 7.26

```
                    Specify Report Column Formatting

Type information, press Enter.
  Column headings: *NONE, aligned text lines

          Column
Field     Spacing    Column Heading            Len   Dec   Edit
SUPCTY      2        CITY_____       15    __
                     _____
                     _____
SUPST       2        STATE_____        2    __
                     _____
                     _____
SUPZP       2        ZIPCODE_____         5    0
                     _____
                     _____

                                                          More...

F3=Exit      F5=Report    F10=Process/previous  F12=Cancel
F13=Layout   F16=Edit     F18=Files             F23=Long comment
```

FIGURE 7.27

```
                    Describe Numeric Field Editing

Field . . . . . . : SUPZP

Type choices, press Enter.
  Decimal point . . . . . . . .1      1=. 2=, 3=: 4=$    5=None
  Thousands separator . . . . .2      1=. 2=, 3=' 4=Blank 5=None
  Show negative sign . . . . . .Y     Y=Yes, N=No
    Left negative sign . . . . .____
    Right negative sign . . . .-___
  Show currency symbol . . . . .N     Y=Yes, N=No
    Left currency symbol . . . .$___
    Right currency symbol . . . '   ___
  Print zero value . . . . . . .Y     Y=Yes, N=No
  Replace leading zeros . . . .Y      Y=Yes, N=No
    Replace with . . . . . . . .1     1=Blanks
                                      2=Asterisks
                                      3=Floating currency symbol
  Single leading zero. . . . . .N     Y=Yes, N=No
F3=Exit      F5=Report        F10=Process/previous  F12=Cancel
F13=Layout   F16=Remove edit  F18=Files
```

The changes are now complete, so exit the query definition by pressing F3. The Exit this Query screen will be displayed. This screen provides the options to:

- Save the new query under a new name
- Replace the old query
- Run the new query and not save it

Since the old query had commas in the zip code and, therefore, is of no use, replace it with the new query. Select that option and run the query. The result will look like Figure 7.28.

FIGURE 7.28

```
                                 Display Report
Query . . . : YOURLIBXX/INVQRY    Report width . . . . . :  133
Position to line . . . . .  _____   Shift to column . . . . . . ____
   Line...+....7....+....8....+....9....+...10....+...11....+...12....+...13...
              STATE  ZIPCODE  ITEM        EOQ    UNIT          ORDER
                              NAME       AMOUNT  PRICE          COST
   000001      ME    11111   TURNIP       25     .22           5.50
   000002NT    TX    44444   RADISH       75     .06           4.50
   000003      GA    33333   ONION        50    3.50         175.00
   000004
   000005                                       FINAL TOTALS
   000006                                       TOTAL         185.00
   ************ End of report ********
```

Tips for Using Query/400

Query/400 is very easy to use, but it does not force the user to select the options in a specific order. Here are several tips on how to use Query/400 effectively and how to avoid some inadvertent errors.

1. Define result fields before selecting and sequencing the fields. If fields are selected and sequenced before result fields are defined, there is no opportunity to include result fields in the output.

2. Use only sort fields as break fields. Using nonsort fields will result in meaningless groups of records with nonsensical subtotal data.

3. Format columns after selecting and sequencing fields. If fields are selected after formatting, they will not be formatted.

4. Whenever you create or make changes to definitions, use F5 (report) and F13 (layout) to see the result of definition changes

immediately. F5 displays a sample report with data, and F13 displays the layout of the report. Using these functions allows you to see the results of the changes without having to save and run the definition.

5.   Rather than writing programs to sort data files, you can use Query/400 to quickly create a sorted data file. Simply start query, specify the file to be sorted, choose the sort field, specify the "send to" file, and run the query.

Summary

Query/400 is another example of the AS/400's concentration on user-friendly interfaces. Unlike many report generators or query languages, the user is spared from having to memorize commands, file names, and file structures. Query/400 provides users with screens, menus, and options that allow them to quickly and easily specify the data to be used and its format. Query/400 also provides summarization functions and allows users to choose the medium for the results—display, paper, or disk.

There are, however, limitations to Query/400's capabilities. Any complex logic (if-then-else), higher calculations (square roots, exponents), or advanced printing (elaborate headers, bar coding) would have to be handled by higher-level programming languages or specialized software. Query/400 is, however, an easy-to-learn utility that provides fast access to stored data.

LAB EXERCISES

These exercises will create two queries that run against several files. The files to be queried are the ITEM, BATCH, and CARTON files that were loaded with data in the lab exercise of Chapter 6.

EXERCISE 1

1.   Invoke Query/400 by typing **STRQRY** at any command line and pressing ENTER.
2.   At the Query Utilities screen, select option 1, Work with queries.
3.   At the Work with Queries screen, select option 1, Create.
4.   At the Define the Query screen, notice that option 1 has already been entered for the Specify file selections prompt. Press ENTER.
5.   At the Specify File Selections screen, enter **ITEM** at the File prompt and **YOURLIBXX** at the Library prompt.
6.   Press F9 to specify a second file to be queried.
7.   At the new File ID prompt, type over the system-supplied value of T01 with the letter **A**.

8. Enter **BATCH** as the second file. If necessary, specify **YOURLIBXX** as the library and **B** as the `File ID`.

9. Press F9 a third time and specify **CARTON, YOURLIBXX,** and **C** (as the `File ID`). Press ENTER twice.

10. At the `Specify Type of Join` screen, make sure option 1, `Matched records`, is specified and press ENTER.

11. At the `Specify How to Join Files` screen, enter the following two conditions: **A.ITMNUM EQ B.ITMNUM** and **B.BCHNUM EQ C.BCHNUM.**

12. Press ENTER to save the conditions and exit.

13. At the `Define the Query` screen, choose the `Select and sequence fields` option.

14. At the `Select and Sequence Fields` screen, choose carton number from the CARTON file, item name from the ITEM file, and expiration date from the BATCH file by entering **1, 2,** and **3,** respectively, next to the field names. Press ENTER twice.

15. At the `Define the Query` screen, press F3 to exit.

16. At the `Exit this Query` screen, specify **1** at the `Run option` prompt and at the `Query` and `Library` prompts specify **CARTONQRY** and **YOURLIBXX.**

17. Press ENTER.

18. Notice that the results are a record for each carton number in the CARTON file.

19. Exit the display screen by pressing F3.

20. Exit the `Work with Queries` screen by pressing F3 again.

21. Type **WRKOBJ** at the command line and press F4.

22. Specify **YOURLIBXX** at the `Library` prompt and ***ALL** for the other prompts. Press ENTER.

23. Notice in the object list that there is a new object called CARTONQRY with a type of *QRYDFN (query definition). Query/400 created this object when steps 16 and 17 were performed.

EXERCISE 2 This second query will perform the same function as the query in the first exercise. However, it will use the logical file ITBATCAR that was defined in Chapter 5.

1. Perform steps 1 through 4 from exercise 1.

2. At the `Specify File Selections` screen, enter **ITBATCAR** at the `File` prompt and **YOURLIBXX** at the `Library` prompt. Press ENTER twice.

3. At the `Define the Query` screen, press F3 to exit.

4. At the `Exit this Query` screen, specify **1** at the `Run option` prompt and **N** at the `Save definition` prompt.

5. Press ENTER.

Notice that the data retrieved is the same as the first exercise's query, CARTONQRY. This is because Query/400 lets the user dynamically join files for a query. This same function is provided by DDS through its join specification. If a logical file does not exist, Query/400 allows the user to easily define a path through the files for the query. In a sense, Query/400 acts as a user-friendly menu interface for defining logical files. The difference is that Query/400 creates the file definition within the query—the file is internally defined, and therefore, the file definition cannot be accessed by other programs or queries. DDS provides users with externally defined files and all the associated benefits.

(If you noticed the difference in the order of the data, it is the result of defining different primary files for the joins. In ITBATCAR, CARTON was specified as the primary file in the JFILE keyword. In CARTONQRY, the ITEM file was the first file specified; therefore, it was the primary file for the query join. This resulted in CARTONQRY displaying the records in the arrival sequence order of the ITEM file records versus the query using ITBATCAR displaying the records in the arrival sequence order of the CARTON file records.)

REVIEW QUESTIONS

1. What options are available for sending output with Query/400?

2. Is Query/400 limited to displaying only stored data? If not, give an example of nonstored information that can be displayed using Query/400.

3. Why might a Query/400 user want to override DDS-defined field characteristics?

4. What are the differences between detail and summary reports?

5. What are the advantages and disadvantages of using Query/400 versus user-written applications to generate reports?

6. Why should a user format columns after selecting and sequencing fields?

7. Explain what is meant by a nonprocedural versus a procedural language.

8. What is the difference between report writers and query languages?

DISCUSSION QUESTIONS

1. Explain the three joins available with Query/400 and the possible uses of each.

2. Discuss in terms of function how logical files and Query/400 overlap.

3. Explain the importance of using sort fields as report break fields.

PC
Support

8

Overview

PC Support is a collection of programs that allow users to: store and access information on the AS/400 from a PC; transfer data between a PC and the AS/400; use a PC as an AS/400 workstation; use both PC; and AS/400 printers from a PC; and communicate between workstations.

This chapter discusses in detail PC Support's architecture, explains how PC Support performs the first three functions listed, and walks through the PC Support menus that enable users to execute those functions.

After finishing this chapter, you will understand:

- Distributed processing
- How PC Support can facilitate distributed processing
- The strengths and weaknesses of the various PC Support functions
- How PC Support interacts with application and communication software
- The advantages of using PC Support

You also will be able to:

- Access and use PC Support screens
- Transfer data between the AS/400 and a PC
- Define and access data in an AS/400 shared folder from a PC
- Create and modify a workstation configuration

Personal Computers and Distributed Processing

With the growth of personal computers over the last decade, there has been a growing trend toward *distributed processing.* Distributed processing means having the actual data processing occur at the point where the information is needed rather than at a central data processing location. Computer users want the programs and data to be at their fingertips, yet getting the data into their computers in a timely manner and keeping it accurate are often problems.

For instance, a manager for a local convenience store executes sales transactions and stores the resulting information on his in-store PC. Processing the sales transaction consists of:

- Multiplying each item's price (which is stored in a file) by the quantity of items sold
- Storing a record of the sale
- Decreasing the amount in inventory for each item sold

The manager uses his PC to perform this operation and keeps a record of the inventory quantities so that he can check them when ordering more supplies.

The problem with this arrangement is that prices are determined at corporate headquarters. To support each store's computer processing, the prices must be mailed to all the stores whenever the prices are changed. Each time a new price list comes out, the store manager must go to his PC and change the appropriate price file. This procedure must be followed by each manager at all 19,999 other branches of our fictional convenience store chain.

There are several problems with this system. First, it is inefficient to have 20,000 employees perform the same operation—for instance, updating the price of a 12-ounce can of soda. Second, given human fallibility, there inevitably will be mistakes in some of the prices entered. (You can be sure that on the next business day, in locations throughout the country, cans of soda will be rung up for prices ranging from $50 to $.05.) There is also a problem with the timeliness of the updating. If the competition has just instituted a sale on soda, how long will it take headquarters to counter with their own promotion? Mailing out the new prices will take three days, and then there is a delay until the price updating is done. Some of the stores will process the new prices right away, but others may forget to do it entirely. Meanwhile, the competition is stealing away customers and making sales.

PC Support software facilitates distributed processing by enabling data to be easily and accurately accessed and transferred between a PC workstation and the AS/400.

Networks and PC Support

For a PC workstation and the AS/400 to communicate, they need to be on the same network. (They can be on separate networks if the networks are linked by a bridge or a gateway.) Many different networking systems are available today that enable users to do this. These networking systems, consisting of both hardware and software, provide the means to transmit signals over a physical line from one computer to another. If a piece of data is to be sent from a PC to the AS/400, a communications program within the networking software is activated (Figure 8.1). As input to this program, a user will have to provide the information that is being sent and, at least, the destination address.

FIGURE 8.1
Non-PC Support Network Configuration

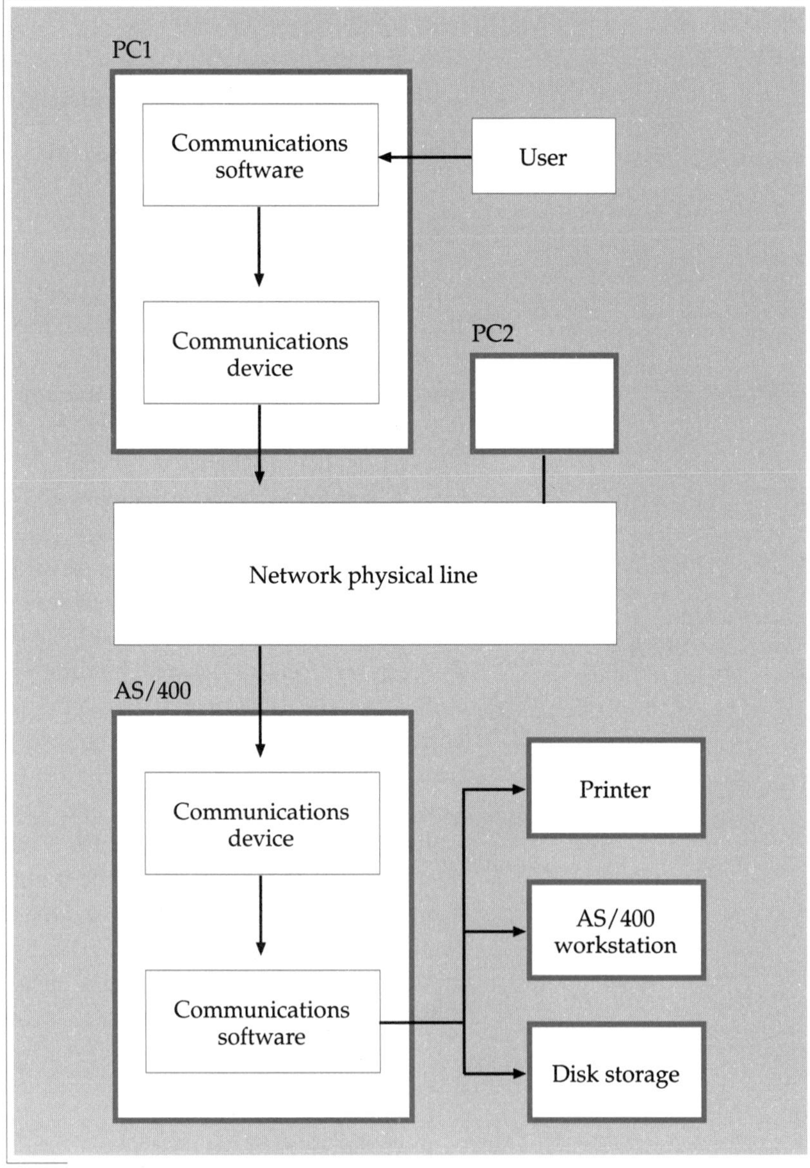

The networking software then sends commands to a physical communications device that issues the actual signals to be sent over the "wire." These electrical impulses travel over the wire and are received at the destination by that computer's communications device. This device initiates another communications program, which determines the actions to be taken based on the information received.

A user can send information from computer to computer by working directly with the communications software. The problem is that most communications software is fairly complex and far from user friendly. The user must remember the commands for each particular networking system and its syntax. For instance, the syntax of the command may dictate that the destination address, a four-character field consisting of one letter and three numbers, be provided first followed by the actual data to be sent. Another network may have a different command that requires the data first, a plus sign, and then the address enclosed in parentheses. Working with several different systems can quickly make things quite confusing.

PC Support acts as a buffer between the networking software and the user and his or her applications. A user who wishes to send information from his or her PC to the AS/400 can interact with a PC Support program. The PC Support program, in turn, interacts with the appropriate networking program (Figure 8.2).

Reasons for Using PC Support

There are several advantages to using PC Support rather than dealing directly with the communications software.

First, PC Support provides an easy-to-use interface consisting of menus, screens, on-line help, and the like. Nonprogrammers can readily learn and use the PC Support functions. The on-line help facility explains all the functions available, and each function can be easily accessed through menus. To perform a PC Support activity, you can simply select the appropriate menu item and enter all the required information at the easy-to-use system prompt screens.

Second, PC Support supplies an alternative way to activate its functions. This other interface is PC Support's API (application program interface), which can be used in user-written programs. The PC Support API is a set of commands that will activate associated PC Support programs. If an application program needs to perform a communications function, the programmer inserts the appropriate API command in the program. When the user program is run and the API command is executed, a PC Support program is called to perform the desired function.

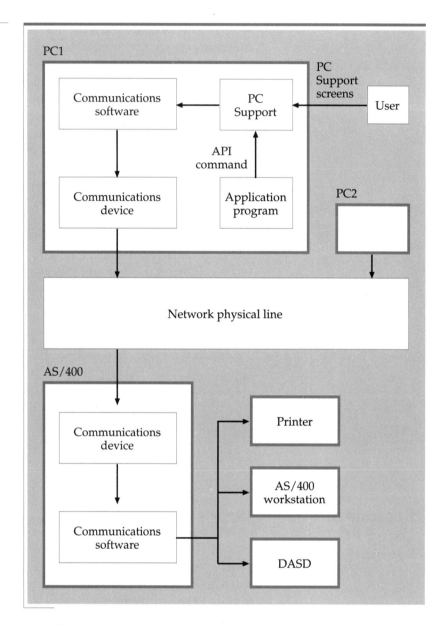

The biggest advantage of PC Support is that by using the API, the application program's portability is increased. When applications are written using a particular network's commands to perform the communications functions, the program cannot be run on a different network. The program is limited to only those computers that use the same network software. PC Support, on the other hand, provides a uniform set of commands and syntax that work across a variety of PC networking systems (Token Ring, TDLC, ASYNC, SDLC). When an API command is issued, PC Support selects the correct command for the network. The information provided with the API command is translated into the correct syntax for the particular communications software. The PC Support program then sends that command to the networking software, and the communication is completed as outlined earlier. The application program can be run on any network system as long as PC Support is resident on the workstation (see Figure 8.2).

PC Support Architecture

Until now, we have talked about PC Support as a monolithic entity. In actuality, PC Support comprises many interrelated programs that call and pass information between themselves.

The *Router* is a key piece of software because it performs several important functions within PC Support.

First, it is the interface to the network software. All communications between the PC Support functions (like data transfer) or a user application (like a payroll program) and the communications software (the Adapter handler or OS/2) are sent through the Router (Figure 8.3).

Second, the Router receives all incoming data and determines which application should be given the data.

Finally, PC Support's API enables application programs to send information to each other through the router. Other PC Support functions allow information to be transferred between the AS/400 and a workstation. For instance, with the PC Support transfer function, information can be sent from a file on the workstation to a member on the AS/400. The Router not only allows information to be sent between the two machines but will also pass information to applications on the AS/400. In other words, a program on the workstation can send information and invoke a program on the AS/400 using the Router. This feature allows the programmer to create programs for the PC that can activate jobs on the AS/400. This significantly enhances the functions performed from the PC.

Essentially, the Router acts as the clearinghouse and distributor for all information into and out of the workstation. The application programs do not have to worry their pretty little logic about communication syntax and addressing schemes. Programs provide the information to be sent to the Router, which handles all communications complexities. In addition, the Router manages the data within the workstation by directing information back to the correct application. The Router "remembers" which PC Support or application program requested data and routes the data to the correct program when the communications software returns with the data.

FIGURE 8.3
Router's Function Within PC Support

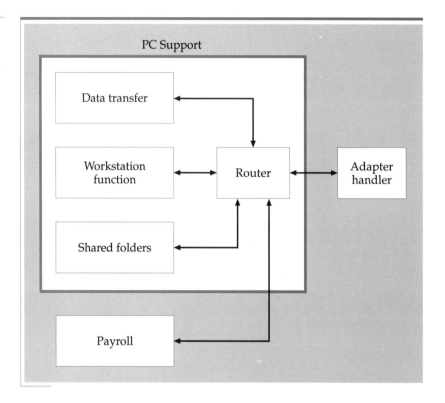

In a DOS environment, the Router communicates with the Adapter handler software, which must be loaded separately if PCLP (PC Lan Program) is being used. When OS/2 is the operating system, the Router communicates with the OS/2 Communications Manager.

Storing Data on the AS/400

PC Support allows users to store and access data on the AS/400 in objects called *folders*. By storing information in folders, users have access to the AS/400's larger storage capacity, and storage space on the PC is freed up.

Once a folder is created on the AS/400, files can be copied between the PC and the shared folder on the AS/400. (Remember, when creating the folder, make sure the proper authority has been specified. If the shared folder's object authority is defined as EXCLUDE, access to the folder from the workstation will be denied.)

One of the easiest ways to manipulate the folder is to define it as a drive, such as the C or A drive, on the PC. This can be done through the PC Support/400 Menu or by directly editing a configuration file on the PC.

Accessing Shared Folders Through the PC Support/400 Menu

From the AS/400 Main Menu, choose option 11, PC Support tasks. The PC Support Tasks screen will be displayed (Figure 8.4). Select option 5, PC Support Organizer. From the PC Support/400 Organizer screen (Figure 8.5), choose option 4, PC Support PC Tasks. This will display the PC Support/400 Menu (Figure 8.6).

FIGURE 8.4

```
PCSTSK                    PC Support Tasks
                                           System: CHICAGO
Select one of the following:

  User Tasks
          1.   Copy PC document to database
          2.   Copy database to PC document
          3.   Work with documents in folders
          4.   Work with folders
          5.   PC Support Organizer

  Administrator Tasks
         20.   Work with PC Support administrators
         21.   Enroll PC Support users
         22.   Configure PC connections

         30.   Change keyboard and conversion tables

Selection or command
===>_____


F3=Exit   F4=Prompt   F9=Retrieve   F12=Cancel   F13=User support
F16=AS/400 Main menu
```

FIGURE 8.5

```
PCOMNU                 PC Support/400 Organizer

Select one of the following:

Office Functions
     1. OfficeVision/400
     2. Work with documents in folders
     3. Select editor of choice

PC Support
     4. PC Support PC Tasks
     5. PC Support host system tasks
     6. PC command prompt
     7. Start a PC command

    90. Sign off

===>_____


F3=Exit      F4=Prompt      F9=Retrieve      F12=Cancel
F13=User support             F16=System main menu
```

FIGURE 8.6

```
                        PC Support/400 Menu

       Select one of the following

         Learn About PC Support
               View PC Support Introduction

         Perform PC Support Tasks
               Go to PC command prompt
               Use printers on host system
               Use folders on host system
               Transfer data
               Send and receive messages
              *Go to Organizer menu
               Submit host system command

         Manage Your PC Support Environment
               Configure PC Support
               Administer PC Support
               View PC Support Error Log
       _____

       Enter       Esc=Cancel        F1=Help        F3=Exit
```

Using the PC Support/400 Menu, which is controlled by a program that is running on the PC, choose the Use folders on host system option. This can be done either by moving the cursor to the option and pressing ENTER or by typing the highlighted letter in the option.

This will pop up the Work with Folders screen, which will already be displaying all the current drives defined on the PC (Figure 8.7). Notice that the I drive has already been defined for the system. The I drive identifies the AS/400 system and a folder that contains the PC Support programs, which we have been talking about.

When PC Support is initially loaded onto the PC from a diskette, only enough programs to enable the PC to make contact to the AS/400 are loaded. Once contact is made, other PC Support programs are retrieved from the AS/400's storage as needed through the shared folders function. (System performance can sometimes be improved by forcing the PC Support programs to be loaded onto the C drive. This decreases the access time to the needed programs; this, however, is far beyond the scope of our discussion.)

A folder on the AS/400 contains most of the PC Support programs. The PC loads the programs from the folder, as it would from the C drive or any other storage location, when a function is requested.

At the Work with Folders screen, another drive can be specified (for example, G). To relate that drive to a folder, the user would simply enter the folder name and the system name, where the folder resides, next to the chosen drive. To do this, the user needs to know how to operate the PC Support screens.

FIGURE 8.7

```
 Assign Release Exit Help
                        Work with Folders
 To select an action shown above, first press F10.

 Drive      System Name        Assignment
    E           -                  -
    F           -                  -
    G           -                  -
    H           -                  -
    I        CHICAGO             QIWSFLR
    J           -                  -
    K           -                  -
    L           -                  -




 Enter   Esc=Cancel   F1=Help   F3=Exit   F10=Actions
```

Using the PC Support Screens

The PC Support screens are a little quirky. To select a function (such as Create, Change, or Exit), you must first press F10. After pressing F10, you can select a function by either pressing the highlighted character corresponding to the function (for example, pressing **g** for Change) or moving the cursor to the command and pressing ENTER.

Assigning a Shared Folder

At the Work with Folders screen:

- Press F10.

- Select the Assign function.

- Choose option 1, Assign a drive (Figure 8.8).

The Assign a Drive screen will be displayed (Figure 8.9). At this screen, enter the drive letter, system name (if not the default system name), and folder name (to be shared).

Press ENTER to establish the folder as a drive, then press ESC to exit to the previous screen. A message should appear saying that the drive was successfully assigned (Figure 8.10). Exit to the PC Support/400 Menu and choose the Go to PC command prompt option. This will result in a DOS-like prompt where many common DOS commands can be issued. Users can manipulate all the documents within the shared folder by using DOS commands and identifying the files as residing on the G drive.

So, the command COPY A:SHARE.FIL G: would result in a copy of the file SHARE.FIL on the diskette in the A drive being copied to the shared folder INTRO99 on the AS/400.

FIGURE 8.8

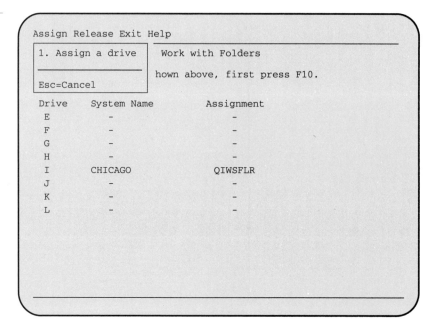

```
 Assign Release Exit Help

 ┌─────────────────┐
 │ 1. Assign a drive │   Work with Folders
 ├─────────────────┤
 │                 │   hown above, first press F10.
 │ Esc=Cancel      │
 └─────────────────┘
     Drive     System Name          Assignment
       E          -                    -
       F          -                    -
       G          -                    -
       H          -                    -
       I        CHICAGO              QIWSFLR
       J          -                    -
       K          -                    -
       L          -                    -
```

FIGURE 8.9

```
                        Assign a Drive
       Drive     System Name          Assignment
         E          -                    -
         F          -                    -
         G          -                    -
         H          -                    -
         I        CHICAGO              QIWSFLR
         J          -                    -
         K          -                    -
         L          -                    -

   Select options, press Enter

   Drive. . . . . . . . [G] (E F G H I J K L)

   System Name. . . . . . [CHICAGO ]

   Folder . . . . . . . . [INTRO99                           >


   Enter   Esc=Cancel  F1=Help  F3=Exit  F4=Prompt
```

The only problem with defining a shared folder as a drive through the PC Support menus is that the preceding steps must be executed each time the user signs on. The connection to the shared folder is maintained only for the length of the session. As soon as sign-off occurs, the shared folder connection is broken. An alternative to using the menus to establish the shared folder connection is to insert a command into the CONFIG.PCS file on the PC.

FIGURE 8.10

```
                        Assign a Drive
      Drive     System Name      Assignment
        E           -                 -
        F           -                 -
        G        CHICAGO           INTRO99
        H           -                 -
        I        CHICAGO           QIWSFLR
        J           -                 -
        K           -                 -
        L           -                 -

    Select options, press Enter

    Drive . . . . . . . [E]    (E F G H I J K L)

    System Name . . . . . [CHICAGO ]

    Folder . . . . . . . .[                             >

    ┌──────────────────────────────────────────────────────┐
    │  Drive G was successfully assigned to system CHICAGO   │
    └──────────────────────────────────────────────────────┘

    Enter   Esc=Cancel   F1=Help   F3=Exit
```

Modifying CONFIG.PCS

The CONFIG.PCS file is automatically read when the AS/400 work session is started. By inserting an establish shared folder connection command into CONFIG.PCS, the connection will be made each time at sign-on. The command to be added (after the line that defines the PC Support folder on the I drive) is

```
SFLR 1,dl,foldername,systemname
```

where

- SFLR is the establish shared folder connection command.
- 1 specifies that the function to be performed is "assign a drive" (a 2 would mean "release a drive").
- *dl* is the drive letter to use. Up to eight drives can be specified. The seven letters following the last letter used to define a drive on the PC are valid (only seven because I is already being used). If the PC had two disk drives (specified by the letters A and B) and a hard drive (specified by the letter C), the valid drive letters for specifying shared folders would be D, E, F, G, H, J, and K.
- *foldername* is the name of the folder on the AS/400 to be accessed (for example, INTRO99).
- *systemname* is the name of the system the folder resides on (for example, CHICAGO).

Folders Within Folders

On the AS/400, folders can be defined within folders, just as directories can be defined within directories on the PC. New folders can also be created within the shared folder by using the MKDIR command.

Typing **MKDIR G:SEYMOUR** at the DOS prompt would create a folder within INTRO99 called SEYMOUR.

The AS/400 also has a function to lock up the folder. If changes are going to be made to it, locking the folder stops any other updates to the folder until it is unlocked. This cuts down on updating errors due to timing.

For instance, any program that updates a savings account's balance will read the account balance, add the deposit amount, and write the new balance to the file. Say you participate in an automatic payroll deposit plan and your employer has just sent a payroll deposit transaction of $200 to the bank. The program to perform payroll updates is invoked and reads your current account balance of $300. Right at the same moment, you are at the bank depositing the traditional $5 birthday check from your loving grandmother. The personal deposits program is invoked and reads the account balance of $300.

Meanwhile, the payroll program adds the $200 to the $300, resulting in a new balance of $500, which it then writes out as the account balance. Next, the personal deposit program adds Grandmother's $5 to what it thinks is the current balance, $300. The personal deposit program comes up with a new balance of $305, which it proceeds to write out as the account balance, replacing the $500 that the payroll update had just written.

The net result is that your $200 paycheck has been lost. If the payroll program had locked the data, the personal deposit program would have been forced to wait until the correct balance of $500 was written. The personal deposit program would then have correctly updated the account, and you would not be out $200.

The command to lock folders is CHKFIL. (See the IBM manuals for more information on the use and maintenance of shared folders.)

Using Folders for Distributed Processing

How can shared folders help with distributed processing? In our convenience store example at the beginning of the chapter, there was a problem with maintaining timely and accurate price data for each store's PC to process. What if, instead of having the prices stored on each of the 20,000 convenience stores' individual PCs, we kept it in a shared folder on an AS/400?

Advantages. First, this would greatly decrease the amount of data stored. Instead of duplicating all the prices on 20,000 PCs, there would be only one copy of the prices, and it would reside on the AS/400. This would result in a considerable savings of storage space.

Second, updating would be faster. A price change would not require mailing notices to all the stores. The change in price would be made at the central data location, thereby eliminating the three-day mail delay.

Third, updating would be more efficient and accurate. Instead of 20,000 store managers—many of whom have pressing day-to-day emergencies, like exploding slurpie machines, that take their minds off less urgent matters, such as data integrity—updating the prices, there would be one person (whose focus is pricing and maintaining accurate price files) updating the price in the shared folder. The number of mistakes and employee hours spent would decrease because 19,999 fewer updates are being performed. Moreover, the chance of prices being different between stores—because some do their computer updates at night, some in the morning, some only on Thursdays—would be eliminated.

Finally, this solution would decrease the time spent tracking down pricing mistakes and would avoid any customer dissatisfaction arising from pricing errors.

Disadvantages. Now that you are totally mesmerized by the benefits of shared folders, you should also know that there are some costs. There are several points to consider before implementing a shared folders solution. For instance, several changes would be needed on every store's PC. Using shared folders would require changing the sales transaction program at each store. Instead of reading a file on the PC's hard drive, each program would now access a price file on the shared drive. All the programs would have to be updated to do this.

Each PC's CONFIG.PCS file would have to be updated with the SFLR command to establish the shared folder connection each time someone signed on. PC Support would also have to be loaded onto each PC. This would require extra storage space and memory to run the programs. Depending on the size of the price file, the addition of PC Support will decrease or negate any storage benefits achieved by eliminating the price file.

There are other costs to consider when using centralized data in a distributed processing environment. Each time a sales transaction is executed at one of the convenience stores, a request for data is sent, and a second transaction containing the requested data is sent back over the physical line. Common carriers, such as the phone companies, charge for every transaction sent over their communications lines. The cost of these price requests needs to be determined. The old transaction cost, a 29-cent stamp for each price list, has been eliminated; however, the number of price transactions that will occur between the stores and corporate headquarters has been greatly increased. Even though you can be sure that the transaction cost will be much less than 29 cents, the phone companies are not philanthropic organizations (even though their warm and caring commercials might lead you to believe otherwise). They are providing a faster, more accurate medium and will be charging accordingly.

Finally, consider the time required to send and receive the data from the widely dispersed stores to the central data location. Telecommunications signals are fast, but line traffic and different software and hardware configurations could have unanticipated slowing effects. Also the impact of 20,000 PCs trying to access the same file needs to be determined. Keeping data on one machine is similar to a bank keeping all its money in one vault. Much better control over the money is achieved, but can the bank handle 20,000 customers at one location? There are only 6 tellers, the lobby holds a maximum of 50 people, and the door to the bank is only 3 feet by 7 feet. Can all the customers get timely access to their money?

Transferring Data

Besides sharing a common storage area, users can work with data on both the AS/400 and the PC by transferring files between the two systems. To access the data transfer function, go to the PC Support/400 Menu and choose the Transfer data option. This will pop up a window (Figure 8.11) where the type of transfer is specified.

FIGURE 8.11

```
                      PC Support/400 Menu
      Select one of the following

         Learn About PC Support
              View PC Support Introduction

         Perform PC Support Tasks
              Go to PC command prompt
              Use printers on host system
              Use folders on host system
              Transfer data
              Send and r┌──────────────────────────────────────────────┐
             *Go to Orga│ 1. Transfer data from host system to PC       │
              Submit hos│ 2. Transfer data from PC to host system       │
                        │                                               │
         Manage Your PC│   Enter Esc=Cancel F1=Help                    │
                        └──────────────────────────────────────────────┘
              Configure PC Support
              Administer PC Support
              View PC Support Error Log
```

Traditionally, transferring information from a large computer to a smaller computer is called *downloading*. If data is sent from a small machine to a larger one, it is called *uploading*. Regardless of the choice, the next screen gives the options to Create a transfer or Recall a saved transfer.

Creating a Download Transfer

Choose the `Transfer from host system to PC` option, then select the `Create` function from the `AS/400 System-to-PC Transfer` screen (Figure 8.12). When creating a transfer request, the FROM and TO destinations must be specified. The `Create an AS/400 System-to-PC Transfer` screen provides this capability (Figure 8.13).

In a download transfer, the system, library, file, and member names on the AS/400 identify the FROM destination. If the file contains data, a record format name can be specified. For files with more than one record format (a multiple-format logical file), a record format

FIGURE 8.12

```
┌──────────────────────────────────────────────────────────────┐
│ Create Recall Exit Help                                        │
│ ─────────────────────────────────────────────────────────     │
│                    AS/400 System-to-PC Transfer                │
│                                                                │
│                                                                │
│                                                                │
│                                                                │
│                                                                │
│            There is no current transfer request at this        │
│            time. You can use the create or recall actions      │
│            to establish the current transfer request. To       │
│            select an action from the top of the display,       │
│            press F10.                                           │
│                                                                │
│                                                                │
│                                                                │
│ ─────────────────────────────────────────────────────────     │
│ Enter    Esc=Cancel   F1=Help   F3=Exit   F10=Actions          │
└──────────────────────────────────────────────────────────────┘
```

FIGURE 8.13

```
┌──────────────────────────────────────────────────────────────┐
│        Create an AS/400 System-to-PC Transfer Request          │
│  Select options and then press Enter                           │
│                                                                │
│    System name . . . . . . .    [CHICAGO]                      │
│                                                                │
│    FROM. . . . . . . . . . .    [                         ]    │
│                                                                │
│    SELECT. . . . . . . . . .    [*                        ]    │
│                                                                │
│    WHERE . . . . . . . . . .    [                         ]    │
│                                                                │
│    ORDER BY. . . . . . . . .    [                         ]    │
│                                                                │
│    Output device . . . . . .    1. Display                     │
│                                 2. Printer                     │
│                                 3. Disk                        │
│                                                                │
│                                                                │
│                                                                │
│ ─────────────────────────────────────────────────────────     │
│ Enter  Esc=Cancel  F1=Help  F3=Exit  F4=Prompt  Shift+F4=Group functions │
└──────────────────────────────────────────────────────────────┘
```

must be specified. The specified record format would define which records would be sent. Consider a file that contained the following two types of records:

Summary Record

Field Name	Field Definition
Prtnum	Part number
Prtnam	Part name
Prtdsc	Part description
Invqty	Total inventory quantity
Cost	Cost of part
Suppl	Part supplier

Detail Record

Field Name	Field Definition
Prtnum	Part number
Prtloc	Part location
Locqty	Location quantity

If the summary-record format was specified in the FROM destination, no detail-record data would be sent with the transfer.

The syntax to specify the FROM destination is:

```
Library-name/File-name(member-name,format-name)
```

The data sent can be further restricted in the transfer by using the SELECT and WHERE options on the Create an AS/400 System-to-PC Transfer Request screen.

SELECT and WHERE

Like the record format, the SELECT option allows users to pick which fields to send in the transfer. However, the SELECT option allows the selection to be done on an ad-hoc, field-by-field basis rather than choosing among predefined record formats.

Next to the SELECT prompt, specify the field names to be sent in the transfer. If Prtnam, Invqty, and Cost were specified (Figure 8.14), only the part name, inventory quantity, and cost data would be sent in the transfer. The part description, part number, and part supplier information would be excluded by the SELECT (just as location and location quantity were excluded by choosing the summary-record format).

WHERE conditions determine which records should be transferred based on individual field values. Only records meeting the conditions of the WHERE statement will be sent. For instance, if a condition specified Cost > 5.00 and Prtnam = "screwdriver," only part name, inventory quantity, and cost information for screwdrivers that cost more than $5.00 would be sent.

Specifying the TO Destination

In a download transfer, the TO destination is always the workstation from which the transfer is requested. Therefore, when specifying the

FIGURE 8.14

```
          Create an AS/400 System-to-PC Transfer Request
                                                       More:
     Select options and then press Enter

       System name  . . . . . . . [CHICAGO]

       FROM . . . . . . . . . . . [PROD/INVDAT(DETAIL,PART)          ]

       SELECT . . . . . . . . . . [PRTNAM,INVQTY,COST               ]

       WHERE. . . . . . . . . . . [COST>5.00                        ]

       ORDER BY . . . . . . . . . [                                 ]

       Output device  . . . . . . 1. Display
                                  2. Printer
                                  3. Disk

       To . . . . . . . . . . . . [C:EXPORT.DAT                     >

       Replace
       old file . . . . . . . . . 1. Yes
                                  2. No

     ──────────────────────────────────────────────────────────────
     Enter  Esc=Cancel  F1=Help  F3=Exit  F5=Run  Shift+F4=Group functions
     Spacebar
```

TO destination, only the device type along with, possibly, a specific device id is being defined. The device type options are Display, Printer, and Disk.

Display, of course, means the information will be sent to the workstation screen. Printer will require more specifics on how the information is to be printed and, if more than one printer is defined for the workstation, which specific printer. Disk will send the data to a drive on the PC. When Disk is chosen, the drive, file name, and file type have to be specified (see Figure 8.14), as do:

- Whether to replace the file if it already exists on that drive
- What type of file is being sent (BASIC, DOS random, ASCII) (Figure 8.15)
- Whether to send a transfer description file

The transfer description file defines the structure of the file being downloaded. When data is uploaded to the AS/400, a transfer description file must be sent. In downloading, it is optional. If data is going to be downloaded, modified, and then sent back to the AS/400, a transfer description will have to be sent back with the modified file. If that is the case, it's a good idea to say yes to the Save transfer description prompt at this time.

Supply a file name at the Description file name prompt. (The traditional file extension for a description file is FDF.) By doing this, the required description file will be available when it is time to upload.

Press ENTER. The transfer is now defined.

FIGURE 8.15

```
          Create an AS/400 System-to-PC Transfer Request
                                                      More: ↑
   Select options and then press Enter

     PC file type  . . . . .  ▶ 1. ASCII text
                                2. DOS random
                                3. BASIC sequential
                                4. BASIC random
                                5. DIF(TM)
                                6. No conversion
                                7. DOS random type 2

   Show format of
   transferred data . . . . .  1. Display
                                2. Print
                              ▶ 3. None

   Save transfer
   description. . . . . . . .▶1. Yes

   Description
   file name. . . . . . . . .  [A:\STUFF.FDF                    >

   Enter Esc=Cancel F1=Help F3=Exit Shift+F4=Group functions Spacebar
```

Running a Transfer

From the Create an AS/400 System-to-PC Transfer Request screen, a transfer can be run in either of two ways:

- Press **F5**.

  or

- Press **F10**.
- Select the Run function.

Saving, Recalling, and Modifying a Transfer

If this data is going to be sent more than once, saving the transfer frees the user from having to redefine it every time data is sent. A transfer can be saved after it has been defined by simply pressing **F10** on the Create an AS/400 System-to-PC Transfer Request **screen** and choosing the Save function. The next screen that appears will prompt for information about saving the transfer (for example, the file name under which to store the transfer definition).

After the transfer has been saved, it can be recalled and run again by selecting the Recall and Run functions from the same screen.

If a mistake was made while defining the transfer or a change needs to be made to a saved transfer, select the Modify function to change any of the parameters. Modify walks through each of the define transfer screens. The previously specified values will be displayed and can be edited.

Uploading Files

To upload a file, select the Transfer data from PC to host system option at the window where the type of transfer to be created is specified (see Figure 8.11). The AS/400 System-to-PC Transfer screen will be displayed. Choose the `Create` function, and the `Create an AS/400 System-to-PC Transfer Request` screen will be displayed. This screen allows entry of the TO and FROM destinations for the upload transfer. In this case, the file on the PC is the FROM location, and the TO destination is a member on the AS/400. (The same syntax used during the download transfer creation is used to specify the PC file and the AS/400 member.) If a data file is being sent, the name of a description file must also be supplied; in our case, it would be the file specified in the download.

When uploading, it must be specified whether the AS/400 should create the TO file and member or, if they already exist, the member should be written over. If a new AS/400 file is being created, the type of file, either source or data, must be entered.

If a data file is being created during the transfer, several other pieces of information must be given:

- **Field reference file name.** A data file must have a field reference file associated with it. The field reference file contains the field descriptions—type of data, length (Character 15, Numeric 6.2, and so on)—for all the data elements within the file. In our case, we would specify the library and file names of the original downloaded file. This tells the AS/400 that we want to use the same field reference file.

- **Authority for the object.** What will other users be able to do with this file (for example, READ, WRITE, ALL)?

- **Text.** This is free-format information associated with the new member or file.

Pressing F5 will run the transfer.

Using the Transfer Function in Distributed Processing

How could the transfer function be applied to our convenience store example? The original manual system of supplying price changes had several problems:

- It took too much manpower to update 20,000 files.
- There was a high risk of errors.
- The elapsed time to change prices was too long, and the time varied between stores.

The shared folders solution solved these problems but carried several other costs:

- Changes had to be made to each store's sales transaction program and CONFIG.PCS file.
- Centralized data caused a major increase in the telecommunications line transmission rate.
- Centralized data also caused the sales transaction programs to take longer because they had to access the remotely stored price data.

The transfer function could be applied two different ways to the problem. If the telephone company's charges weren't that bad and charge projections seemed reasonable, we could just apply the transfer function to the problem of updating each store's software and files. Instead of sending a copy of the new program and the CONFIG.PCS file to each manager and having him or her type it into the system, why not ship the new program and file to each store location using the transfer function?

Each manager could be given a procedure to create a download transfer. The managers would select the `Transfer data from host system to PC` option and specify a member on the AS/400 that contained the new PC sales transaction program. The TO destination would be the C drive on the PC. The managers would then follow the same procedure for the CONFIG.PCS file. This would simplify what the managers had to do and certainly be better than sending a programmer to each store to update the machines.

However, if the telephone company's charges were too much, we could always go back to the distributed data approach but use the transfer function to send the data, that is, have duplicate price files on each PC but use the transfer function to get new prices down from the AS/400 to each PC.

The price expert at corporate would create a new file that contained each item's price changes. The programmers would create a new update price program that ran once a night on the PC. This update price program would first download the price change file by issuing the correct transfer function API download command. Once the file was downloaded to the C drive, the program would read the items contained in the change file and update the master price file with the information.

The nice thing about this solution is that all the manual system problems have been solved, and the centralized data disadvantages of the shared folder solution have been eliminated. Moreover, the communications line traffic has been cut by distributing copies of the price data to all the stores. The only communication required is to transfer the price change file. Given the number of sales per store, this should result in a tremendous decrease in the telecommunications costs.

This transfer solution also takes very little time to update the prices since it is done by a program, and no manual data entry is required. By having the program kick on automatically each night, it ensures that each store's prices are updated at the same time. The transfer function can also be used to download any software changes, just as described in the first transfer solution combining both shared folders and transfer.

The only disadvantage is the increased PC storage space needed. Not only is space still required for the 20,000 copies of the price file, but extra space is needed for PC Support and the price update program.

Transfer Tips

The transfer function is very obliging about sending files from a PC to the AS/400. However, accessing the files on the AS/400 is another story. When using the AS/400 utilities—OfficeVision/400, SEU, and so on—there may be trouble accessing or manipulating data that came from a PC. For instance, files created using some word processing applications cannot be accessed using SEU. The applications insert control characters that SEU cannot process. Further, a file's record length must be less than 240 characters to display them using SEU.

Of course, the main advantages of the transfer function are that it facilitates distributed processing and provides an easy and secure method to back up data on the AS/400's larger storage capacity. If data is being transferred to the AS/400 for backup purposes only, accessing the data with the AS/400 utilities will not be an issue.

Distributed processing is complicated, and tight control over access and modification of distributed data must be exercised. The transfer function and its associated API can greatly ease this process; however, advanced programming knowledge will be needed to use PC Support effectively and securely.

Workstation Function

PC Support, through the workstation function, enables users to define PC systems and printers to the AS/400 so that they can be used as AS/400 workstations and printers. To access the workstation function from the PC Support/400 Menu:

- Choose the Configure PC Support option.

  or

- Choose the Go to PC command prompt option.

- Change the drive to the shared folder drive (I).

- Type **CFGWSF**.

- Press ENTER.

Either method will start the CFGWSF program that allows the workstation to be configured. Configuring a workstation using PC Support means selecting options such as the colors and window sizes for the display screen and functions for each key on the keyboard.

After starting the CFGWSF program, a window will be displayed with the options PC Support configuration (which lets users change the colors and window sizes) and Work station function configuration (which lets users change keyboard functions and other display characteristics). The characteristics and functions chosen are stored in keyboard and session profiles.

The *session profile* defines the type of session (screen or printer) and its characteristics (132 characters to a screen versus 80 characters). The *keyboard profile* defines the keys. A key's function (delete a character, page down, print screen, and so on) or its playback characters (what character or characters will appear at the cursor when the key is pressed) can be modified.

A *master profile* contains other workstation parameters and the file names of the keyboard and session profiles that will define the workstation at sign-on. Many different keyboard profiles can be created, but only one can be active. The active keyboard profile is the one listed in the master profile. Up to five different session profiles can be defined in the master profile. These will all be activated at sign-on, and a user can "hot key" between the different sessions at the workstation.

Reconfiguring the Workstation

Often during a computer session, the same information is entered many times during a day—a particular customer's name and address, an often used command, and so on. This process can be sped up by redefining a key's playback characters as the commonly entered character sequence. As an example, let's redefine the Alternate state of F12 as the frequently entered characters SIGNOFF.

To change a key's function, choose the `Configure PC Support` option from the `PC Support/400` Menu. Then select option 2, `Work station function configuration`, from the window that appears (Figure 8.16). The next screen provides options for the type of function to be performed (Figure 8.17). To change a profile, press F10 and select the `Change` function.

A window will be displayed where the type of profile to be changed—session, keyboard, or master—is selected (Figure 8.18). Choose option 2, `Change keyboard profile`. A new window will appear prompting for the keyboard profile name and path (Figure 8.19). Let's assume that a keyboard profile already exists on the C drive within a directory called PCS. In this case, enter `C:\PCS\KEYBD.KBD`.

The `Define Keyboard` screen, which shows a layout of the keyboard, will be displayed (Figure 8.20). To change a particular key's function or playback characters, move the cursor to that key's position on the layout and press ENTER. For our example, move the cursor to the F12 spot on the keyboard layout and press ENTER.

A window at the bottom of the screen will appear showing the current definition of that key in its various states (Figure 8.21). Valid states are:

- `Base state`. The key's definition when it is pressed by itself (for the F12 key, it is F12).

FIGURE 8.16

```
                    PC Support/400 Menu
Select one of the following

   Learn About PC Support
      View PC Support Introduction

   Perform PC Support Tasks
      Go to PC command prompt
      Use printers on host system
      Use folders on host system
      Transfer data
      Send and r ┌─────────────────────────────────────────┐
     *Go to Orga │ 1. PC Support Configuration              │
      Submit hos │ 2. Work station function configuration   │
                 │                                          │
   Manage Your PC│ Enter Esc=Cancel F1=Help                 │
                 └─────────────────────────────────────────┘
      Configure PC Support
      Administer PC Support
      View PC Support Error Log
```

FIGURE 8.17

```
Create Change Exit Help

             Work Station Function Configuration

To select an action shown above, first press F10.

This program allows you to build the following profiles for use
with the work station function program:

—Session profiles, which define the type of workstation or
 printer a session will imitate.

—Keyboard profiles, which define the type and style of keyboard
 you will use in a session.

—Master profiles, which contain a keyboard profile and information
 to be used by up to five session profiles.

You should complete the work station function checklist found in
the PC Support/400 DOS Installation and Administration Guide
before continuing program.


Enter  Esc=Cancel  F1=Help  F3=Exit  F10=Actions
```

- Shift state. The key's definition when it is pressed at the same time as the SHIFT key (for F12, it should be F24).

- Alt state. The key's definition when it is pressed at the same time as the ALT key (for F12, it should be blank).

- Alt Graphics state. The key's definition when its pressed at the same time as the ALT GRAPHICS key (for F12, it also should be blank).

FIGURE 8.18

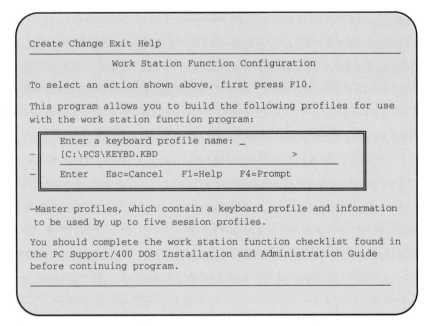

```
Create Change Exit Help
                 ┌─────────────────────────┐
                 │ 1. Change session profile │ ion Configuration
                 │ 2. Change keyboard profile│
       To selec  │ 3. Change master profile  │ ess F10
                 │ Esc=Cancel                │
                 └─────────────────────────┘
This program allows you to build the following profiles for use
with the work station function program:

—Session profiles, which define the type of workstation or
 printer a session will imitate.

—Keyboard profiles, which define the type and style of keyboard
 you will use in a session.

—Master profiles, which contain a keyboard profile and information
 to be used by up to five session profiles.

You should complete the work station function checklist found in
the PC Support/400 DOS Installation and Administration Guide
before continuing program.
```

FIGURE 8.19

```
Create Change Exit Help

                Work Station Function Configuration

To select an action shown above, first press F10.

This program allows you to build the following profiles for use
with the work station function program:
 ┌─────────────────────────────────────────────────────┐
 │  Enter a keyboard profile name: _                     │
─│  [C:\PCS\KEYBD.KBD                           >        │
 │                                                       │
─│  Enter   Esc=Cancel   F1=Help   F4=Prompt            │
 └─────────────────────────────────────────────────────┘

—Master profiles, which contain a keyboard profile and information
 to be used by up to five session profiles.

You should complete the work station function checklist found in
the PC Support/400 DOS Installation and Administration Guide
before continuing program.
```

To define a function for the `Alt state` of **F12**, type in the appropriate function command after the opening bracket on the `Alt state` line. To find the valid function commands, press **F4**. This will bring up a list of all available functions. Select a function by scrolling through the list, placing the cursor on the desired option, and pressing **ENTER**.

For this exercise, we want to change the playback characters for the `Alt state` of **F12**. Do this by moving the cursor to the space after the opening bracket on the `Alt state` line and entering the playback character string enclosed in single quotes. For our example, type in

FIGURE 8.20

```
 Options  Layout  Exit  Help
 ──────────────────────────────────────────────
                    Define Keyboard
 □  □□□□  □□□□  □□□□   □□□
 □□□□□□□□□□□□□□   □□□    □□□□
 □□□□□□□□□□□□□□   □□□    □□□▯
 □□□□□□□□□□□□□          □□□
 □□□□□□□□□□□□      □     □□□▯
 □  □ □□□□□□□□ □  □    □□□    □□▯

 Move the cursor to the key to be defined, press Enter
   or
 Press the key to define while holding the shift key down.

 To save the profile, press F10 and select the Exit action.
 ──────────────────────────────────────────────
 Enter  Esc=Cancel  F1=Help  F3=Exit  F10=Actions
```

FIGURE 8.21

```
 Options  Layout  Exit  Help
 ──────────────────────────────────────────────
                    Define Keyboard
 □  □□□□  □□□□  □□□□   □□□
 □□□□□□□□□□□□□□   □□□    □□□□
 □□□□□□□□□□□□□□   □□□    □□□▯
 □□□□□□□□□□□□□          □□□
 □□□□□□□□□□□□      □     □□□▯
 □  □ □□□□□□□□ □  □    □□□    □□▯

 ┌──────────────────────────────────────────┐
 │ Base state. . . . . . . . . . [[F12]    > │
 │ Shift state . . . . . . . . . [[F24]    > │
 │ Alt state . . . . . . . . . [         > │
 │ Alt Graphics state. . . . . . [        > │
 ├──────────────────────────────────────────┤
 │ Enter  Esc=Cancel  F1=Help  F4=Prompt  F5=Extended input │
 └──────────────────────────────────────────┘
```

'SIGNOFF' (Figure 8.22) and press ENTER. This will change the keyboard profile and bring back the Define Keyboard screen.

To save the newly defined keyboard profile, press F10 and select the Exit function. A window will appear prompting for the keyboard profile name—in our case, the original one typed in will be displayed. Change this name or leave the original one. For our example, leave the original one and press ENTER, which will overwrite the previous definition. To save a previous definition, a new name should be typed in at this prompt.

FIGURE 8.22

```
 Options  Layout  Exit  Help
 ───────────────────────────────────────────────────────────
                     Define Keyboard
  □   □□□□  □□□□  □□□□     □□□
  □□□□□□□□□□□□□□□□□□       □□□   □   □□□□
  □□□□□□□□□□□□□□□□□□       □□□       □□□□
  □□□□□□□□□□□□□□□□□□                 □□□
  □□□□□□□□□□□□□□□          □         □□□
  □   □□ □□□□□□□□□□ □□  □  □   □□□    □□□

  ┌─────────────────────────────────────────────────────────┐
  │ Base state. . . . . . . . . . [[F12]                   > │
  │ Shift state . . . . . . . . . [[F24]                   > │
  │ Alt state . . . . . . . . . . ['SIGNOFF'               > │
  │ Alt Graphics state. . . . . . [                        > │
  │                                                          │
  │ Enter  Esc=Cancel  F1=Help  F4=Prompt  F5=Extended input │
  └─────────────────────────────────────────────────────────┘
```

The `Add Keyboard Profile to Master Profile` screen will appear. At this point, a new keyboard profile has been created and saved. It will be active only if it is defined in the master profile. This screen lets users add the newly defined keyboard profile to the master profile. Currently, the master profile name should be displayed. If it is not, type in the correct name and press ENTER; otherwise, just press ENTER. This will update the master profile.

The next time the workstation is booted, the new keyboard profile will be read. Prove this by pressing ALT-F12. The characters SIGNOFF should be displayed at the cursor. If the cursor was positioned on the command line, pressing ENTER would result in signing off.

The workstation function allows users to customize their workstation session so that it is more efficient and user friendly. In a bizarre way, the workstation function also encourages users not to leave their workstations unattended after they have signed on. In general, leaving a signed-on workstation unattended is considered a breach of security because anyone passing could sit down and run amok in the system. Now with the workstation function, there is a more personal reason to be careful. If you happen to leave your signed-on AS/400 workstation to get a quick bite to eat, anyone who has read this chapter (one of your classmates, maybe even your instructor?) could invoke PC Support and change the keyboard profile. When you come back and press E, a Z might print out. Pressing ENTER may result in the `Exit` function being performed. Or pressing the spacebar may result in the first line of the "Pledge of Allegiance" being displayed. To avoid pranks and having to go back and check every key to see if any of the various states have been changed, never leave a signed-on workstation unattended. Remember, you are surrounded by potential keyboard terrorists.

Summary

PC Support is a collection of programs that enable the PC to interact with the AS/400 as an intelligent workstation. It provides utilities that:

- Identify and define the PC and its printer as an AS/400 workstation and printer
- Transfer data between machines and application programs that are on the same network
- Allow data to be stored and accessed on the AS/400 from the PC workstation

PC Support, like all functions on the AS/400, can be accessed through a series of easy-to-use menus and is supported by on-line help.

Most PC Support utilities can also be executed from user-defined programs. Each utility has an API, a command or set of commands with associated syntax, keywords, and parameters that can be inserted into a user's program. These commands, when executed within the user application, will kick in the associated PC Support program. The PC Support program will execute according to the parameters set.

Most important, PC Support provides a common user interface across different communications networks. All users will see the same menus and be able to perform the same functions regardless of the type of network. By using the API provided by PC Support, customers insulate their application programs from any changes that occur in the physical or logical network structure. If there is a change in networking software or hardware, PC Support is changed on the affected workstation not user applications. No application programs or user files need to be changed or compiled because of network hardware or software changes. This saves the AS/400 users time and effort and cuts down on confusion as their network environment changes to satisfy business needs.

LAB EXERCISE

This lab exercise will create a host-to-PC transfer of a data file. The download will simulate a real-world transfer of data between the dairy in the previous chapters' examples and a store to which milk has been shipped.

Instead of each individual grocery store updating its inventory file by entering the carton number, expiration date, and product name of each carton received, a transfer file could be sent to the store's PC. After the file was received, an application program could read the transfer file and update the store's inventory data. By using the PC Support transfer function and an application program, time would be saved and the accuracy of updating the store's inventory records increased.

ITBATCAR will be the logical file used in this exercise. If ITBATCAR was not created earlier, it must be created to perform this exercise.

1. At any command line, type **GO PCOMNU** and press ENTER.

2. At the PC Support/400 Organizer screen, choose option 4.

3. From the PC Support/400 Menu, choose the Transfer data option.

4. From the window, choose option 1, Transfer data from host system to PC.

5. At the AS/400 System-to-PC Transfer screen, press F10 and choose the Create function.

6. Specify:

   a. **YOURLIBXX/ITBATCAR** at the FROM prompt

   b. **CRTNUM, ITMNAM, EXPDTE** at the SELECT prompt

   c. **STORE = '2894628'** at the WHERE prompt

   d. **3** at the Output device prompt

   e. **A:\DAIRY** at the To prompt

   f. **1** at the Replace old file prompt

   g. **1** at the PC file type prompt

(If this information was really to be used in an application program, the type chosen in step 6 would depend on the application environment.)

7. Press ENTER.

8. Press F10 and choose the Save option.

9. Choose the Save the current transfer request option and save the transfer as **A:\DAIRYDLD**.

10. Press F10 and choose the Run option (make sure you have a disk in the A drive).

11. Press ESC, then F3, and choose option 1.

12. At the PC Support/400 Menu, choose the Go to PC command prompt option.

13. At the prompt, specify **DIR A:DAIRY.*** and press ENTER.

14. File information should be displayed regarding the data file DAIRY and the file definition file sent with it, DAIRY.FDF.

15. To see the contents of the file, enter **TYPE A:\DAIRY** and press ENTER.

REVIEW QUESTIONS

1. What is the function of the Router within PC Support?

2. What object stores information that can be accessed from both the AS/400 and a PC?

3. Explain the purpose of and relationship between session, keyboard, and master profiles.

4. How many active sessions can PC Support maintain?

5. What is the difference between distributed processing and distributed data?

6. How does PC Support enhance the portability of application programs between different networks?

7. How is the CONFIG.PCS file used by PC Support?

8. What are the major functions provided by PC Support?

9. What is the advantage of assigning a drive to a shared folder by modifying the CONFIG.PCS file over dynamically working with folders?

10. How many active keyboard definitions can PC Support maintain for a workstation?

DISCUSSION QUESTIONS

1. Where do PC Support programs reside?
2. What are the benefits and costs associated with distributed processing?
3. Compare the advantages and disadvantages of the transfer function to the shared folders function in a distributed processing environment.
4. What are some of the advantages of using PC Support?

OfficeVision/400

9

This chapter focuses on OfficeVision/400. There is a short explanation of the different types of business systems concentrating on office automation systems and their functions. The chapter then explores OfficeVision/400 and demonstrates how the AS/400 provides the most common office automation functions.

After finishing this chapter, you will understand:

- The four major types of business systems
- The major features of an office automation system

You also will be able to:

- Access and change your calendar
- Set up a meeting and update other users' calendars
- Send and receive electronic mail
- Create documents
- Create documents containing data from queries or physical file members

Business Systems

There are four types of business systems:

- Transaction processing systems (TPS)
- Management information systems (MIS)
- Computer-aided design and manufacturing systems (CADAMS)
- Office automation systems (OAS)

Each system enables businesses to perform common business functions. For instance, all businesses perform transactions. Every activity that occurs at a business is a transaction. Every time a customer buys something at a convenience store, an employee performs a sales transaction. The sales transaction consists of:

- Identifying the item to be purchased
- Calculating a subtotal amount by multiplying each item's price by the quantity being sold
- Generating a total sales amount by adding up all the subtotals
- Recording the amount paid
- Generating the amount of change that should be returned to the customer
- Recording the sale
- Decreasing the amount in inventory for each item sold

The convenience store also performs receiving transactions when they receive goods from their suppliers, and they perform a pay transaction when they pay their employees. Each of these transactions consists of many steps that use and create information. Application software packages can be bought or developed that help the business perform generic business transactions such as sales, payroll, or billing faster and more accurately. Other transaction processing systems may be more industry specific (reservation systems for airlines, patient registering and tracking systems for hospitals, and so on). Each TPS enables a company or organization to perform day-to-day operations more efficiently.

Management information systems, on the other hand, provide information that enables management to make decisions on problems that are beyond day-to-day operational concerns. As an example, consider a convenience store chain that is growing rapidly. Overall, sales are increasing 50 percent a year. Management is trying to decide where to open new stores and, for existing stores, where to hire new employees. The TPS would not help management with that decision. The TPS helps store employees perform and track sales. However, an MIS will often use information generated by a TPS. An MIS will process transaction data and present it in a way that will help management make a decision. In our example, if the sales data being generated by each store was summarized monthly for the last two years, it would show which stores have been growing the fastest. This would help management identify high-growth regions and, based on the amount of growth, decide which areas could support new stores and which stores simply need extra help. This is the goal of the MIS: to help management make the tactical and strategic decisions that will affect the company for years to come.

A CADAMS is completely different from an MIS and a TPS. This software helps companies design, test, and control the manufacturing of new products. For instance, a car parts designer could enter specifications for a new tire into the computer and generate an image of what the tire would look like. Once the initial design specifications have been entered, he or she would simulate the wear and tear of 60,000 miles of use. Based on the results of the simulation, the designer would then make changes to the design and rerun the simulation. This process would continue until the designer is satisfied with how the tire holds up after 60,000 miles of use. The tire specifications would then be sent to computer-controlled equipment that would manufacture the tire based on the final specifications.

A CADAMS speeds up the design and manufacturing processes and ensures a smooth and accurate transfer of data. In addition, computer-controlled manufacturing frees people from mundane, repetitive tasks, and it removes them from dangerous or hazardous manufacturing environments.

The fourth type of business system, an OAS, allows users to perform many tasks commonly associated with an office environment. Normal administrative and secretarial tasks such as creating business documents, sending memos, or maintaining an appointment calendar can be performed on a computer with an OAS.

Many application packages are available from software vendors that provide each of these business systems on the AS/400. IBM supplies an AS/400 OAS called OfficeVision/400. OfficeVision/400 is tightly coupled to OS/400 and its many utilities, thereby providing added functions and versatility.

OfficeVision/400

OfficeVision/400 enables a user to perform the common OAS tasks mentioned. It also provides software to maintain the automated office environment (for example, programs to enroll userids in OfficeVision/400, utilities to search for documents based on selected characteristics, and the ability to protect and restrict access to OfficeVision items). The rest of this chapter covers accessing and using the following three OfficeVision/400 features:

- Calendars
- Word processing
- Electronic mail

  To access OfficeVision/400 from the AS/400 Main Menu screen:

- Choose option 2, Office tasks.

- Press ENTER. The Office Tasks screen will appear (Figure 9.1).

- From the Office Tasks screen, choose option 1, Office-Vision/400.

- Press ENTER. The OfficeVision/400 screen will be displayed (Figure 9.2).

  or

- Type **STROFC**.

- Press ENTER.

FIGURE 9.1

```
                              Office Tasks
OFCTSK                                                    System: CHICAGO

Select one of the following:

        1. OfficeVision/400
        2. PC Support tasks
        3. Decision support
        4. Office security
        5. Work with system directory
        6. Documents
        7. Folders

       70. Related commands

Selection or command
===>_____

_____


F3=Exit  F4=Prompt   F9=Retrieve   F12=Cancel   F13=User support
F16=AS/400 Main menu
```

FIGURE 9.2

```
                        OfficeVision/400
                                              System: CHICAGO

   Select one of the following:

         1. Calendars                              Time: 12:44
         2. Mail
         3. Send message                 December          1992
         4. Send note                    S   M   T   W   T   F   S
         5. Documents and folders                    1   2   3   4   5
         6. Word processing              6   7   8   9  10  11  12
         7. Directories/distribution lists   13  14  15  16  17  18  19
         8. Decision support            20  21  22  23  24  25  26
         9. Administration              27  28  29  30  31

        90. Sign off
                                        Bottom

   Press ATTN to suspend a selected option.
   Selection
   ___
   F3=Exit       F12=Cancel      F19=Display messages
```

Calendars

If you have never worked in an office environment, it may be difficult to appreciate the benefits of an electronic calendar. Often "new hires" starting their first job try to keep their appointments in their head. If the job requires even a small number of meetings or any advanced planning, the beginner quickly learns that an appointment calendar is a necessity of business life. The problem with a physical calendar is that if it is forgotten or lost, no plans or appointments can be made. Moreover, anyone who wants to set up a meeting must contact the person that maintains the calendar to arrange it. Traveling or simply being very busy can make it exceedingly difficult to reach a particular person. This is a real problem when trying to schedule a meeting. The OfficeVision/400 electronic calendar offers a solution to these problems.

OfficeVision/400 creates a calendar for each user when he or she is enrolled into OfficeVision/400. Calendar functions allow users to access and change their calendars and access other OfficeVision/400 users' calendars to schedule meetings and appointments.

Calendar functions can also set up system reminders. System reminders are messages sent to a user's screen at a specified time or at continual intervals for a specified period. Another useful feature of calendars is the ability to schedule the running of programs. By specifying CL commands, system functions can be executed or application programs "kicked off" without a user submitting the commands directly.

To access the calendar functions, choose option 1, Calendars, from the OfficeVision/400 screen. Depending on how the system is set up, one of three calendar displays will appear. A daily, weekly, or six-month calendar will be shown. Figure 9.3 shows the

Weekly Calendar screen. To change between the three types of calendars press F11. This will bring up the Change Calendar View display on the bottom half of the screen (Figure 9.4). You can then:

- Type 1 and press ENTER to display the Daily Calendar screen (Figure 9.5).

  or

- Type 2 and press ENTER to switch to the Six Month Calendar screen (Figure 9.6).

FIGURE 9.3

```
                          Weekly Calendar
Function . . . . _____      Calendar. . .INTRO99  CHICAGO_____
MON            TUE            WED            THU            FRI
11/30/92       12/01/92       12/02/92       12/03/92       12/04/92
8a_____     8a_____     8a_____     8a_____     8a_____
_____      _____      _____      _____      _____
9a_____     9a_____     9a_____     9a_____     9a_____
_____      _____      _____      _____      _____
10a_____    10a_____    10a_____    10a_____    10a_____
_____      _____      _____      _____      _____
11a_____    11a_____    11a_____    11a_____    11a_____
_____      _____      _____      _____      _____
12n_____    12n_____    12n_____    12n_____    12n_____
_____      _____      _____      _____      _____
1p_____     1p_____     1p_____     1p_____     1p_____
_____      _____      _____      _____      _____
2p_____     2p_____     2p_____     2p_____     2p_____
_____      _____      _____      _____      _____
3p_____     3p_____     3p_____     3p_____     3p_____
_____      _____      _____      _____      _____
4p_____     4p_____     4p_____     4p_____        More...
F3=Exit           F4=Prompt   F6=Add item    F9=Display item
F10=Change item   F12=Cancel  F16=Remove item  F24=More keys
```

FIGURE 9.4

```
                          Weekly Calendar
Function . . . . _____      Calendar. . .INTRO99  CHICAGO_____
MON            TUE            WED            THU            FRI
11/30/92       12/01/92       12/02/92       12/03/92       12/04/92
8a_____     8a_____     8a_____     8a_____     8a_____
_____      _____      _____      _____      _____
9a_____     9a_____     9a_____     9a_____     9a_____
_____      _____      _____      _____      _____
10a_____    10a_____    10a_____    10a_____    10a_____
_____      _____      _____      _____      _____
11a_____    11a_____    11a_____    11a_____       More...

                     Change Calendar View

Type choices, press Enter.
  Calendar view  . . . . 2          1=Daily, 2=Weekly, 3=Group
                                    4=Composite, 5=Six month

  Calendar . . . . . .   INTRO99 CHICAGO_____ F4 for list
  Date . . . . . . . .   12/01/92__  MM/DD/YY

F3=Exit     F4=Prompt     F5=Refresh   F12=Cancel   F24=More keys
```

FIGURE 9.5

```
                              Daily Calendar
Function . . . . _____   Calendar. . .   INTRO99 CHICAGO_____

Type information, press Enter to schedule.
Nbr From To Text                                                     Type
               12/01/92 Tuesday

____ __  _____
         _____
         _____
         _____
         _____
         _____
         _____
         _____
         _____
         _____
         _____
         _____
         _____
                                                            Bottom
F3=Exit           F4=Prompt    F6=Add item      F9=Display item
F10=Change item   F12=Cancel   F16=Remove item  F24=More keys
```

FIGURE 9.6

```
                            Six Month Calendar
Function . . . . _____   Calendar. . .   INTRO99 CHICAGO_____

November        1992  December        1992  January         1993
 S  M  T  W  T  F  S   S  M  T  W  T  F  S   S  M  T  W  T  F  S
 1  2  3  4  5  6  7         1  2  3  4  5                     1  2
 8  9 10 11 12 13 14   6  7  8  9 10 11 12   3  4  5  6  7  8  9
15 16 17 18 19 20 21  13 14 15 16 17 18 19  10 11 12 13 14 15 16
22 23 24 25 26 27 28  20 21 22 23 24 25 26  17 18 19 20 21 22 23
29 30                 27 28 29 30 31        24 25 26 27 28 29 30
                                            31
February        1993  March           1993  April           1993
 S  M  T  W  T  F  S   S  M  T  W  T  F  S   S  M  T  W  T  F  S
    1  2  3  4  5  6      1  2  3  4  5  6                  1  2  3
 7  8  9 10 11 12 13   7  8  9 10 11 12 13   4  5  6  7  8  9 10
14 15 16 17 18 19 20  14 15 16 17 18 19 20  11 12 13 14 15 16 17
21 22 23 24 25 26 27  21 22 23 24 25 26 27  18 19 20 21 22 23 24
28                    28 29 30 31           25 26 27 28 29 30
                                                         More...
   F3=Exit        F4=Prompt      F6=Add item     F11=Change view
   F12=Cancel     F21=Nondisplay keys           F24=More keys
```

Updating a Calendar

Items can be added to a calendar from any of the three calendar displays:

- Press **F6**. The Add Item window will appear on the bottom of the screen (Figure 9.7).

- Type **1** at the Type of item prompt.

- Press **ENTER**. The Add Event window will appear on the bottom of the screen (Figure 9.8).

FIGURE 9.7

```
                              Weekly Calendar
    Function . . . ._____  Calendar. . .   INTRO99 CHICAGO_____
    MON            TUE            WED            THU            FRI
    11/30/92       12/01/92       12/02/92       12/03/92       12/04/92
    8a_____     8a_____     8a_____     8a_____     8a_____
    _____     _____     _____     _____     _____
    9a_____     9a_____     9a_____     9a_____     9a_____
    _____     _____     _____     _____     _____
    10a_____    10a_____    10a_____    10a_____    10a_____
    _____     _____     _____     _____     _____
    11a_____    11a_____    11a_____    11a_____        More...

                               Add Item

    Type choices, press Enter.
       Type of item . . . . . . 1      1=Event (single calendar)
                                       2=Meeting (multiple calendars)
                                       3=Reminder
                                       4=Job

       Multiple items . . . . . N      Y=Yes, N=No

    F3=Exit  F9=Six month calendar  F12=Cancel  F19=Display messages
```

FIGURE 9.8

```
                              Weekly Calendar
    Function . . . ._____  Calendar. . .   INTRO99 CHICAGO_____
    MON            TUE            WED            THU            FRI
    11/30/92       12/01/92       12/02/92       12/03/92       12/04/92
    8a_____     8a_____     8a_____     8a_____     8a_____
    _____     _____     _____     _____     _____
    9a_____     9a_____     9a_____     9a_____     9a_____
    _____     _____     _____     _____     _____
    10a_____    10a_____    10a_____    10a_____    10a_____
    _____     _____     _____     _____     _____
    11a_____    11a_____    11a_____    11a_____        More...

                               Add Event
    Type choices, press Enter.
       Calendar . . . .   INTRO99 CHICAGO_____ F4 for list
       Date/day . . . .   12/01/92__      MM/DD/YY
       From/to  . . . .   8:00a 9:00a     hh:mmA, hh:mmP
       Description  . .   _____
                         _____
                         _____

       Message  . . . .   N        Y=Yes, N=No
                                                            More...
    F3=Exit      F4=Prompt       F12=Cancel      F24=More keys
```

On this window, specify the date, times (beginning and ending), and a brief description of the event to be scheduled. In Figure 9.9, a notice for the office Christmas party that's scheduled for 3:00 p.m. to 5:00 p.m. on 12/23/93 is being added to the calendar. Don't forget to specify a.m. or p.m. by adding *a* or *p* after the time. If a.m. or p.m. is not specified, the system will make the best guess based on traditional office hours (for example, for 3 to 5, it will assume 3 p.m. to 5 p.m.).

FIGURE 9.9

```
                       Weekly Calendar
 Function . . . . _____  Calendar . . .  INTRO99 CHICAGO_____
 MON            TUE           WED           THU           FRI
 11/30/92       12/01/92      12/02/92      12/03/92      12/04/92
 8a_____     8a_____    8a_____    8a_____    8a_____
 _____       _____      _____      _____      _____
 9a_____     9a_____    9a_____    9a_____    9a_____
 _____       _____      _____      _____      _____
 10a_____     10a_____    10a_____    10a_____    10a_____
 _____       _____      _____      _____      _____
 11a_____     11a_____    11a_____    11a_____         More...
                         Add Event
 Type choices, press Enter.
   Calendar . . . . . INTRO99 CHICAGO_____ F4 for list
   Date/day . . . . . 12/23/93__     MM/DD/YY
   From/to. . . . . . 3:00P 5:00P    hh:mmA, hh:mmP
   Description. . . . XMAS Bash_____
                               _____
                               _____
   Message. . . . . . N              Y=Yes, N=No
                                                         More...
 F3=Exit      F4=Prompt      F12=Cancel     F24=More keys
```

FIGURE 9.10

```
                       Weekly Calendar
 Function . . . . _____  Calendar. . .  INTRO99 CHICAGO_____
 MON            TUE           WED           THU           FRI
 12/20/93       12/20/93      12/22/93      12/23/93      12/24/93
 8a_____     8a_____    8a_____    8a_____    8a_____
 9a_____     9a_____    9a_____    9a_____    9a_____
 10a_____     10a_____    10a_____    10a_____    10a_____
 11a_____     11a_____    11a_____    11a_____    11a_____
 12n_____     12n_____    12n_____    12n_____    12n_____
 1p_____     1p_____    1p_____    1p_____    1p_____
 2p_____     2p_____    2p_____    2p_____    2p_____
 3p_____     3p_____    3p_____    >3:00p**E 3   3p_____
                                            >Xmas Bash
 4p_____     4p_____    4p_____    > 5:00p          More...
 F5=Refresh        F11=Change view F13=More tasks F15=Print
 F17=Earlier days  F18=Later days  F20=Copy item  F24=More keys
```

Figure 9.10 shows how that entry will appear in the weekly calendar. The monthly calendar is not affected by adding items, and the daily calendar would have the full text of the event.

There is a second way to add items to the calendar or look at a different date. There is a Function field in the upper left-hand corner of the screen. Typing in a function code and pressing ENTER causes the appropriate Add screen to be displayed. For instance, typing **AE** (Add Event) and pressing ENTER will bring up the Add Event display, as in Figure 9.8. The function codes allow the user to bypass the Add Item display, where the type of item is specified. A date can also be typed into this field. Entering a date in the MM/DD/YY format and pressing ENTER will result in the calendar orienting itself to that day. (For a list of all the function codes, move the cursor to the Function field and press F4.)

A third way to add to a calendar is to go directly to the Daily Calendar screen and type in the times and description for the event. After entering the information, press ENTER, then change to the Weekly Calendar screen. Notice that the weekly calendar has also been updated.

Changing an already scheduled item can be handled directly from the daily calendar. Simply pull up the Daily Calendar screen for the event and type over any of the information. For instance, if an event time has been changed, type the new times over the old times and press ENTER. The calendar will be updated.

To delete an item from the calendar, bring up the Daily Calendar screen. Move the cursor to the event to be deleted and press F16. The Confirm Remove of Calendar Item screen will be displayed. Press ENTER to delete the item or press F12 to leave the item on the calendar.

Updating Other People's Calendars

To update another person's calendar, the owner of the calendar has to grant potential updaters authority to access his or her calendar. This is similar to granting object authorities, as discussed in previous chapters. OfficeVision/400, however, has special calendar authorities that define the access and functions used against a calendar. It also provides a screen to easily assign these authorities. Initially, when a user is enrolled into OfficeVision/400, a calendar is created, and a default authority is assigned. The user, however, can change the authority for the calendar at any time. To change the authority from any calendar display:

- Press F13. The More Calendar Tasks screen will appear (Figure 9.11).

- At the More Calendar Tasks screen, choose option 2, Work with calendars. The Work with Calendars screen will appear (Figure 9.12).

- Type **14**, for the Change authority option, in the space next to the calendar name.

- Press ENTER. The Change User Authority to Calendar screen will be displayed (Figure 9.13).

If the calendar authority has never been specified, the only userid displayed should be *PUBLIC. This is a catchall id used to define all other users' access to the calendar. If someone's userid is not explicitly specified in the list, the authority specified for *PUBLIC is used.

FIGURE 9.11

```
                    More Calendar Tasks

Select one of the following:

         1. Change calendar session
         2. Work with calendars
         3. Work with groups
         4. Copy calendar items
         5. Remove calendar items
         6. Work with distribution lists
         7. Work with meetings
         8. Search remote calendars
         9. Work with user defined functions




Selection
  _
F3=Exit  F9=Six month calendar  F12=Cancel  F19=Display messages
```

FIGURE 9.12

```
                    Work with Calendars

Position to . . . . . ._____        Starting characters

Type options, press Enter.
   2=Change   4=Delete   14=Change authority

                ------Owner------
Opt   Calendar   User ID   Address   Calendar Description
 __    INTRO99    INTRO99   CHICAGO   student id






                                                      Bottom
F3=Exit  F5=Refresh  F6=Create new calendar  F9=Six month calendar
F11=Display authorities  F12=Cancel  F19=Display messages
```

FIGURE 9.13

```
                    Change User Authority to Calendar

  Calendar . . . . . . . :    INTRO99

  Type choices, press Enter. Press F6 to authorize distribution list.
  Authority: 1=Exclude 2=Times 3=Use 4=Add item 5=Change

                          -----Authority-----
  User ID     Address   Unclass   Conf    Pers   Description
  *PUBLIC_     _____     1        1       1    Public authorities
  _____     _____     _        _       _
  _____     _____     _        _       _
  _____     _____     _        _       _
  _____     _____     _        _       _
  _____     _____     _        _       _
  _____     _____     _        _       _
  _____     _____     _        _       _
  _____     _____     _        _       _
  _____     _____     _        _       _
                                                                More...
  F3=Exit   F4=Prompt      F5=Refresh   F6=Authorize distribution list
  F9=Six month calendar   F12=Cancel   F19=Display messages
```

There are five levels of authority, ranging from 1 to 5, with 1 corresponding to the least amount of access and functional capability. These authority levels are assigned for each type of calendar item. Item types can be unclassified, confidential, or personal. The ability to assign authority by the type of event provides another level of control over the functions others can perform against your calendar. For instance, users can be allowed to view nonpersonal items and change only unclassified items.

The five authority levels are:

1. Exclude. Stops all access to the events specified.

2. Times. Allows the specified user to see the weekly calendar and the times that have an item scheduled. However, no details regarding the items can be viewed. The calendar's description can also be viewed.

3. Use. Grants all the functions that the Times authority does and allows the scheduled items' details to be seen.

4. Add item. Grants all the functions that the Use authority does and allows the specified user to add items to the calendar. The user can also change any items that he or she has added to the calendar.

5. Change. Allows the specified user to perform all the Add item functions as well as change all items on the calendar, including deleting.

Typically, OfficeVision/400 users grant Add item authority, not Change authority, for the public id. Change authority is reserved for the calendar owner or administrative personnel who are in charge of setting up and maintaining the owner's calendar. These people's responsibility would be to resolve any calendar conflicts for the owner.

Typing in a **4** for each *PUBLIC event type would grant all OfficeVision/400 users the authority to add items to the calendar. Each calendar custodian would then need to be added individually and granted Change authority by specifying a **5** for each event type (unclassified, confidential, personal).

Setting Up Meetings

OfficeVision/400 also allows users to update multiple calendars at the same time by scheduling a meeting. To schedule a meeting from the Add Item display (see Figure 9.7):

- Specify **2** at the Type of item prompt and press ENTER.

or

- Type **AM** (Add Meeting) in the Function field and press ENTER.

This will bring up the Add Meeting screen. From this screen, a meeting description can be specified just like an event description. More important, more than one calendar can be identified for updating.

For instance, say the boss has requested that you schedule a Christmas carol practice prior to the Christmas party (last year's warbling left quite a bit to be desired). Type in the appropriate meeting time, place, and purpose. Then specify all the carolers' userids (Figure 9.14). As long as all the carolers have granted you Add Item authority, pressing ENTER will update each specified user's calendar with the meeting information.

FIGURE 9.14

```
                          Add Meeting
Type choices, press Enter.
   Requester . . .    INTRO99_ CHICAGO___   student id
   Date/day  . . .    12/23/93__            MM/DD/YY
   From/To . . . .    1:00P 3:00P           hh:mmA, hh:mmP...
   Subject . . . .    Christmas carol practice_____
   Place . . . . .    Conference room 99_____
   Purpose . . . .    Tune up those vocal chords_____
   Status. . . . .    1             1=Tentative, 2=Confirmed
   Security. . . .    1             1=Unclassified, 2=Confidential
                                    3=Personal

Type invitee calendars, press Enter.
Invitee Calendars           Conflict Status
INTRO35_____
INTRO34_____
_____
_____
_____
_____
                                                     More...
F3=Exit F4=Prompt F5=Refresh F11=Display descriptions F12=Cancel
F13=Find place F14=Extended entry F15=Find free time F24=More keys
```

Calendar Jobs

Probably the most powerful feature of the OfficeVision/400 calendar is the ability to schedule programs to be run automatically from the calendar. A new type of item, called a *job*, can be added to any calendar. A job is made up of a CL command and its associated keywords and parameters. Now, being able to run CL commands may not sound like much, but the CL command CALL can invoke any program on the system. Adding a job to the calendar to run a program at 6 a.m. every Monday means that when the sun comes up at the start of the work week, the AS/400 will automatically execute that command, and you can stay snugly tucked in bed.

For instance, imagine the situation of a restaurant manager. Division headquarters requires that all data on the previous week's sales, purchases, and inventory be received by 8 a.m. Tuesday. This requires the manager to "close the books" after the end of business on Sunday night. Closing the books means running a series of programs that read, record, and summarize all the sales, purchases, and inventory transactions for that week. After the books are closed, another series of programs are run that update the financial records and produce cost reports, inventory balances, and the like. It takes about five hours to run all these programs.

The manager then reviews all the data, checking on missing sales slips, correcting data that was entered incorrectly, and so on. He reruns some of the programs to capture the corrected information. Finally, a program is executed to send this information to divisional headquarters.

Usually, the manager has to stay till 1 a.m. Monday to submit the job to close the books. He then comes in around 8 a.m. Monday to start the update job. The reports are printed about 10:30 a.m., which is when he can start making the corrections and rerun the programs. Traditionally, he gets to leave about 8 p.m. Monday. Sometimes, however, he has actually been there till 7:59 a.m. Tuesday! Can you see a use for the calendar function that may enable the manager to sleep a little later on Monday mornings and get home at a decent hour on Sunday and Monday nights?

What if a CL program was created that called the close the books and financial update jobs that take five hours to run? The CL program could be scheduled to kick off at 3 a.m. Monday through the calendar.

This would mean that the manager would not have to stick around till closing, and when he arrived at 8 a.m. Monday, the reports and data would be all ready. He could then start reviewing the data instead of waiting till 10:30 a.m. This would mean he would start getting home around 5:30 p.m. instead of 8 p.m. on Mondays.

But what about the transfer program that sends the data to division headquarters? There have been several times in the past that the manager, because of sleep deprivation, has forgotten to send the data. With the calendar function, a job could be scheduled for 7:59 a.m. every Tuesday to call the transfer program that sends the data to division headquarters. The manager would be relieved of having to remember to send the data; it would be sent every Tuesday automatically.

Scheduling a Job

To schedule a job, go to the Add Item screen and type **4**, Job, as the type of item. (Alternatively, from any of the calendar displays, type **AJ** in the Function field and press ENTER.) This will bring up the Add Job window in the bottom half of the screen (Figure 9.15). Fill out the time and date the job is supposed to execute, just as you would schedule any other event. If a program is being called, the library that contains the program and any keywords and values will have to be specified. To prompt for the command's keyword and values, enter the command and press F4. If you are not sure of the commands available, simply move the cursor to the command line and press F4. The Major Command Group screen will be displayed.

FIGURE 9.15

```
                          Weekly Calendar
  Function . . . .  _____ Calendar . . . . INTRO99 CHICAGO_____
  MON            TUE            WED            THU            FRI
  11/30/92       12/01/92       12/02/92       12/03/92       12/04/92
  8a_____     8a_____     8a_____     8a_____     8a_____

  9a_____     9a_____     9a_____     9a_____     9a_____

  10a_____     10a_____     10a_____     10a_____     10a_____

  11a_____     11a_____     11a_____     11a_____         More...
                                 Add Job
  Type choices, press Enter.
    Calendar . . . . . .    INTRO99 CHICAGO_____ F4 for list
    Date/day . . . . . .    12/01/92__   MM/DD/YY
    Time . . . . . . . .    8:00a        hh:mmA, hh:mmP
    Job description. . .    _____    Name
      Library. . . . . .    _____    Name
    Command. . . . . . .    _____

  F3=Exit      F4=Prompt      F12=Cancel     F24=More keys
```

After the job is entered, the `Calendar` function will take over. When the designated date and time arrive, the command will be executed.

Jobs can also be scheduled to execute regularly (daily, weekly, monthly, and so on). To do this, the user would enter a **Y** in the `Multiple items` prompt on the `Add Item` screen. This will bring up the `Add Multiple Jobs` screen (Figure 9.16), which looks similar to the `Add Job` screen except that there is a `Sequence` prompt. This prompt allows the user to specify the regularity of the run (for example, every other week) or the specific dates and times for each execution.

FIGURE 9.16

```
                          Add Multiple Jobs

   Type choices, press Enter.

         Calendar . . . . .    INTRO99 CHICAGO_____
         Date/day . . . . .    12/01/92__     MM/DD/YY
         Time . . . . . . .    8:00a          hh:mmA, hh:mmP...
         Job description. .    QDFTJOBD__     Name
           Library. . . . .       QGPL_____  Name
         Command  . . . . .    _____
                                                1=Daily, 2=Weekly
         Sequence . . . . .    _              3=Every other week
                                               4=Monthly, same date
                                               5=Monthly, same relative
                                                 day and week
                                               6=Individual dates and times


                                                                  Bottom
       F3=Exit  F4=Prompt  F5=Refresh  F9=Six month calendar  F12=Cancel
       F14=Extended entry  F19=Display messages
```

Word Processing

OfficeVision/400 provides a word processor that is integrated with several of the other AS/400 utilities. Documents can be created and edited using any of several editors, but more important, the word processing system allows information stored in files or generated by queries to be included in these documents. Before we cover how to create these documents, several unique aspects of the AS/400's word processing functions need to be covered.

First, all documents are stored in *folders*. When a userid is enrolled in OfficeVision/400, a folder is created for that id. The name of the folder is the same as the id (for example, userid INTRO99 has a folder called INTRO99). When a document is created, the folder that it will reside in must be specified, just as the library must be specified when an object is created.

OfficeVision/400 offers the ability to edit documents, as well as manipulate them as a whole within the folder (delete, print, and so on). Most common formatting features such as margin setting, spacing, and indexing are also supported. The AS/400, however, stores this data differently from most word processing packages. Rather than embedding formatting codes or descriptive information in the document itself, OfficeVision/400 allows the user to create two separate objects— a text profile and a document's details—to contain this information.

A *text profile* contains format parameters for a document. Unlike many other word processing packages, where the margins and headers are inserted in the document itself, OfficeVision/400 allows the user to set up a separate profile that contains format characteristics. The text profile can be created separately from any document and then assigned to a folder. All documents within that folder will then be printed according to the parameters specified in the text profile. Using text profiles in this way creates a common profile that can be assigned to many documents, thereby saving the user from having to respecify the formatting parameters each time a new document is created.

A *document's details* are information about a document not related to its appearance (for example, a description of the document's contents, the author's name, or a due date associated with the document). OfficeVision/400 allows the user to search for documents or keep track of them by these characteristics rather than by name alone.

Shell Documents

As mentioned earlier, OfficeVision/400 has the capability to retrieve information from outside sources and place it inside a document. Text from other documents can be retrieved, and variable data from files or queries can be included. For instance, rather than retyping a document with new sales figures each month, a user can set up a report that has a defined format and some standard text. Included in the document are commands to retrieve and insert specified data elements each time the document is generated. A document that contains standard text and variable data commands is called a *shell document*, and it can retrieve data from three sources: a fill-in document, a file, or a query.

A *fill-in document* contains a data structure definition and data. It is created just as any other document. When it is time to print the shell document, the fill-in document's name is specified as the source of the data, and it is merged with the shell document. To create a fill-in document, simply list the field names on the first x number of lines, one field name per line preceded by an ampersand. This is the structure of the data. Skip a line and begin entering the "records." A data element value is entered on each succeeding line, and a blank line is placed before the start of a new record. The data element names specified in the fill-in document must match the variable names specified in the shell document.

Although a fill-in document is handy, the question becomes how is the document created? Is it typed in by hand? If so, maintenance of the data may become an issue if the data is changeable. Because of this, there is an option to merge data from a file. Files can be updated by application programs, DFU (Data File Utility), or SQL (Structured Query Language). In addition, information generated on a PC can be uploaded to an AS/400 data member through the PC Support transfer option.

When a shell document is merged with a file, the variable names specified in the DDS (Data Description Specification) must be used in the document. At the time of printing, the library, file, and member name where the data is stored are specified.

However, there may be a problem with the data in a file. What if the data is not in the correct format or not grouped according to how the data needs to appear in the document? This is where merging from query-generated data can help. If data is needed from more than one file, only certain records are needed, or the data needs to be sorted in a certain order, a query can be written to retrieve the correct data and format it.

A query creates a spool file containing the query report before it is printed, sent to a file, or displayed. OfficeVision/400 intercepts that data before it goes to its destination and incorporates it into the document. In this way, the query acts as a tool to select and sequence the specific records desired for the document.

If the query, fill-in document, or file contains multiple records, two types of shell documents can be created: a multi-letter document or a multi-line document.

A *multi-letter document* will result in a separate document being generated for each data record. This multi-letter feature allows users to create customized form letters. For instance, a late billing notice could be sent to each customer that contains that person's balance due.

A *multi-line document* will result in a single document with a separate line for each record. This type of document is good for summary accounting. For instance, a letter containing a line for each overdue account balance and the owner's name could be sent to the collections department.

Creating a Document

The first step in creating a document is to choose option 1, Documents and folders, from the OfficeVision/400 screen. The Documents and Folders screen will be displayed. Choose option 1, Work with documents in folders. The Work with Documents in Folders screen will be displayed (Figure 9.17). To create a document, type 1 in the Opt field, type a document name in the Document field, and press ENTER.

FIGURE 9.17

```
                  Work with Documents in Folders
Folder . . . INTRO99_____
Position to . . . . . . _____ Starting characters

Type options (and Document), press Enter.
  1=Create  2=Revise     3=Copy      4=Delete      5=View
  6=Print   7=Rename     8=Details   9=Print options 10=Send
  11=Spell  12=File remote 13=Paginate 14=Authority


Opt    Document   Document Description    Revised    Type

__     _____

   (No documents in folder)




                                                    Bottom
F3=Exit    F4=Prompt    F5=Refresh  F10=Search for document
F11=Display names only  F12=Cancel  F13=End search  F24=More keys
```

As an example, we are going to create a multi-letter shell document called REORDLET. Enter this name in the `Document` field. REORDLET is going to be an order letter to the suppliers of our produce market. One letter will be generated for each item for which the quantity in stock is below the reorder point. To get the record for each item, we will use the data generated by the query created earlier. REORDLET will also include the unit price for each item, so the query will have to be changed to include the unit price field. Go back to the query definition menus and change the query to include unit price. In addition to each item's unit price, REORDLET will contain a header, some standard text for ordering an item, and instructions to retrieve the item name, reorder quantity, supplier name and address, and the total order cost for each item being ordered.

After entering option 1 and the document name, press ENTER. The `Create Document Details` screen will be displayed (Figure 9.18). This is the first of two screens where information about the document as a whole can be specified. For instance, the document can be assigned a description, an expiration date, an author's name, keywords, and a subject.

Once all the details have been specified, press ENTER. OfficeVision/400 will save all the information and bring up the main document edit screen (Figure 9.19). From this screen, the shell document text and commands can be entered.

FIGURE 9.18

```
                    Create Document Details            Page 1 of 3
     Profile being used . . . . . : SYSTEM          (User)

     Type choices, press Enter.
        Document . . . . . . . . . REORDLET____    Name
        Document description . . . . _____
        Subject . . . . . . . . .   _____
     _____
        Document to copy . . . . . _____
          From folder . . . . . . .
     _____
        Authors . . . . . . . . Intro99_____
        Keywords. . . . . . . . _____
     _____
     _____     F4 for list
        Document class. . . . _____     F4 for list
        Print as labels . . . N                  Y=Yes, N=No
                                                            More...
     F3=Exit    F4=Prompt    F10=Bypass text entry    F12=Cancel
     F20=Change format/options
```

FIGURE 9.19

```
     Create Document     |Page End    |Ins| |          |Pg 1
     REORDLET,INTRO99                 |Typestyle 86 (12p) |Ln 7
     «2...:...3...:...4...:...5........6...:...7...:...8...:...9». ..:




     _____
     1=Copy       7=Window      15=Table      21=Spell Opt. J=End Und/Bold
     2=Move       8=Cancel      16=Adjust/Pag 22=Add to Dct P=Page End
     3=Exit/Save  9=Instructions 17=Query File 23=Synonym   S=Stop
     4=Find Char 11=Hyphenate   18=Search/Rep 24=Spell Aid  U=Underline
     5=Goto      13=Edit Options 19=Print/View B=Bold       W=Word Und
     6=Find      14=Get Options 20=Chg Formats C=Center     Y/H=Up/Down
```

The numbers at the bottom of the screen specify function keys and the associated function of each. However, just pressing a function key will not result in the function being performed. Many of the OfficeVision/400 function keys work in block mode. Individual keys do not perform the operation, they activate the blocking function. For instance, 1 equals Copy, but pressing F1 activates the copy block mode. When block mode is activated, the beginning of the block is set to the location of the cursor. OfficeVision/400 then instructs the user to move the cursor to the end of the text to be blocked. After that is done, pressing ENTER confirms and blocks the text. Another prompt will instruct the user to move the cursor to the location the block is to be copied to. When ENTER is pressed, the data will be copied.

Even keys like DEL operate in this manner. Pressing DEL also invokes the blocking function. The information is deleted only after the blocked area is specified and ENTER is pressed. To delete a single character with one keystroke, BACKSPACE can be used.

The letters at the bottom of the screen also control edit and format functions. These letters, in conjunction with ALT, will perform the operations listed. Again, many of them invoke the block function but with a different twist. For instance, pressing ALT-U will underline everything from the cursor position to the end of the document. Moving the cursor to the end of the area to be underlined and pressing ALT-U a second time signifies the end of the block to be underlined. The underlining will stop at the second cursor position.

Not all the letter functions work like this. For instance, pressing ALT-C and designating the block of text to be centered does *not* center the text. Pressing ALT-C marks the spot on the line around which the text will be centered. For example, to center text on the line, move the cursor to column 55 and press ALT-C. This marks column 55 as the centering point. Type in the text to be centered, and the editor will orient it around the centering function code. (For a more thorough coverage of the editing function keys and letters, see the *Using OfficeVision/400 Word Processing* manual.)

The centering function hints at the method used to implement functions. The AS/400 word processor embeds codes into the text. Choosing an option like centering results in a nondisplayed function code being placed inside the document. These embedded codes can be seen by placing the cursor over their location in the document and looking at the *audit window* (the area at the top of the screen in Figure 9.19 where it says Page End). The audit window will display text that describes the function code. To delete a function code, move the cursor to the function code's location in the text, press DEL and then ENTER. If the function code is coupled (that is, it has a start and an end), then move the cursor to the space that contains the end function code. Again look at the audit window to find the location. Press DEL and then ENTER again to delete the ending function code.

In addition to the function keys and letters, a series of text instructions can be inserted into the document. Pressing F9 displays a list of available functions (Figure 9.20), including:

- Skip a specified number of lines or to a new page
- Insert the current date or time
- Create a table of contents

- Create an index
- Change fonts
- Create a footnote

Selecting an option will result in a further definition of that option. For instance, choosing the Skip function will result in a screen that requests the number of lines to be skipped. Pressing ENTER twice will result in the instruction being inserted at the cursor position. Text instructions can also be inserted directly into the document if the text instruction code is known. For instance, to insert a skip code, simply type **.sk(#)** on a line (substituting a number for #). When ENTER is pressed, the . will be changed into another symbol signifying that the instruction has been accepted. (The symbol that replaces the . depends on the type of terminal you are working on.)

To start creating the document, move the cursor to the upper left-hand corner of the entry area and press F9. From the screen that appears, choose option 3, Date, and press ENTER. Accept all the defaults for the date parameters, then press ENTER again. Move to the next line, mark the center of the line as described earlier, and type the header **XXXXXX PRODUCE MARKET** (substituting your name for XXXXXX). Move back to the first line and then to the end of the line and type **.time** (as in Figure 9.21). The .time text instruction tells the system to insert the current time at that location in the document. This is the alternative method of inserting text instructions. Move to the line following the header and either type in the Skip command or press F9 to insert the Skip command, specifying that three lines be skipped.

FIGURE 9.20

```
Create Document          |Page End    |Ins | |            |Pg 1
REORDLET,INTRO99                       |Typestyle 86 (12p) |Ln 7
«2...:...3...:...4...:...5...:...6...:...7...:...8...:...9»...:...

                      Select Text Instruction            Page 1 of 2

Select one of the following:
  Instruction to be Inserted at Cursor Position
      1. Start new page                8. Numbered list
      2. Keep                          9. Running headings
      3. Date                         10. Conditional text
      4. Time                         11. Include
      5. Document ID                  12. Data field
      6. Skip                         13. Table of contents/
      7. Change font                      Outline headings

                                                       More...



Selection
___
F3=Exit      F12=Cancel
```

FIGURE 9.21

```
Revise Document       |          |Ins|  |              |Pg 1
REORDLET,INTRO99                 |Typestyle 86 (12p)   |Ln 8
«2...:...3...:...4...:...5...:...6...:...7...:...8...:...9»..:.
.date                                        .time
                    your name Produce Market




_____
1=Copy       7=Window      15=Table       21=Spell Options J=End Und/Bold
2=Move       8=Cancel      16=Adjust/Pag  22=Add to Dct    P=Page End
3=Exit/Save  9=Instructions 17=Query File 23=Synonym       S=Stop Code
4=Find Char  11=Hyphenate  18=Search/Rep  24=Spell Aid     U=Underline
5=Goto       13=Edit Options 19=Print/View B=Bold          W=Word Und
6=Find       14=Get Options 20=Chg Formats C=Center        Y/H=Up/Down
```

Creating a Shell Document

If the document is going to be merged with data, the data field names to be merged must be specified. The names used are the names as defined in the source of the data (that is, a fill-in document, query, or database file). When identifying data fields in a shell document, the first data field also specifies information regarding how all the data fields are going to be used throughout the document. In our example, each reorder letter is going to start with the appropriate supplier's name and address. The data for this shell document is going to be supplied by the query used as an example in Chapter 7. To specify the Supplier Name field, move the cursor to the position for the supplier's name and press F5 (GOTO). Type .& at the prompt and press ENTER. The .& tells OfficeVision/400 that a data field name will be entered, so the Data Field Instruction screen is displayed (Figure 9.22). On this screen, the data field name must be specified, as well as where the data for this field will come from. For our example, we will specify SUPPL as the data field name. We will also specify *print as the data field source, meaning that the location of the data (that is, the query) will be specified at print time. For our example, we will also specify that this document will generate multiple letters. (Typing 1 in the Letters or list option will do this.) Press ENTER to return to the main document edit screen.

FIGURE 9.22

```
Revise Document  |Carrier Return  |Ins |    |            |Pg 1
REORDLET,INTRO99                  |Typestyle 86 (12p) |Ln 9
«2..:...3...:...4...:...5...:....6...:...7...:...8...:...9»..:...
.date                                           .time
                    your name Produce Market

.&                      Data Field Instruction

This instruction prints the value of a data field from a described
datafile, Query, or document.

Type choices, press Enter.
     Data field  . . . .  _____   Name
        Data field source  2       1=From Merge Data Options
                                    2=*PRINT, 3=*NOTE
   Letters or list . . .  1         1=Multiple letters, 2=Column list
   File ID for Query . .  ___
   Instruction length. .  12        1-255, Blank=Entire instruction



F3=Exit                   F5=Numeric editing   F6=Character editing
F9=Date/time editing   F12=Cancel              F24=More keys
```

For all data fields specified later in the document, this information does not have to be reentered. All other data fields in this document can be identified by simply typing in .& followed by the field name. Continue entering the data as shown in Figure 9.23. If ENTER is pressed, the .& preceding the field name may be changed to other characters. The replacement characters will depend on the type of terminal you are working on. Also, if you are working from an AS/400 terminal, the appearance of the SUPPL field may not be the same as in Figure 9.23.

FIGURE 9.23

```
Revise Document  |              |Ins | |            |Pg 1
REORDLET,INTRO99                |Typestyle 86 (12p)  |Ln 17
«2...:...3...:...4...:...5...:...6...:...7...:...8...:...9»...:...
.date                                           .time
                    your name Produce Market
.sk(3)
.&SUPPL(P,,,
.&SUPADD
.&SUPCTY,.&SUPST .&SUPZP
.sk(2)
Dear Sir,
.sk(2)
    Please ship .&EOQ units of .&ITMNME's at the current unit cost
of .&UNTPRC for a total cost of .&ORDCST.
.sk(2)
Sincerely,
.sk(2)
yourname
```

FIGURE 9.24

```
                          Exit Document

Type choices, press Enter.

Save document  . . . . . . .    Y              Y=Yes, N=No
   Document . . . . . . . . .    REORDLET____   Name, F4 for list
      Folder . . . . . . . .                   Name, F4 for list
   INTRO99_____


   Display save options . . .    N              Y=Yes, N=No

Print document . . . . . . .     N              Y=Yes, N=No

   Display print options. . .    N              Y=Yes, N=No




F4=Prompt        F6=Print queue        F12=Cancel
```

After entering the document, press **F3** to exit and save the document. This will bring up the Exit Document screen (Figure 9.24), where the name of the document and the folder it is to be stored in can be specified. Enter **Y** to save the document and specify **reordlet** for the document name. Specify **N** for all other options and press ENTER. The Work with Documents in Folders screen will be redisplayed. From this screen (as well as the previous screen), the document can be printed. There are also many options to choose from regarding printing. Typing **9** next to the document name and pressing ENTER will bring up the first of four Print Options screens. From these screens, a variety of parameters regarding the document appearance can be set, and the printer id can be specified. Most important, on page 3, the user must specify **Y** for the Place on job queue prompt for the document to be printed. For our example, specify the options as shown in Figures 9.25 through 9.28.

If the document is going to include outside data, the merge data options must be specified. Pressing **F15** (from any Print Options screen) will display the Merge Data Options screen (Figure 9.29). From this screen, the user can specify the query, file, or other document to be merged. For our example, merge the document with the query created previously, INVQRY in YOURLIBXX. Enter **1** as the merge data source. Since the document will result in a separate letter being generated for each reorder, specify **N** for the Multiple line report option. Pressing ENTER will result in a second prompt area being displayed in the middle of the screen where the library and query name can be specified. (When a query is specified as the data source, the document will take longer to print than when a file is used as the source. This is because the merge must wait for the query to process.) Pressing ENTER will result in the print job being added to the processing queue and the documents being printed out as seen in Figures 9.30(A), 9.30(B), and 9.30(C).

FIGURE 9.25

```
                              Print Options              Page 1 of 4
        Document . . . . . . . . : REORDLET

        Type choices, press Enter.
           From page . . . . . .     1___          1-9999
           Through page  . . . . .   9999          1-9999
           Number of copies. . . .   1_            1-99
           Output device . . . . .   1             1=Printer, 2=Display
                                                   3=File
             Printer . . . . . . .   *WRKSTN___    *USRPRF, *SYSVAL, *WRKSTN
                                                   Printer ID
             Output queue. . . . .   *DEV_____   Name, *DEV, *FILE, *WRKSTN
               Library. . . . . . .  *LIBL_____    Name, *LIBL
             Output file . . . . .   *DOC_____   Name, *DOC, *FILE
             Form type . . . . . .   _____    Printer form
             Printer file  . . . .   QSYSPRT___    Name
               Library. . . . . . .  *LIBL_____    Name, *LIBL


                                                              More...
        F3=Exit    F6=Print queue    F12=Cancel
        F15=Merge data options       F18=Additional page ranges
```

FIGURE 9.26

```
                              Print Options              Page 2 of 4
        Document . . . . . . . . . . . . : REORDLET

        Type choices, press Enter.
           Delay printing . . . . . . . . . . N         Y=Yes, N=No
           Draft spacing  . . . . . . . . . . N         Y=Yes, N=No
           Print line numbers . . . . . . . . N         Y=Yes, N=No
           Resolve instructions . . . . . . . Y         Y=Yes, N=No
           Print with large print . . . . . . N         Y=Yes, N=No
           Print separator page . . . . . . . N         Y=Yes, N=No
           Adjust line endings. . . . . . . . N         Y=Yes, N=No
           Adjust page endings  . . . . . . . Y         Y=Yes, N=No
             For choice Y=Yes:
               Allow widow lines  . . . . . . N         Y=Yes, N=No
             For choice No=No:
               Renumber system page
                 numbers  . . . . . . . . . . Y         Y=Yes, N=No
           Print quality  . . . . . . . . . . 1         1=Letter, 2=Text
                                                        3=Draft
                                                              More...
        F3=Exit    F6=Print queue    F12=Cancel
        F15=Merge data options       F18=Additional page ranges
```

FIGURE 9.27

```
                        Print Options              Page 3 of 4
     Document . . . . . . . . . . : REORDLET

     Type choices, press Enter.
       Place on job queue . . . . . Y            Y=Yes, N=No
         For choice Y=Yes:
           Send completion
             message . . . . . . . N            Y=Yes, N=No
         Job description. . . . . . QBATCH_____  Name
           Library . . . . . . . . *LIBL_____   Name, *LIBL
       Cancel on error. . . . . . . N            Y=Yes, N=No
       Print error log . . . . . . N            Y=Yes, N=No
         For choice Y=Yes:
             Form type . . . . . . . _____   Printer form
       Save resolved output . . . . N            Y=Yes, N=No
         For choice Y=Yes:
           Document. . . . . . . . . _____ Name, F4 for list
           Folder. . . . . . . . .               Name, F4 for list
       _____
                                                      More...
     F3=Exit      F4=Prompt       F6=Print queue      F12=Cancel
     F15=Merge data options       F18=Additional page ranges
```

FIGURE 9.28

```
                        Print Options              Page 4 of 4
     Document . . . . . . . . . . : REORDLET

     Type choices, press Enter.
       Print revisions symbols. . . . N       Yes=Yes, No=No
         Symbols to be printed. . . . -----
       Additional spaces to left. . . 0       0-99
       Graphic character set. . . . . _____   Identifier
       Type of page printing. . . . . 1       1=Single-sided
                                               2=Double-sided
                                               3=Double-sided tumble

         For choice 2 or 3:
           Adjust margins for
             page binding. . . . . . Y        Y=Yes, N=No
         For truncated text:
           Shift left margin . . . . . N      Y=Yes, N=No


                                                      Bottom
     F3=Exit     F6=Print queue     F12=Cancel
     F15=Merge data options       F18=Additional page ranges
```

A multi-line document with a list of all the order records can also be generated; however, each field must be defined as a column list item on the Data Field Instruction screen (see Figure 9.22). Unlike the multiple letters document, where only the first field had to

FIGURE 9.29

```
                          Merge Data Options

Document . . . . . . . . . . . . . : REORDLET

Type choices, press Enter.
  Multiple line report. . . . . .  N        Y=Yes, N=No
  Merge data source . . . . . . .  _        1=Query
                                            2=Document
                                            3=File















F3=Exit        F12=Cancel
```

FIGURE 9.30(A)

```
   DECEMBER 4, 1993                                    04:50:25 PM
                      your name Produce Market

   AMERICAN TURNIP CORP
   101 VEGETABLE LANE
   BANGOR,ME 11111


   Dear Sir,

        Please ship 25 units of TURNIP's at the current unit cost of
   .22 for a total cost of 5.50.


   Sincerely,


   yourname
```

be defined as a multi-letter document field, a column list document requires each field to be specified as a multi-list item. To do this, type **2** at the `Letters or list` prompt on the `Data Field Instruction` screen. The fields should be specified one after the other, as in Figure 9.31.

FIGURE 9.30(B)

```
DECEMBER 4, 1993                                       04:50:25 PM
                       your name Produce Market

RADISHES 'R US
1 DIRT ST
LARCHMONT,TX 44444

Dear Sir,

    Please ship 75 units of RADISH's at the current unit cost of
.06 for a total cost of 4.50.

Sincerely,

yourname
```

FIGURE 9.30(C)

```
DECEMBER 4, 1993                                       04:50:25 PM
                       your name Produce Market

STINKY'S
PEA-YEW DR
VADALIA,GA 33333

Dear Sir,

    Please ship 50 units of ONION's at the current unit cost of 3.50
for a total cost of 175.00.

Sincerely,

yourname
```

When it comes time to specify merge options, the Multiple line report option should be specified as Yes (not as in Figure 9.29, where it is specified as No). Assuming that the document was entered correctly, the results would appear as in Figure 9.32. (Notice the grand total field from our query summary specification.)

Electronic Mail

Electronic mail systems enable users to send notes, messages, and documents to one another on the computer. A user does not have to be signed on to the system to receive electronic mail. When a person is

FIGURE 9.31

```
Revise Document          Date        Ins              Pg 1
REORDLST,INTRO99                      Typestyle 86 (12p) Ln 7
2...:...3...:...4...:...5...:...6...:...7...:...8...:...9...:...
.date                                          .time
                    your name Produce Market
.sk(3)
Dear Boss,
.sk(2)
    The following is a list of this weeks orders.

.&SUPPL(P,,, .&ITMNME(P,, .&EOQ(P,,,,C .&UNTPRC(P,, .&ORDCST(P,,
.sk(2)
Sincerely,
.sk(2)
yourname
```

FIGURE 9.32

```
DECEMBER 4, 1993                              04:50:25 PM
                    your name Produce Market


Dear Boss,

    The following is a list of this weeks orders.


AMERICAN TURNIP CORP      TURNIP    25      .22      5.50
RADISHES 'R US            RADISH    75      .06      4.50
STINKY'S                  ONION     50     3.50    175.00

                                         FINAL TOTALS

                                         TOTAL    185.00
Sincerely,

yourname
```

enrolled in OfficeVision/400, a mail log is set up for his or her userid. This mail log acts as an electronic mailbox. Just as people don't have to be home to receive mail from the postal carrier, a user doesn't have to be signed on to receive electronic mail. The mail log stores any electronic notes that are sent whether the user is signed on or not. When a user accesses OfficeVision/400, a message underneath the monthly calendar that says New mail means that new mail has been received since the last time the mail log was checked (Figure 9.33).

FIGURE 9.33

```
                          OfficeVision/400
                                                    System: CHICAGO
        Select one of the following:

             1. Calendars                                Time: 4:47
             2. Mail
             3. Send message            December              1992
             4. Send note                    S  M  T  W  T  F  S
             5. Documents and folders         1  2  3  4  5  6  7
             6. Word processing               6  7  8  9 10 11 12
             7. Directories/distribution lists 13 14 15 16 17 18 19
             8. Decision support             20 21 22 23 24 25 26
             9. Administration               27 28 29 30 31

            90. Sign off                   New mail
                                                            Bottom
        Press ATTN to suspend a selected option.
        Selection
        __
        F3=Exit       F12=Cancel      F19=Display messages
        (C) COPYRIGHT IBM CORP. 1985, 1991.
```

Sending Mail

Three types of electronic mail can be sent in OfficeVision/400: messages, notes, and documents. The screens to actually send all three are much the same, but there are major differences in what each mail item is and how it is created.

We discussed what a document is and how it is created in the "Word Processing" section of this chapter. Notes and messages are created when a user is ready to send them. There are two major differences between notes and messages. First, messages are shorter in length than notes. Notes have no length restriction; however, the maximum length for a message is 256 characters. Second, received notes can be saved, whereas messages cannot. When a message is received, it can be read; it cannot be filed or printed. (We cover the differences regarding receiving electronic mail in more detail at the end of the chapter.)

Sending Documents. To send a document to another user:

- Select option 5, Documents and folders, from the OfficeVision/400 screen (see Figure 9.2).

- Select option 1, Work with documents in folders, from the Documents and Folders screen.

- On the Work with Documents in Folders screen (Figure 9.34), move the cursor next to the document to be sent and type **10**.

- Press ENTER.

The Send Document screen will be displayed (Figure 9.35). This screen is similar to the screens used to send messages and notes. At

FIGURE 9.34

```
                    Work with Documents in Folders
Folder . . .
INTRO99_____
Position to . . . . . . _____ Starting characters


Type options (and Document), press Enter.
  1=Create  2=Revise        3=Copy       4=Delete        5=View
  6=Print   7=Rename        8=Details    9=Print options 10=Send
  11=Spell  12=File remote  13=Paginate 14=Authority

Opt Document      Document Description      Revised    Type
__  _____
__  REORDLET      Supplier reorder letter   12/01/92   RFTAS400
__  REORDLST      Supplier reorder list     12/01/92   RFTAS400




                                                          Bottom
F3=Exit     F4=Prompt     F5=Refresh F10=Search for document
F11=Display names only  F12=Cancel F13=End search  F24=More keys
```

FIGURE 9.35

```
                        Send Document
Document description . . . . . :  Supplier reorder letter
Document . . . . . . . . . . :  REORDLET
  Folder . . . . . . . . . . :  INTRO99

Type distribution list and/or addressees, press F10 to send.
  Distribution list. . . . .    _____ _____ F4 for list

-----Addressees------
User ID     Address      Description
_____    _____
_____    _____
_____    _____
_____    _____
_____    _____
_____    _____
_____    _____
_____    _____

                                                      More...
F3=Exit     F4=Prompt F9=Attach memo slip F10=Send F11=Change details
F12=Cancel F13=Change defaults F18=Sort by user ID F24=More keys
```

the top of the screen, the folder and document name are listed. The bottom half of the screen is used to specify the userids to send the document to. Simply type in the userids under the appropriate heading and press **F10**. The document will be sent.

Using Distribution Lists. To send electronic mail to many ids at once, each id can be typed in as we stated. An alternative is to use a *distribution list* to specify the many users to receive the document. A distribution list is simply a list of userids. To create a distribution list:

- Select option 7, `Directories/distribution lists`, from the `OfficeVision/400` screen.

- Select option 3, `Distribution lists`, on the `Directories and Distribution Lists` screen (Figure 9.36).

- Select option 1, `Create list`, on the `Work with Distribution Lists` screen (Figure 9.37) and enter a list name.

On the Create a New Distribution List screen, the system id and some optional descriptive information can be assigned. After this

FIGURE 9.36

```
                    Directories and Distribution Lists

Select one of the following:

           1. Personal directories
           2. System directory
           3. Distribution lists
           4. Nicknames
           5. Search system directory
           6. Departments
           7. Locations




Selection
  _
F3=Exit       F12=Cancel       F19=Display messages
```

FIGURE 9.37

```
                    Work with Distribution Lists

Type options, press Enter.
  1=Create list 4=Delete list 5=Display entries 6=Print entries
  8=Work with entries

Opt  -----List ID-----       Description
 _   _____ _____




                                                        More...
   F3=Exit       F5=Refresh      F9=Work with nicknames  F12=Cancel
   F13=Display departments       F17=Position to
```

data is entered, press ENTER. The `Add Distribution List Entries` screen will be displayed. At this screen, the series of userids that will make up the distribution list is specified. This group of userids can be referenced by the list name identified on the previous screen. If electronic mail needs to be sent to this group of users, simply enter the distribution list id at the prompt on any send mail screen and press ENTER.

Sending a Note. To send notes and messages, they must first be created. To create and send a note:

- Select option 4, `Send note`, from the `OfficeVision/400` screen.

- Press ENTER.

The `Send Note` screen will be displayed (Figure 9.38). Just as on the `Send Document` screen, the userid(s) or a distribution list must be specified on this screen. After the distribution information is entered, press F6 to begin writing the note.

FIGURE 9.38

```
                            Send Note
Type mailing information, press F6 to type note.
Press F10 to send.

     Subject  . . . . . .    _____

     Personal . . . . . .    N            Y=Yes, N=No

-----Addressees------
User ID      Address      Description
_____      _____      
_____      _____
_____      _____
_____      _____
_____      _____

                                                    More...
F3=Exit   F6=Type note   F10=Send   F12=Cancel   F14=Specify copy list
F20=Specify distribution list F21=Select assistance level F24=More keys
```

Unlike a document, where the creator has a great deal of control over the format, notes have limited formatting capability. A note is more like a letter. When a note is created, only the contents of the note are entered and formatted. The header and the trailer of the note are preformatted, and each note's unique text is filled in. This text, however, can be manipulated quite extensively. For instance, both documents and file members can be copied into a note. Further, many of the common word processing functions (search and replace, spell check, and so on) can be used on the note's text. Once the contents of the note have been entered, press F10, and the note will be sent.

Sending a Message. To send a message:

- Select option 3, `Send message`, from the `OfficeVision/400` screen.

- Press ENTER.

The `Send Message` screen will be displayed. The `Send Message` screen, looking suspiciously like all the other send screens, is broken into two halves. The first half is where the message is defined. Simply type in the message, up to 256 characters, at the `Type message` prompt. The second half of the screen is for entering the distribution information. The same rules apply as for the `Send Document` and `Send Note` screens. Pressing F10 will send the message to the designated userids.

Receiving Mail

Receiving mail is even simpler than sending it. Select option 2, `Mail`, from the `OfficeVision/400` screen. Any mail items will be displayed on the `Work with Mail` screen (Figure 9.39). This screen lists all mail items in order of the date and time received, from newest to oldest. It also displays a status for each mail item. For notes and documents, the status can be new or opened. For messages, the status is always message.

From this screen, several options can be exercised regarding mail items.

To *view* the contents of a mail item, type **5** in the `Opt` area next to the name of the item and press ENTER. The contents of the item will be displayed. If the mail item was a note or document, its status will be changed from new to opened when the display screen is exited. The status is changed so that when the mail log is reentered at a later date, it is obvious which mail items have already been read.

FIGURE 9.39

```
                          Work with Mail

Type options below, then press Enter.
   4=Delete  5=View  6=Print  10=Forward  11=Reply  13=File
           ------From------                              Date
Opt Status  User ID  Address  Description               Received
__  MESSAGE BJANSON  CHICAGO  Who has been stealing company p 11/18/92
__  OPENED  BJANSON  CHICAGO  Real Important Stuff        11/18/92
__  OPENED  BJANSON  CHICAGO  Important stuff             11/18/92




                                                          Bottom
F3=Exit  F5=Refresh  F10=Display new mail  F12=Cancel
F21=Select assistance level
```

A *reply* can also be made to a note. The Reply function lets users quickly send a response note to the person who sent the original. The same screens are displayed as when a new note is created; however, no destination information is needed. The userid of the note sender is stored with the mail item, so this information does not need to be reentered. To reply to a note, simply type **11** in the data area next to the name of the note. The Reply to Mail screen will be displayed (Figure 9.40) with all the addressing, subject, and reference fields filled in. Press **F6** to compose the reply text and press **F10** to send it.

Forwarding a note enables a user to send the note to other users without reentering the note into the system. To forward a note, type **10** in the Opt area next to the mail item's name. The Forward Mail screen will be displayed with the subject and reference fields already filled in. Fill in the userids or distribution list to whom the note should be forwarded. When a note is forwarded, there is an option to precede the forwarded note with some extra text or comments. To attach a memo to the beginning of the note, press **F6**. Type in the memo text, then press **F10** to send the note with the attached memo.

To delete a mail item, type **4** in the Opt area next to the mail item and press **ENTER**. The Confirm Delete of Mail Entries screen will be displayed. Press **ENTER** to delete the mail item or press **F12** to cancel the delete. Items should be deleted from the mail log after they have served their useful purpose. Never deleting mail will increase the mail log size, which, depending on the machine and the volume of mail, could lead to performance degradation.

FIGURE 9.40

```
                          Work with Mail
 Type ...................................................................
    4=D:                        Reply to Mail                         :
        :                                                             :
        :   Description . . . . : Real Important Stuff           :e
 Opt    :                                                        :eived
    __  :   Type information below, press F6 to type note.       :18/92
    11  :   Press F10 to send.                                   :18/92
    __  :                                                        :18/92
        :      Personal . . . . . . .   N        Y=Yes, N=No     :
        :                                                        :
        :   -----Addressees-----                                 :
        :   User ID      Address      Description                :
        :   BJANSON_     Chicago___   Rebel trainee              :
        :   _____     _____                                :
        :   _____     _____                                :
        :   _____     _____                                :
        :   _____     _____                     More... :
        :  F4=Prompt    F5=Refresh    F6=Type note  F10=Send   :ottom
 F3=Ex: F12=Cancel   F14=Copy list  F20=Distribution list      :
 F21=S:                                                         :
        :.............................................................:
```

Summary

The four major business systems are: transaction processing systems, management information systems, computer-aided design and manufacturing systems, and office automation systems. OfficeVision/400 is the AS/400's office automation system. It provides each user with an electronic calendar, a word processor, and electronic mail.

As with all the utilities on the AS/400, OfficeVision/400 is integrated with the other system functions. For instance, data in files or data generated from a query can be incorporated into OfficeVision/400 documents. Moreover, programs and job streams can be scheduled to run on the AS/400 from the OfficeVision/400 calendar. Features such as these give the AS/400 office system a distinct advantage over stand-alone word processors and other office automation systems.

LAB EXERCISE

In this exercise, you will be creating a multi-letter shell document that will incorporate data from the query created in the exercise in Chapter 7. Before creating the shell document, go back and change CARTONQRY to include the `STORE` and `AMOUNT` fields. After you have changed the query, perform the following steps.

1. Issue the STROFC command to start OfficeVision/400.

2. Choose the `Documents and folders` option from the `OfficeVision/400` screen.

3. From the `Documents and Folders` screen, choose option 1, `Work with documents in folders`.

4. At the `Work with Documents in Folders` screen, type **1** in the `Opt` field, type the document name **STORELET** in the `Document` field, and press **ENTER**.

5. At the `Create Document Details` screen, specify your name as the author and press **ENTER**.

6. At the document edit screen, move the cursor to the upper left-hand corner of the entry area and press **F9**. At the `Select Text Instruction` screen, choose option 3, `Date`, and press **ENTER**. Accept all the defaults for the date parameters and press **ENTER**.

7. Move to the next line and type **.sk(3).**

8. Move to the next line and enter **XXXXXXX's Dairy** (substituting your name for XXXXXXX).

9. Move to the next line and type **.sk(3)**.

10. Move to the next line, type **Dear Store #**, and press **F5** (GOTO). Type **.&** and press **ENTER**.

11. At the `Data Field Instruction` screen, specify **STORE** at the `Data field` prompt, **2** at the `Data field source` prompt, and **1** in the `Letters or list` prompt. Press **ENTER**.

12. At the main document edit screen, move to the next line and type `.sk(2)`.

13. Move to the next line and type `You will be receiving carton number .&CRTNUM. It is a .&AMOUNT container of .&ITMNAM. Thank you for choosing our company to supply your dairy needs.`

14. Move to the next line and type `.sk(3)`.

15. Move to the next line and type `Yours truly,`.

16. Move to the next line and type `.sk(3)`.

17. Move to the next line and type your name.

18. Press F3 to exit and save.

19. At the `Exit Document` screen, make sure STORELET is specified for the document name and Y is specified at the `Save document` prompt. Select **Y** for the `Print document` and `Display print options` prompts and **N** for all other prompts. Press ENTER.

20. At the first of four `Print Options` screens, specify **MYQ** at the `Output queue` prompt and **YOURLIBXX** at the `Library` prompt.

21. Press PAGE DOWN twice to get to the third `Print Options` screen. Make sure a Y is specified at the `Place on job queue` prompt. Accept all other defaults. Press F15.

22. At the `Merge Data Options` screen, make sure N is specified for the `Multiple line report` option and type **1** at the `Merge data source` prompt.

23. At the new prompt, specify **CARTONQRY** (which was created in the exercise in Chapter 7) at the `Merge data source` prompt and **YOURLIBXX** at the `Library` prompt.

24. Press ENTER to submit the print job to the processing queue.

25. The documents will be sent to your output queue. To verify that the letters were created successfully, access your output queue and display the spool file.

REVIEW QUESTIONS

1. What is the difference between a calendar event and a meeting?

2. Explain how a calendar item update affects the monthly, weekly, and daily calendars.

3. What are the four types of business systems? Describe the function of each.

4. What type of business system is OfficeVision/400?

5. Explain the five levels of calendar authority.

6. What type of object are documents stored in?

7. Define a shell document.

8. What are the three objects from which a shell document can retrieve information?

9. What is a text profile?

10. What type of information is stored in a document's details?

11. Explain the difference between a multi-letter and a multi-line document.

12. Compare documents, notes, and messages.

13. What composes a distribution list, and what does a distribution list enable a user to do?

14. What is the difference between forwarding a note and replying to a note?

15. What are the three types of electronic mail handled by OfficeVision/400?

DISCUSSION QUESTIONS

1. Discuss how ObjectVision/400's calendaring function can control the execution of application and system programs.

2. Explain the advantages of an electronic calendar over a physical calendar.

3. Compare the OfficeVision/400 editor to a common PC-based word processing program's editor.

4. Discuss the advantages of the OfficeVision/400 word processor over standalone word processing applications.

DEBUG

10

This chapter covers the interactive DEBUG facility available on the AS/400. The pertinent CL commands (and their parameters) for creating a DEBUG environment will be discussed, as well as some general debugging techniques. Several CL commands that are valid only when in DEBUG mode will also be explained.

After finishing this chapter, you will understand:

- The concept and uses of tracing
- The concept and uses of breakpoints

You also will be able to:

- Run a program in DEBUG mode
- Activate tracing
- Set breakpoints
- Specify breakpoint display parameters

Starting DEBUG

Unlike most of the other AS/400 utilities, the debugging functions on the AS/400 cannot be accessed through PDM. To invoke a DEBUG function, the user must remember the specific DEBUG command or, alternatively, display a menu of DEBUG commands by issuing the command GO CMDDDBG. Because of the limited access, the user may feel that the DEBUG functions are clumsy to use. Remember, it only seems clumsy in comparison to the previous functions' tie-in with the menu system. We have been using the PDM menu system as a "road map" to find the correct function. DEBUG, unfortunately, requires the user to issue the individual commands. Also, there are no screens that provide easy access to common DEBUG functions. Unlike PDM's handling of the other system functions (where the user can delete, create, compile, or edit a member from one screen), the DEBUG functions cannot be executed through function keys or option numbers. All DEBUG commands, however, are supported with prompt screens.

To start the DEBUG function (or, phrased differently, to run the program in DEBUG mode), type in **STRDBG** and press F4. This will bring up the Start DEBUG (STRDBG) prompt screen (Figure 10.1). On this screen, identify the program to be tested at the Library and Program prompts. Notice the other parameters available on the screen. For instance, the user can control whether a program in DEBUG mode can update production level databases. As mentioned earlier, many information system organizations group their databases into development, test, and production libraries. When a library is created on the AS/400, it can be identified as a production library. Specifying *NO in the Update production files prompt will stop updates to any file in a production library. This ensures that any erroneous processing by the untested program will not corrupt production data. Specifying *NO also means that any files updated by the program during debugging must reside in a test library. (The other parameters available on this screen will be discussed in the next section.)

After specifying the program to be tested, press ENTER. This will add the program to the *DEBUG stack*, a list of all programs currently in DEBUG mode. (You can display this list by entering DSPDBG, the display debug command, at the command line and pressing ENTER.) A maximum of ten programs can be in DEBUG mode at a time. After DEBUG has been started, programs can be added and deleted from the DEBUG stack with the ADDPGM and RMVPGM commands.

FIGURE 10.1

```
                    Start Debug (STRDBG)

Type choices, press Enter.

Program . . . . . . . . . . .    *NONE_____    Name, *NONE
   Library . . . . . . . . .     _____    Name, *LIBL, *CURLIB
              + for more values  _____
                                 _____

Default program . . . . . .     *PGM_____    Name, *PGM, *NONE
Maximum trace statements  . .   200_____      Number
Trace full  . . . . . . . . .   *STOPTRC      *STOPTRC, *WRAP
Update production files . . .   *NO_          *NO, *YES




                                                          Bottom
F3=Exit F4=Prompt F5=Refresh F12=Cancel F13=How to use this display
F24=More keys
```

Tracing

Tracing is a feature that records the order of statement execution when
a program is run. Turning tracing on for a program causes a trace file
to be built for that program. When the program is run, each statement
that is executed results in an entry being made to the trace file. The
entry comprises the program name, the statement number executed,
the recursion level, and a sequence number. (Using recursive logic is
an advanced programming topic, so we ignore DEBUG's ability to
track the recursion level in this discussion.) The sequence numbers
indicate the order in which the statements were executed. At the end of
program execution, the programmer can display the contents of the
trace file and see the statement path that was followed by the program.

Being able to trace the statements executed by the program can
be very useful if the program is yielding unexpected results. When the
cause of a problem is unknown, the first thing a programmer tries to
do is narrow down the location of the error within the program. By
tracking which statements are executed, Trace eliminates the unexe-
cuted statements as possible sources of the error.

For instance, the CL program in Figure 10.2 calculates an
employee's net pay. Net pay is calculated by subtracting federal and

state taxes from gross pay. Federal withholding tax is based only on the amount of gross salary, whereas the state tax rate depends on the state of residence and the gross salary. (For instance, Florida and Washington have no state income tax, but New York does.) When the program is called, the employee's gross salary and the state he or she works in must be supplied to the program.

FIGURE 10.2

```
Columns . . . :  1 71            Edit              YOURLIBXX/CLSRC
 SEU==> _____  PAY
 FMT **  ...+... 1 ...+... 2 ...+... 3 ...+... 4 ...+... 5 ...+... 6 ...+... 7
 ************** Beginning of data *********************************
0001.00 /*****************************************************************/
0002.00 /* THIS PGM CALCS NET SALARY.                                    */
0003.00 /* LINES 10 THRU 17 CALCULATE NET SALARY AFTER FEDERAL WITHHOLDING. */
0004.00 /* LINES 18 THRU 21 CALCULATE NET SALARY AFTER STATE WITHHOLDING.   */
0005.00 /*****************************************************************/
0006.00 START:      PGM        PARM(&SAL &STATE)
0007.00             DCL        VAR(&NETSAL) TYPE(*DEC) LEN(7 2)
0008.00             DCL        VAR(&SAL) TYPE(*DEC) LEN(15 5)
0009.00             DCL        VAR(&STATE) TYPE(&CHAR) LEN(2)
0010.00             IF COND(&SAL)> 50000) +
0011.00                        THEN(CHGVAR VAR (&NETSAL) VALUE(&SAL * .65))
0012.00             IF COND(&SAL > 25000 *AND &SAL <= 50000) +
0013.00                        THEN (CHGVAR VAR (&NETSAL) VALUE(&SAL * .75))
0014.00             IF (&SAL > 15000 *AND &SAL <=25000) +
0015.00                        THEN (CHGVAR VAR(&NETSAL) VALUE(&SAL * .85))
0016.00             IF (&SAL <= 15000 +
0017.00                        THEN (CHGVAR VAR (&NETSAL) VALUE(&SAL)
0018.00             IF (&STATE = 'NY') DO
0019.00                IF (&SAL > 25000) CHGVAR &NETSAL VALUE(&NETSAL * .90)
0020.00                IF (&SAL <= 25000) CHGVAR &NETSAL VALUE(&SAL * .95)
0021.00             ENDDO
0022.00 END:        ENDPGM
 **************** End of data ****************************************

 F3=Exit  F4=Prompt  F5=Refresh   F9=Retrieve  F10=Cursor
 F16=Repeat find    F17=Repeat change        F24=More keys
```

A person living in New York and making $20,000 should have a net pay of $16,000. However, when the program is run, the result is a net salary of $19,000. To find the problem, the first step should be to set up a trace on the program. To do this, the program would have to be placed in DEBUG mode. First, issue the following command:

STRDBG PGM YOURLIBXX/PAY

Next, type **ADDTRC** and press **F4** to display the Add Trace (ADDTRC) prompt screen (Figure 10.3). On this screen, a subset of program statements to be traced can be selected, or the default of *ALL—meaning trace all the program statements—can be accepted. Also on this screen, program variables can be specified. If a program variable is specified, its value will be included in the trace file. The starting values of the program variables will be the first entries into the trace file. Each time a value is changed during program execution, another entry will be made. Therefore, the trace data will consist of program variable values and statement entries intermixed.

FIGURE 10.3

```
                           Add Trace (ADDTRC)

Type choices, press Enter.

Statements to trace:                      _
   Starting statement identifier       *ALL_____   Character value, *ALL...
   Ending statement identifier .       _____   Character value
                 + for more values _
 Program variables:                      _
   Program variable . . . . . . .
                                      *NONE_____
_____

 _____
   Basing pointer variable . . .      _____

 _____

 _____
                 + for more values      _____

 _____
                 + for more values _
   Output format . . . . . . . .      *CHAR          *CHAR, *HEX
                                                            More...
F3=Exit    F4=Prompt   F5=Refresh   F10=Additional parameters  F12=Cancel
F13=How to use this display         F24=More keys
```

The order in which Trace stores the program variables and statement entries, however, is slightly misleading. In the trace data, the line that changes the value is not the line that immediately precedes the variable value. The statement previous to the statement that immediately precedes the program value is the statement that changed the value. For instance, if the trace data consisted of three statements and then a variable value, the second statement would be the one that changed the variable, not the third. This peculiarity can sometimes lead to confusion when interpreting the trace data.

For the sample program, specify &SAL as a variable to be displayed and press ENTER. Reissue the ADDTRC command and specify &NETSAL. Then run the program by issuing the following command:

```
CALL PGM(YOURLIBXX/PAY) PARM(20000 NY)
```

Trace data will be generated as in Figure 10.4. The command to display trace data is DSPTRCDTA.

Looking at the trace data shows that, after the declare statements, the values for &SAL and &NETSAL are correct (0 and $20,000). The program then checks the conditions in each of the IF statements and executes correctly. (That is, only after the condition is met in line 14 does the value of net salary finally change. You can see from the trace data that it is correctly set to $17,000.)

The program then encounters the IF condition that checks the value of the state variable on line 18 and again executes the appropriate statements. However, notice that statement 20 (the statement two lines before the net salary variable's value display) is incorrectly setting &NETSAL to $19,000. This would lead the tester to a closer inspection of line 20. Notice that &NETSAL is being set to 95 percent of the gross salary. This is incorrect. Net salary should equal gross salary minus *both* state and federal taxes, not just state taxes. The state tax should be calculated as 5 percent of gross salary and then subtracted from net salary. The statement in line 20 should read:

```
IF (&SAL <= 25000 CHGVAR &NETSAL VALUE(&NETSAL - (&SAL * .05))
```

A look at line 19 shows that it also should be changed.

By using DEBUG and adding trace program variables, the line that contained the incorrect calculation was quickly pinpointed. You will find tracing to be very useful in any application development effort on the AS/400.

FIGURE 10.4

```
                        Display Trace Data
Program          Instruction        Recursion Level      Sequence Number
PAY              NETSAL                  1                     1
  Start position . . . . . . . . . . . : 1
  Length . . . . . . . . . . . . . . . : *DCL
  Format . . . . . . . . . . . . . . . : *CHAR
  *Variable. . . . . . . . . . . . . . : &NETSAL
    Type. . . . . . . . . . . . . . . : PACKED
    Length. . . . . . . . . . . . . . :  7 2
     '        .00'
  Start position . . . . . . . . . . . : 1
  Length . . . . . . . . . . . . . . . : *DCL
  Format . . . . . . . . . . . . . . . : *CHAR
  *Variable . . . . . . . . . . . . . . : &SAL
    Type . . . . . . . . . . . . . . . : PACKED
    Length . . . . . . . . . . . . . . :  15.5
     '      20000.00000'
                   Statement/
Program          Instruction        Recursion Level      Sequence Number
PAY              1000                    1                     2
PAY              1200                    1                     3
PAY              1400                    1                     4
PAY              1600                    1                     5
  Start position . . . . . . . . . . . : 1
  Length . . . . . . . . . . . . . . . : *DCL
  Format . . . . . . . . . . . . . . . : *CHAR
  *Variable . . . . . . . . . . . . . . : &NETSAL
    Type . . . . . . . . . . . . . . . : PACKED
    Length . . . . . . . . . . . . . . :  7 2
 ' 17000.00'
                   Statement/
Program          Instruction        Recursion Level      Sequence Number
PAY              1800                    1                     6
PAY              1900                    1                     7
PAY              2000                    1                     8
PAY              2100                    1                     9
  Start position . . . . . . . . . . . : 1
  Length . . . . . . . . . . . . . . . : *DCL
  Format . . . . . . . . . . . . . . . : *CHAR
  *Variable . . . . . . . . . . . . . . : &NETSAL
    Type . . . . . . . . . . . . . . . : PACKED
    Length . . . . . . . . . . . . . . :  7 2
 ' 19000.00'
                   Statement/
Program          Instruction        Recursion Level      Sequence Number
PAY              2200                    1                     10
```

There are a couple of other Trace features you should be aware of. We already pointed out that when trace data is displayed, the statement immediately preceding the program variable information is not the statement that changed the variable's value. The statement before the immediately preceding one is the culprit.

Another point is that the trace file has a limit of 200 statements. When the limit is reached, the AS/400 continues program execution, but no more data is entered into the trace file. The problem with this limit is that often with a complex or long program many more than 200 statements will be executed before the error is encountered. Fortunately, the action the program takes on reaching that limit can be changed. On the Start Debug prompt screen (see Figure 10.1), notice the parameter Trace full. At this prompt, the action to take when the 200-statement maximum is reached is defined. If *WRAP is specified for the Trace full parameter, the last 200 statements executed will be saved in the trace file. In other words, the latest Trace file entries will begin to replace the earlier ones. When the 201st statement is executed, the 1st statement will be dropped from the trace file. The *WRAP option is also useful for programs that are looping and then abending (abnormally ending).

The maximum number of statements recorded at any time can also be changed from the Start Debug screen (or with the CHGDBG command). Simply type in a new number over the default of 200 at the Maximum trace statements prompt. The new number, however, cannot be greater than 200.

Once the program has been executed, traced, and recoded, the old trace information is no longer needed. All trace data can be erased from the trace file with one CL command, CLRTRCDTA (clear trace data).

Breakpoints

When a program is in DEBUG mode, programmers can define breakpoints inside a program. A *breakpoint* is a point in a program where program execution is suspended and control is returned to the programmer at the workstation. When a breakpoint is reached, the Display Breakpoint screen is shown.

For a breakpoint to be set, DEBUG must be active. The command ADDBKP allows the user to specify a condition, statement number, or statement name within a program at which the breakpoint is to occur. Figure 10.5 shows the Add Breakpoint screen with the associated parameter prompts to do this. If a particular statement is identified as the breakpoint, it will be the first statement executed after the program is reactivated. This, of course, implies that program execution stops at the statement number before the one identified as the breakpoint. In other words, if statement number 100 is identified as the breakpoint (entering '/100' at the Statement identifier prompt in Figure 10.5), all statements up to and including 99.99 will be executed. When the program is reactivated, statement 100 will be the first statement executed.

The ADDBKP command also lets the user specify program variables to be displayed when the breakpoint is reached. The program variable values will be displayed on the `Display Breakpoint` screen, which is automatically shown when the breakpoint is reached.

```
                      Add Breakpoint (ADDBKP)

Type choices, press Enter.

Statement identifier . . . . . . _____        Character value

             + for more values _____
Program variables:                  _
  Program variable . . . . . . . *NONE_____
_____

  Basing pointer variable . .    _____

_____

             + for more values _____
_____

             + for more values _
Output format . . . . . . . . .   *CHAR     *CHAR, *HEX
Program . . . . . . . . . . . .   *DFTPGM___ Name, *DFTPGM
                                                    Bottom
F3=Exit F4=Prompt F5=Refresh F10=Additional parameters F12=Cancel
F13=How to use this display F24=More keys
```

The data on the `Display Breakpoint` screen is similar to the information on the `Display Trace Data` screen. The difference is that the breakpoint values displayed are the current values for the program variables. Trace data is a picture of what the values were. A breakpoint stops program execution and displays the current values of the breakpoint variables.

The user has several options at a breakpoint: The program can be restarted by pressing ENTER; program execution can be ended (not suspended) by pressing F3; or the user can press F10 and go into command entry mode. Pressing F10 results in a screen where the user can execute CL commands. A number of breakpoint-specific CL commands provide unique functions that can be executed only during a breakpoint.

For instance, if the debugger forgot to specify a breakpoint variable in the ADDBKP command, there's no need to worry. Any program variable's value can also be displayed at a breakpoint by using the DSPPGMVAR (display program variable) command.

From the `Display Breakpoint` screen, press F10 to go into command entry mode. Then enter the **DSPPGMVAR** command with the variable name. The program variable definition and value will be displayed.

Another special CL command that can be executed during a breakpoint is the CHGPGMVAR (change program variable) command. This command allows the user to change a variable value at a breakpoint. As with the DSPPGMVAR command, the program and variable names must be specified. After a program variable has been viewed and changed, the program can be reactivated. First, exit from command entry mode by pressing F3. Then press ENTER at the `Display Breakpoint` screen. The program will restart execution at the breakpoint statement.

An interesting use of breakpoints and the CHGPGMVAR command is in testing partially written programs. For instance, if two-thirds of a program had been written (the first third and the last third) and the programmer wanted to see if those portions were working correctly, processing of the middle third could be simulated through the use of a breakpoint and the CHGPGMVAR command. By placing a breakpoint at the end of the first third of the program and then issuing CHGPGMVAR commands to set the program variable values to appear as if processing of the middle third had occurred, a programmer could test the final third.

For instance, say the first third calculates an employee's pay, the middle third updates files with the pay information and retrieves the employee's address, and the final third prints out a check and an addressed envelope. At the end of the pay calculation, a breakpoint would be inserted. When the breakpoint is reached, the programmer would make sure that the pay has been calculated correctly. If so, the program's address variable could be set to some value, and the program would be allowed to continue executing. The paycheck and envelope would be printed and checked to see if they are correct. In this way, a programmer doesn't have to wait till the program is completely written or the data files are established in order to start testing. By stopping execution and manipulating the data, breakpoints and the CHGPGMVAR command can also test programs that call other programs or use, as of yet, unwritten subroutines.

As mentioned earlier, breakpoints can also be set to occur conditionally. The breakpoint condition prompt, which is displayed by pressing F10 on the `Add Breakpoint` screen (see Figure 10.5), allows the programmer to specify a variable, an operand, and a value that must be true in order to invoke the breakpoint. For instance, if during program execution, some employees' pay calculations are coming out negative, a conditional breakpoint can be set to stop execution at that time. The condition can be written as follows:

*PGMVAR1 *LT 0

When the variable is less than zero, the program will be stopped, and the programmer can begin displaying other program variables to determine why a negative number is being generated.

Besides LT (less than), the list of valid operands includes:

*EQ   equal

*NE   not equal

*GT   greater than

*GE   greater than or equal to

*LE   less than or equal to

*CT   contains

The *CT operand is used for comparisons between character strings. It checks to see if the second string is contained in the first. The condition *PGMVAR1 *CT PGMVAR2 would require that the character string value of PGMVAR2 be contained within PGMVAR1 for the breakpoint to be activated. The *CT operand is also case sensitive.

Summary

The AS/400 provides several debugging tools for programmers. These utilities include:

- A Trace feature that allows programmers to record and view the logic path followed by a program. It also provides information regarding the definition and value of program variables.
- A Breakpoint function that stops program execution and displays the current values of program variables.

Several special DEBUG CL commands also allow the programmer to monitor, maintain, and manipulate the DEBUG environment. These commands allow the user to:

- Add and delete programs from the DEBUG stack
- Display the DEBUG stack
- Clear out the trace file
- Display and change program variables during breakpoints

Together, these functions provide an effective environment to test programs and identify program problems.

LAB EXERCISE

This lab exercise will set up breakpoints within a program and then perform some of the CL commands specific to breakpoints and DEBUG. The program to be used is CRTMBR, which was created in the lab exercise to Chapter 3.

To define a breakpoint:

1. Start DEBUG by typing **STRDBG** at any command line and pressing **F4**.

2. Specify:

a. **CRTMBR** at the `Program` prompt. (This will add CRTMBR to the DEBUG stack.)

b. **CRTMBR** at the `Default program` prompt. (This will save you from having to specify the program name every time a CL DEBUG command is executed.)

c. ***YES** at the `Update production files` prompt. (This will allow CRTMBR to create a new member in INVSRC, a production file, while in DEBUG mode.)

3. Press ENTER.

4. To confirm that CRTMBR has been added to the DEBUG stack, type **DSPDBG** at the command line and press ENTER. Look for CRTMBR at the end of the list of programs. After confirming that the program is on the list, press ENTER to return to the command line.

5. At the command line, type **ADDBKP** and press F4.

6. At the `Add Breakpoint` screen, enter **'/7'** at the `Statement identifier` prompt and **'&MEM'** at the `Program variable` prompt. Press ENTER.

To change program variable values at a breakpoint:

1. Execute the create member program by typing **CALL CRTMBR ('NEW' 'PF')** at any command line and pressing ENTER.

2. Notice at the `Display Breakpoint` screen that the current value of the member name variable is 'NEW', exactly as was specified in the CALL command.

3. Press F10 to go into command entry mode.

4. Display the value of the member type field by typing the display program variable command as follows: **DSPPGMVAR '&MTYP'**. Press ENTER.

5. Notice that the member type field also contains the correct value, PF. Press ENTER to return to command entry mode.

6. Change the two program variable values by issuing the following change program variable commands: **CHGPGMVAR '&MEM' SLICK** and **CHGPGMVAR '&MTYP' CLP**.

7. Press F3 to exit command entry mode and return to the `Display Breakpoint` screen.

8. Continue executing the create member program by pressing ENTER.

9. When the program executes the STRSEU command, the SEU `Edit` screen will be displayed. Notice that the member being edited is SLICK. The CHGPGMVAR commands changed the file name and type values that were specified in the initial call of the program to SLICK and CLP.

10. Exit and save member SLICK.

11. To remove CRTMBR from the DEBUG stack and end DEBUG, type **ENDDBG** and press ENTER.

REVIEW QUESTIONS

1. What information is contained in trace data?

2. What is the DEBUG stack?

3. Explain tracing.

4. What is the difference between a program variable value displayed through Trace and one displayed through breakpoints?

5. Is the breakpoint statement executed before program execution is suspended or after execution is resumed?

6. What is a conditional breakpoint?

7. How is production level data safeguarded by DEBUG?

8. What is the purpose of the `Trace full` parameter?

DISCUSSION QUESTIONS

1. Discuss the uses of tracing and breakpoints in finding program errors and testing.

2. Discuss some of the limits and peculiarities of the AS/400 Trace function.

3. Describe several functions that can be executed at a breakpoint.

Screen Design Aid

11

Overview

In this chapter, we explore Screen Design Aid (SDA), a utility that enables programmers to quickly and easily create screens and menus. As mentioned earlier, DDS can be used to define both files and screens. SDA allows the user to define screens in an interactive hands-on manner. By using SDA, the programmer does not have to know DDS commands, parameter keywords, or their syntax. The user first describes and constructs the screen with SDA. SDA then generates and compiles the DDS specifications, thereby creating a display file. The display file contains the machine-understandable definition of the screen.

SDA also provides several editing functions and commands to easily define and manipulate fields on the screen. For instance, SDA is tightly coupled with the AS/400 database. Fields from existing files can be used to define screen fields. If a field is chosen from a file, it is not necessary to respecify the field characteristics. The field's database definition is used to create the display field.

A final advantage of SDA is that it allows screens to be displayed and tested throughout the development process. User-written programs do not have to be created to do this. Instead, SDA provides a test utility that works with all SDA-defined screens.

After finishing this chapter, you will understand:

- The relationship between display files and DDS source members
- The advantages of using SDA over DDS to define and test screens
- The relationship between SDA and the AS/400 database management system

You also will be able to:

- Define a screen to be used in an interactive program
- Save, compile, and reedit the display definition source member
- Display the screen with test data and check the screen's input buffer
- Create a menu

Starting SDA

SDA, like most AS/400 utilities, can be invoked through a CL command or a series of user-friendly menus. To skip over the non-SDA menus, type **STRSDA** and press ENTER. The AS/400 Screen Design Aid (SDA) screen will appear (Figure 11.1). To create a screen, select option 1. This will result in the Design Screens screen (Figure 11.2). On this display, the user specifies the member that will contain the screen definition source code. Type the member name along with its library and file names and press ENTER. The Work with Display Records screen will be displayed (Figure 11.3).

FIGURE 11.1

```
                    AS/400 Screen Design Aid (SDA)

Select one of the following:

     1. Design screens
     2. Design menus
     3. Test display files




Selection or command
===>_____

F1=Help    F3=Exit    F4=Prompt    F9=Retrieve    F12=Cancel
```

FIGURE 11.2

```
                        Design Screens
Type choices, press Enter.

    Source file  . . . . . . .   INVSRC____   Name, F4 for list

       Library. . . . . . . . .  YOURLIBXX_   Name, *LIBL, *CURLIB

    Member . . . . . . . . . .   INVDSPF___   Name, F4 for list










F3=Exit        F4=Prompt         F12=Cancel
```

FIGURE 11.3

```
                    Work with Display Records
File. . . . . . . :   INVSRC          Member . . . . . . :  INVDSPF

   Library . . . . :    YOURLIBXX    Source type. . . . :  DSPF

Type options, press Enter.
    1=Add                2=Edit comments      3=Copy         4=Delete
    7=Rename             8=Select keywords   12=Design image

Opt   Order   Record     Type  Related Subfile  Date   DDS Error

1_            ITEM_____
   (No records in file)




                                                              Bottom
F3=Exit                 F12=Cancel     F14=File-level keywords
F15=File-level comments F17=Subset     F24=More keys
```

Each screen definition is stored in a *display record*, which will contain the DDS source code that SDA generates based on your screen design. To create a new display record, type 1 in the Opt column and specify a record name in the Record column. Pressing ENTER will bring up the Add New Record screen (Figure 11.4). The name of the record and its type, RECORD, will be displayed. Press ENTER to go to the Work screen (Figure 11.5).

FIGURE 11.4

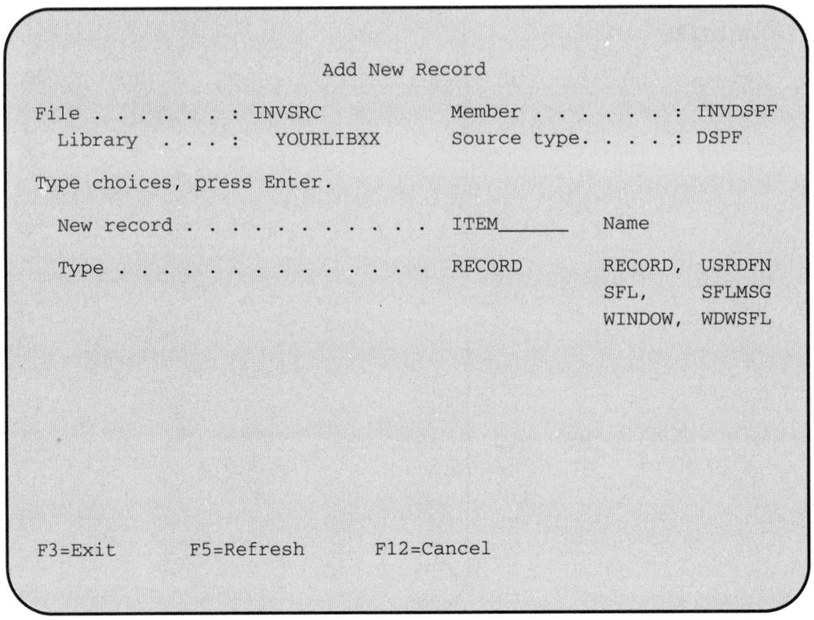

```
                        Add New Record
   File . . . . . . : INVSRC        Member . . . . . . : INVDSPF
     Library  . . . :  YOURLIBXX    Source type. . . . : DSPF

   Type choices, press Enter.

     New record . . . . . . . . . . ITEM_____   Name

       Type . . . . . . . . . . . . . RECORD      RECORD,  USRDFN
                                                  SFL,     SFLMSG
                                                  WINDOW,  WDWSFL




   F3=Exit      F5=Refresh      F12=Cancel
```

FIGURE 11.5

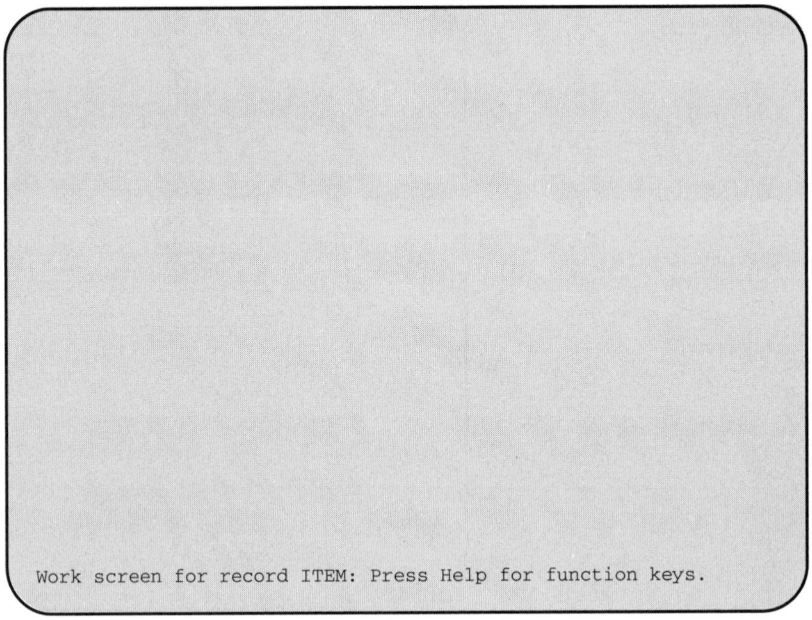

```




                Work screen for record ITEM: Press Help for function keys.
```

Defining a Screen

SDA allows the programmer to define and position three types of display fields: constant text fields, system variable fields, and data fields.

Defining Constant Text Fields

To specify a constant text field, simply type the text at the location on the screen where it should appear. If the constant text contains more than one word, enclosing it in single quotes is often a good idea. If the text is not enclosed in quotes, SDA will treat each word as a field. For a function like highlighting or underlining to be performed on all the text, each word would have to be individually highlighted or underlined. But if the text is enclosed in quotes, all the text can be operated on at once.

For our example, we first want to assign a screen name. A screen name is an example of a screen text constant. Move the cursor to the fourth line on the screen, type **'ITEM UPDATE SCREEN'**, and press ENTER. The single quotes will disappear, and the screen name text will remain.

Defining System Variable Fields

To define a system variable as an output field, the appropriate system variable code has to be entered on the screen. For this screen, specify that two system variable fields—time and date—will appear on the second line of the screen. To do this, move the cursor to line 2, column 1, and type ***TIME**. This system variable code tells the system to display the time at that position on the screen. On the far right-hand side of the line, specify the date by typing ***DATE** at column 63.

Counting off 62 spaces to find column 63 is rather tedious, isn't it? SDA provides a *ruler* to clearly identify line and column numbers. Move the cursor to line 3 and press F14 to display the ruler. The ruler numbers each row and column on the Work screen. The numbers will not appear on the final screen and can be typed over. The ruler makes it much easier to find column 63. To turn the ruler off, press F14 a second time. F14 acts as a toggle switch, turning the ruler alternately on and off when it is pressed.

Some other system variables that can be specified include:

*USER   supplies the userid
*SYSNAME   supplies the name of the system

Defining Data Fields

Fields that will display or accept data can be defined two different ways. If the data element already exists in a database, its DDS definition can define the screen field. If the field is not in a database, it is a user-defined data field.

To add database fields to the screen, press F10 on the Work screen. The Select Database Files screen will be displayed (Figure 11.6). From this screen, the user can select fields from a single file or multiple files. Simply specify the file, library, and record format names in the appropriate columns. There are also four options for each file. Option 1 allows the user to pick selected fields from the file. Options 2, 3, and 4 select all the fields from the file and designate whether the fields will be used for, respectively, input only, output only, or both input and output.

Choosing option 1 will result in the Select Database Fields screen being displayed with all the fields for the database listed

(Figure 11.7). Each field's length, type, and header text will also be displayed. On this screen, fields can be selected by designating them as input, output, or both. Once the options have been typed (as in Figure 11.7), press ENTER twice and the Work screen will reappear. Notice on the Work screen that the selected fields appear at the bottom of the screen (Figure 11.8). They are there to remind the user which database fields have been selected for placement on the screen.

FIGURE 11.6

```
                        Select Database Files

Type options and names, press Enter.
  1=Display database field list
  2=Select all fields for input (I)
  3=Select all fields for output (O)
  4=Select all fields for both (B) input and output

Option  Database File  Library      Record
  1      STOCKQTY__     YOURLIBXX_   STKFMT____
  _      _____       _____     _____
  _      _____       _____     _____
  _      _____       _____     _____




F3=Exit       F4=Prompt        F12=Cancel
```

FIGURE 11.7

```
                        Select Database Fields

Record . . . . : STKFMT

Type information, press Enter.
  Number of fields to roll. . . . . . . . . . . . . .   8
  Name of field to search for . . . . . . . . . . .  _____

Type options, press Enter.
  1=Display extended field description
  2=Select for input (I), 3=select for output (O), 4=Select for both (B)

Option   Field    Length   Type    Column Heading
  4      ITMNUM       6      A      ITEM NUMBER
  4      ITMNME      15      A      ITEM NAME
  _      QTYNST      6,0     P      QUANTITY IN STOCK




                                                          Bottom
F3=Exit    F12=Cancel
```

To place a field on the screen, *work screen symbols* need to be used. An example of a work screen symbol is an ampersand followed by one of the numbers that precedes a database field name at the bottom of the `Work` screen and the letter L (&1L). The ampersand designates the starting location of the field, and the L says that the header text is to appear to the left of the field followed by a colon. Two blank spaces will separate the colon from the start of the screen field. Type **&1L** at row 7, column 25, and type **&2L** at row 10, column 25.

After entering the work screen symbols, press ENTER. The work screen symbols will be replaced by characters that depict the length of the fields and their type. For instance, the character I says the field is for character input only; O, for character output only; and so on. Further, the headers will appear where dictated by the work screen symbol.

FIGURE 11.8

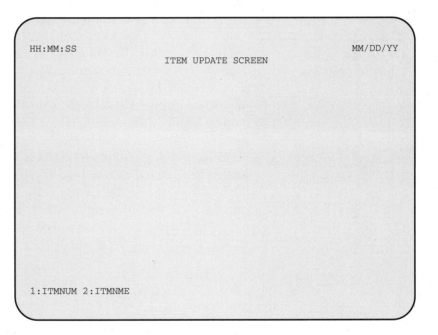

```
HH:MM:SS                                          MM/DD/YY
                      ITEM UPDATE SCREEN




1:ITMNUM 2:ITMNME
```

Creating User-Defined Fields

To add a user-defined field, type + at the position before where the field is to begin on the screen. The plus sign is an *attribute character* that designates the field as user defined.

The next character entered after the plus sign defines the field type. Some codes that can be entered and their definition are:

3	numeric input only
6	numeric output only
9	numeric input and output
I	character input only
O	character output only
B	character input and output

The next characters after the character type define the length of the field and, optionally for numeric fields, how many decimal places will be needed. The length can be denoted by either repeating the field type character the number of times of the length—+IIIIIIIII for a nine-character input-only field—or using a shorthand notation—+I(9). The same holds for numeric fields: +3333333.33 and +3(7,2) both describe a nine-digit numeric input-only field with two decimal places.

For our example, define a message area on the last line of the screen. At column 5, type **+O(70)** and press ENTER. SDA will display the new field as dictated by the plus sign and the length parameters. SDA will also assign the field a name of FLDxxx, where xxx begins with 001 and progresses by one for each user-defined field. Thus, the first user-defined field would be FLD001, the next would be FLD002, and so on. For the message field, define a constant text header to the left of it. Start in the first column and type **MSG:**.

Defining Field Characteristics

As mentioned, each screen field can have attribute characters associated with it. *Attribute characters* define the field and how it will appear on the screen. *Display characters*, which are a type of attribute character, define characteristics such as the field color or whether the field will be highlighted, underlined, or blinking. These attributes can be specified in the space that immediately precedes the field, the *attribute field*. To find the attribute field, press F20. F20 reverse highlights the screen field, including any preceding blank spaces. Through reverse highlighting, the field is clearly defined, and the space immediately preceding the field (the attribute field) can be easily located.

The following codes can be specified in the attribute field:

B   blink
H   highlight
R   reverse image
U   underline

The following color codes can also be specified:

CB   blue
CG   green
CP   pink
CR   red
CT   turquoise
CW   white
CY   yellow

For the screen name, we are going to specify an *action attribute*. Type **AC** starting in the attribute field of the screen header. AC is the code to center a field. The attribute characters will appear to overtype the first letter of the screen name. Press ENTER. The first character of the screen name will be restored, and the screen name will be centered on the line.

Another way to specify a field's attributes as well as define editing and auditing functions is to type * in a field's attribute field and press ENTER. This will invoke a series of prompt screens that allow the user to select a field's attributes or editing functions. The prompt screens free the programmer from having to remember all the attribute characters and symbols.

The first screen to appear, after the user places an asterisk in the attribute field and presses ENTER, is the Select Field Keywords screen. This screen's option list changes based on the type of field being defined. For instance, if the data field was defined as output only, the Input keywords option would not be displayed. Similarly, if the field was defined as character, the Editing keywords option would not be displayed because editing keywords are for numeric fields only. The screen displayed in Figure 11.9 shows all the possible options.

FIGURE 11.9

```
                         Select Field Keywords

  Field . . . . . : FLD008         Usage . . : B
  Length. . . . . : 7,2            Row . . . : 15  Column . . : 16

  Type choices, press Enter.
                                   Y=Yes For Field Type
     Display attributes . . . . .   -    All except Hidden
     Colors . . . . . . . . . . .   -    All except Hidden
     Keying options . . . . . . .   -    Input or Both
     Validity check . . . . . . .   -    Input or Both, not float
     Input keywords . . . . . . .   -    Input or Both
     General keywords . . . . . .   -    All types
     Editing keywords . . . . . .   -    Numeric Output or Both
     Database reference . . . . .   -    Hidden, Input, Output, Both
     Error messages . . . . . . .   -    Input, Output, Both
     Message ID (MSGID) . . . . .   -    Output or Both

     TEXT keyword . . . . . . . .        _____

  F3=Exit      F12=Cancel
```

Choosing an option from the `Select Field Keywords` screen will result in a screen that displays a list of potential attributes and keywords. From these screens, the user can select any attribute he or she likes. For instance, typing **Y** at the `Display attributes` prompt will result in the `Select Display Attributes` screen being displayed (Figure 11.10). From this screen, the field can be underlined, highlighted, and so on. Notice that in the upper left-hand corner there is a space for the name of the field being defined. Other areas show the field's location on the screen, length, and usage (input, output, and so on).

Selecting the `Colors` option will bring up the `Select Colors` screen (Figure 11.11). This screen allows the user to define the color of all characters and numbers that will appear in the field. In addition to allowing the user to define one color for a field, this screen allows a field's color to be controlled by the program that will be using it. This is done by associating an indicator with a color. If the specified indicator is set on, the field will be displayed in the indicator's associated color. The program logic can turn indicators on and off based on conditions.

FIGURE 11.10

```
                    Select Display Attributes

 Field . . . . . :  FLD001      Usage . . :  O
 Length . . . . . :  70         Row . . . :  24  Column . . :  6

 Type choices, press Enter.
                                   Keyword   Y=Yes   Indicators/+
 Field conditioning . . . . . . .            _       __ __ __
 Display attributes:              DSPATR
   High intensity . . . . . . . .   HI       _       __ __ __
   Reverse image . . . . . . . .    RI       _       __ __ __
   Column separators . . . . . . .  CS       _       __ __ __
   Blink . . . . . . . . . . . .    BL       _       __ __ __
   Nondisplay . . . . . . . . . .   ND       _       __ __ __
   Underline . . . . . . . . . . .  UL       _       __ __ __
   Position cursor . . . . . . . .  PC       _       __ __ __


 F3=Exit    F12=Cancel
```

FIGURE 11.11

```
                        Select Colors
    Field . . . . :   FLD001      Usage . . : O
    Length  . . . :   70          Row . . . : 24   Column . . . : 6

    Type choices, press Enter.

                                           Keyword Order Indicators/+
                                                         (1-7)
    Colors:                          COLOR
      Blue . . . . . . . . . . . . . . .   BLU    _     __ __ __
      Green . . . . . . . . . . . . . .    GRN    _     __ __ __
      Pink  . . . . . . . . . . . . . .    PNK    _     __ __ __
      Red . . . . . . . . . . . . . . .    RED    _     __ __ __
      Turquoise . . . . . . . . . . .      TRQ    _     __ __ __
      White . . . . . . . . . . . . .      WHT    _     __ __ __
      Yellow  . . . . . . . . . . . .      YLW    _     __ __ __




    F3=Exit   F12=Cancel
```

For instance, it is customary to display serious error messages in red (the better with which to catch the user's eye!). Typing **30** in the indicator column on the red row would associate indicator **30** with red. Each time the program is about to display a message, it could check the message severity. If the message is concerned with a serious error, the program would turn indicator 30 on, thereby turning the error message field red. Through the use of indicators, an entire error message color scheme could be set up based on the severity of the message. (For example, green messages would mean everything is fine, informational messages would be in white, yellow would be used for minor errors, pink would signal more serious problems, and red would mean, "Step away from the terminal and keep your hands away from the keyboard.")

Choosing the other `Select Field Keywords` options will allow the user to define the following attributes and keywords:

- `Keying options`. For input fields, allows the user to define the fields as mandatory fill or entry. Gives the user the ability to set the justification of all input values and define the fill characters (blanks or zeros). These options correspond to the DDS keyword, CHECK.

- `Validity check`. Allows input values to be compared to a single value, a list of values, or a range of values. This allows the user to define the values to be used in the DDS keywords, RANGE, COMP, and VALUES.

- `Input keywords.` Lets the programmer set up response indicators. These will be turned on if the input field is changed, blanks are entered, or DUP is pressed. The program can check the value of the response indicators to determine if any of these conditions has occurred.

- `General keywords.` Allows the user to set up another name that the field can be referenced by or define a default value that will be shown in the field when the screen is displayed. The default value displayed can be typed over by the user. This corresponds to the functions of the ALIAS, DFT, and DFTVAL DDS keywords.

- `Editing keywords.` Lets the user specify the EDTCDE and EDTWRD parameters for the screen field. These parameters designate numeric formatting functions like suppressing leading zeros; the type of thousands separator to be used; whether the negative sign should be displayed, and if so, where it should be displayed, before or after the number.

- `Database reference.` Allows the user to assign an already defined database field's definition to the current field. This option also allows some overriding of the database definition.

- `Error messages` and `Message ID (MSGID).` Allow the user to define error messages, associate message identifiers with the message, and assign indicators for program control.

Before leaving the `Work` screen, add another text constant field that identifies the F3 key as the exit key. The `Work` screen should look like Figure 11.12.

FIGURE 11.12

```
HH:MM:SS                                                    MM/DD/YY
                          ITEM UPDATE SCREEN

        ITEM NUMBER: BBBBBB

         ITEM NAME: BBBBBBBBBBBBBBBB




            PRESS F3 TO EXIT THIS DISPLAY


MSG: OOOOOOOOOOOOOOOOOOOOOOOOOOOOOOOOOOOOOOOOOOOOOOOOOOOOOOOOOOOOOOOOOO
```

FIGURE 11.13

```
                        Exit SDA Work Screen
Select one of the following:

      1. Save work since last Enter and exit work screen
      2. Exit without saving any work done on the work screen
      3. Resume work screen session




Selection
  _
F12=Cancel
```

Saving and Compiling

To generate and save the DDS for the screen, press **F3**. The Exit SDA Work Screen will be shown (Figure 11.13). For our example, save all the changes by selecting option 1. This will cause the Work with Display Records screen to be displayed (Figure 11.14). Notice there is now a record entry for ITEM, which we just defined. Pressing **F3** again will result in the Save DDS - Create Display File screen being displayed (Figure 11.15). The library, file, and members specified earlier as the destination for the DDS will be filled in on the screen. To save the DDS code, type **Y** at the Save DDS source prompt.

FIGURE 11.14

```
                    Work with Display Records

 File . . . . . . . : INVSRC         Member . . . . . . : INVDSPF
   Library . . . . :   YOURLIBXX     Source type  . . . : DSPF

 Type options, press Enter.
   1=Add       2=Edit comments    3=Copy        4=Delete
   7=Rename    8=Select keywords  12=Design image

 Opt  Order   Record     Type   Related Subfile Date    DDS Error
 __   _____
 __    ___10  ITEM       RECORD                 01/15/93




                                                         Bottom
 F3=Exit                    F12=Cancel   F14=File-level keywords
 F15=File-level comments  F17=Subset    F24=More keys
 Record ITEM added to member INVDSPF.
```

FIGURE 11.15

```
              Save DDS - Create Display File

 Type choices, press Enter.

    Save DDS source . . . . . . . . .  Y         Y=Yes
      Source file . . . . . . . . . .  INVSRC____   F4 for list
        Library . . . . . . . . . .    YOURLIBXX_  Name, *LIBL ...
      Member  . . . . . . . . . . .    INVDSPF___  F4 for list
      Text  . . . . . . . . . . . .    _____
 _____
    Create display file . . . . . . .  Y         Y=Yes
      Prompt for parameters . . . . .  _         Y=Yes
      Display file. . . . . . . . . .  ITEMDSPF__  F4 for list
        Library . . . . . . . . . . .  YOURLIBXX_  Name, *CURLIB
      Replace existing file . . . . .  _         Y=Yes

    Submit create job in batch  . . .  Y         Y=Yes

    Specify additional
      save or create options. . . . .  _         Y=Yes

 F3=Exit      F4=Prompt       F12=Cancel
```

To compile the DDS source code and create the display file, make sure there is a Y at the Create display file and Submit create job in batch prompts. The Library and Display file names can also be specified. Press ENTER. The DDS will be compiled, and the display screen created as specified.

Testing Screens

SDA provides the user with the capability to see screens as they will be displayed at the user's workstation. It also lets the tester specify data for output, manipulate indicators, and see the effect on the screen appearance. For input fields, the tester can enter data in the display fields, test any defined validity checks, and inspect the input buffer that is passed back to the application program.

To go into test mode, choose option 3, `Test display files`, from the `AS/400 Screen Design Aid (SDA)` screen (see Figure 11.1). This will bring up the `Test Display File` screen, where the library, file, and record to be tested are specified (Figure 11.16). Once the information has been entered, press ENTER.

The test facility cycles through three screens (with the third screen being an optional screen to view the input buffer). These three screens are the `Set Test Output Data` screen, the user's screen that was defined through SDA, and the `Display Test Input Data` screen. The user progresses through the screens by pressing ENTER.

FIGURE 11.16

```
                          Test Display File

 Type choices, press Enter.
 Display file. . . . . . . . .     ITEMDSPF__   Name, F4 for list
   Library . . . . . . . . . .     YOURLIBXX_   Name,
                                                *LIBL ...

 Record to be tested . . . . .     ITEM_____   Name,
                                                F4 for list

 Additional records to display .   _____   Name
                                   _____
                                   _____





 F3=Exit        F4=Prompt        F12=Cancel
```

For instance, after the display to be tested has been specified, the Set Test Output Data screen is displayed (Figure 11.17). On this screen, the tester can type in values for any field that has been defined for output and turn any display attribute indicators on or off. After specifying the output information, pressing ENTER will result in the user-defined screen being displayed with the values specified and the attributes dictated by the indicators. In Figure 11.18, the screen has no values displayed because none were specified on the Set Test Output Data screen. The user-defined screen in Figure 11.18 can, however, accept input. Typing in values, as seen in Figure 11.19, and pressing ENTER, will bring up the Display Test Input Data screen (Figure 11.20). This screen displays each input field (notice that FLD001 is not listed—it was defined as output only) and the value contained in that field. To see the input buffer layout and the contents that the application program would receive, press F14.

Pressing ENTER again would redisplay the Set Test Output Data screen, as seen in Figure 11.21. Figure 11.22 simulates the message and what the screen would look like if whole milk was already in the database.

FIGURE 11.17

```
                        Set Test Output Data

     Record . . . : ITEM

     Type indicators and output field values, press Enter.

     Field      Value
     ITMNUM     BBBBBB:_____
     ITMNME     BBBBBBBBBBBBBBB:_____
     FLD001     OOOOOOOOOOOOOOOOOOOOOOOOOOOOOOOOOOOOOOOOOOOOOOOOOOOOO







                                                              Bottom
     F3=Exit    F12=Cancel
```

FIGURE 11.18

```
13:59:48                              .                    1/15/95
                        ITEM UPDATE SCREEN

         ITEM NUMBER: BBBBBB

          ITEM NAME : BBBBBBBBBBBBBBBB




                PRESS F3 TO EXIT THIS DISPLAY


MSG: OOOOOOOOOOOOOOOOOOOOOOOOOOOOOOOOOOOOOOOOOOOOOOOOOOOOOOOOOOOOO
```

FIGURE 11.19

```
13:59:48                                                  1/15/95
                        ITEM UPDATE SCREEN

         ITEM NUMBER: 111111

          ITEM NAME : WHOLE MILK




                PRESS F3 TO EXIT THIS DISPLAY


MSG: OOOOOOOOOOOOOOOOOOOOOOOOOOOOOOOOOOOOOOOOOOOOOOOOOOOOOOOOOOOOO
```

FIGURE 11.20

```
                        Display Test Input Data

       Record . . . : ITEM

       View indicators and input field values.

       Field      Value
       ITMNUM     111111:
       ITMNME     WHOLE MILK :




                                                               Bottom

       Press Enter to continue

       F3=Exit        F12=Cancel      F14=Display input buffer
```

FIGURE 11.21

```
                        Set Test Output Data

       Record . . . : ITEM

       Type indicators and output field values, press Enter.

       Field      Value
       ITMNUM     111111:_____
       ITMNME     WHOLE MILK:_____
       FLD001     ITEM 1111111 - WHOLE MILK - ALREADY EXISTS IN THE DATABASE.







                                                               Bottom

       F3=Exit    F12=Cancel
```

FIGURE 11.22

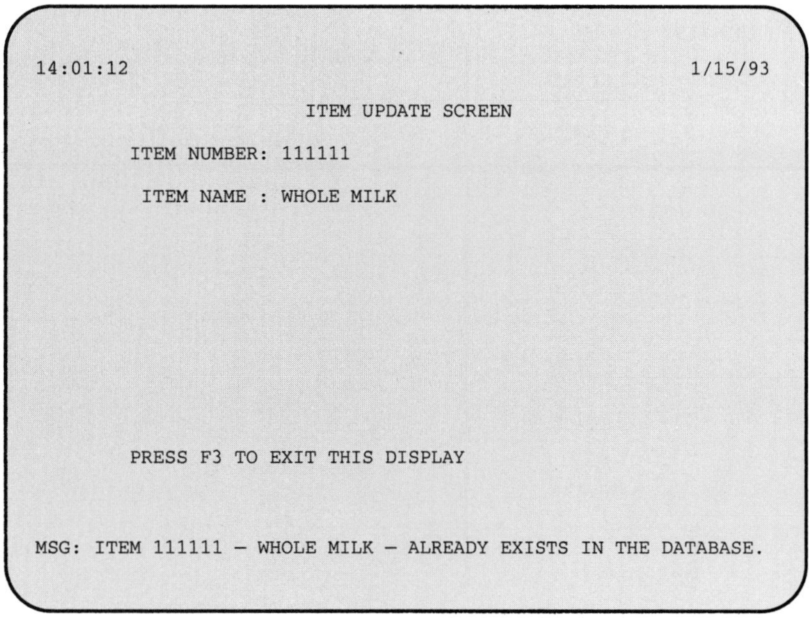

```
14:01:12                                                              1/15/93
                              ITEM UPDATE SCREEN

            ITEM NUMBER: 111111

            ITEM NAME : WHOLE MILK




                     PRESS F3 TO EXIT THIS DISPLAY



MSG: ITEM 111111 — WHOLE MILK — ALREADY EXISTS IN THE DATABASE.
```

Creating Menus

Menus are even easier to create than screens. To create a menu, select option 2, Design menus, from the AS/400 Screen Design Aid (SDA) screen (see Figure 11.1). This will result in the Design Menu screen. At this screen, specify the library, file, and member in which to store the menu definition. (All menu definition members have a type of MNUDDS.) Once the information is entered, press ENTER. The Specify Menu Functions screen is displayed. The user would specify Y for the Work with menu image and commands option. This will result in the menu definition screen being displayed (Figure 11.23). The title of the screen will actually be the member name specified earlier, followed by the word *Menu*. The example menu member was called NEW; therefore, the screen name is NEW Menu. If an inventory functions menu were being defined and the member had been called INVFUNC, the name of the screen would be INVFUNC Menu.

FIGURE 11.23

```
                        Design Menus
NEW                           NEW Menu

Select one of the following:

    1.
    2.
    3.
    4.
    5.
    6.
    7.
    8.
    9.
   10.
Selection or command _
F3=Exit              F10=Work with commands      F12=Cancel
F13=Command area     F20=Reverse                 F24=More keys
Press Help for a list of valid operations.
```

The menu definition screen allows the user to change the menu name by simply typing over the old one. Up to ten menu options can be defined on this screen. Move the cursor next to the option number and type the appropriate text that describes the function that will be offered by that menu option.

To define what each option will do, press **F10**. This will bring up the Define Menu Commands screen (Figure 11.24). This screen allows the user to enter a CL command that will be executed when an option is chosen. For instance, the first menu option could be Start PDM. In this case, the CL command STRPDM would be typed in as the command to be executed. Option 2 could be Update item. The command entered at option 2 of the Define Menu Commands screen would be CALL ITMUPD. Assuming that the ITMUPD program uses the screen defined earlier, when option 2 is chosen, the Item Update screen would be displayed (as in Figure 11.18 without the data fields being filled in).

A system function, a user-defined application program, or a CL job stream can be called and executed from a menu. Moreover, constant text fields can be added to the menu, and all field attribute characters covered earlier in the chapter can be specified for any menu field. Pressing **ENTER** and specifying **Y** at the Create menu prompt will result in SDA building a menu.

FIGURE 11.24

```
                        Define Menu Commands

Menu . . . . . . : NEW        Position to menu option . . . . ._ _

Type commands, press Enter.

Option Command
01
   _____
02
   _____
03
   _____
04
   _____
05
   _____
06
   _____
07
   _____
                                                                More...
F3=Exit    F11=Defined only options    F12=Cancel    F24=More keys
```

Summary

SDA allows users to define and create display files. Through an easy-to-use, menu-driven interface, SDA allows the user to define and control the display characteristics of constant text fields, system variable fields, and data fields. Based on the characteristics specified by the user, SDA then creates the appropriate DDS specifications and stores them in a new type of object called a display record. This source definition of the screen is then compiled into a display file. The display file contains the machine-understandable definition of the screen and is the object that will be used by application programs.

The display file can also be tested using SDA. The SDA test facility allows the user to "send" the screen to a workstation display just as it would appear if an application had sent it. The user can then enter information in areas defined for input. All defined edits and audits will be performed. In addition, the contents of the buffer that would be passed back to the application program can be displayed. The test utility also lets a user set the values of output fields and then send the screen. In this way, the user can see the screen as it would appear with data.

SDA also provides a facility to quickly define menus that can contain up to ten options. These options can be used to invoke system and application programs, as well as other screens and menus.

LAB EXERCISE

This exercise will create a screen that allows the user to pass salary and state information to the CL program PAY. (PAY was used as an example in Chapter 10.) After the screen is created, the CL program will be modified to display and receive the screen. This will be done by changing the program's logic flow and adding CL commands that identify and manipulate a display file.

To create a member to hold the screen source definition:

1. Create a new file called PAYSRC with an attribute of PF-SRC within YOURLIBXX.

2. Create a new member called PAYDSPF with a type of DSPF in file PAYSRC.

To create a display file with SDA:

1. Type **STRSDA** at any command line and press ENTER.

2. Select option 1, Design screens, from the AS/400 Screen Design Aid (SDA) screen.

3. Specify **YOURLIBXX**, **PAYSRC**, and **PAYDSPF** at the appropriate prompts.

4. On the Work with Display Records screen, specify **1** in the Opt column to add a record and enter **NETSALARY** as the record name. Press ENTER.

5. At the Add New Record screen, make sure **RECORD** is specified for the Type prompt and press ENTER.

6. On the Netsalary Work screen:

   a. Move to the second line, column 5, and type ***time**.

   b. On the second line, at column 65, type ***date**.

   c. Move to the third line, column 26, and type **'Net Salary Calculation'**.

   d. Move to line 7, column 10, and type **'Please enter gross salary and state'**.

   e. Move to line 10, column 17, and type **'Gross Salary:'**. On line 10, at column 32, type **+9(6)**.

   f. Move to line 14, column 24, and type **'State:'**. On line 14, at column 32, type **+BB**.

   g. Move to line 20, column 19, and type **'Net Salary:'**. On line 20, at column 32, type **+6(6)**.

   h. Move to line 23, column 10, and type **'To exit, enter -1 in the state field and press Enter'**.

   i. Press ENTER.

   j. Place an asterisk in line 23's constant text field's attribute field (column 10) and press ENTER.

k. On the `Select Field Keywords` screen, specify **Y** for the `Display attributes` prompt and press ENTER.

l. On the `Select Display Attributes` screen, specify **Y** for the `High intensity` prompt. Press ENTER. Press F3 to exit.

m. Place an asterisk in the Net Salary data field's attribute field (line 20, column 32) and press ENTER.

n. On the `Select Field Keywords` screen, specify **Y** for the `Editing keywords` prompt and press ENTER.

o. On the `Select Editing Keywords` screen, specify **4** for the `Edit code` prompt and **$** for the `Replace leading zeros with` prompt. Press ENTER. Press F3 to exit.

p. Place an asterisk in the State data field's attribute field (line 14, column 32) and press ENTER.

q. On the `Select Field Keywords` screen, specify **Y** for the `Validity check` prompt and press ENTER.

r. On the `Valid Check Keywords` screen, specify **'FL' 'NY' 'WA' '-1'** at the `Values list` prompt. Press ENTER. Press F3 to exit.

s. Press ENTER.

t. Press F3.

7. At the `Exit SDA Work Screen`, select option 1.

8. At the `Work with Display Records` screen, press F3.

9. Specify **Y** to both the `Save DDS source` and `Create display file` prompts, then press ENTER twice. This will create the display file object that can be used in the CL program.

10. Exit SDA by pressing F3.

11. Start PDM and look at objects under YOURLIBXX. Notice the new object PAYDSPF with a type of *FILE and an attribute of DSPF. This object was created by SDA in step 9.

12. Also look at members under PAYSRC. Notice the new member PAYDSPF. Display the member. This is the DDS that SDA generated based on the specifications made at the SDA Netsalary `Work` screen in step 5.

To create a CL program to send and receive a screen:

1. Create a new member called PAY with type equal to CLP under PAYSRC and enter the following CL program:

Notice the new DCLF command in line 25. This is used to identify a display file in a CL program. The SNDRCVF command in line 26 will display the screen at the workstation that calls the program and halt execution of the program. When ENTER is

pressed, any information in the input fields will be passed back
to the program, and execution will begin at the statement following the SNDRCVF command.

```
                *************** Beginning of data ****************************************
0001.00 /******************************************************************************/
0002.00 /* THIS PROGRAM CALCULATES NET SALARY.                                        */
0003.00 /* LINE 26 SENDS THE INITIAL BLANK SCREEN TO THE WORKSTATION DISPLAY.         */
0004.00 /* AFTER THE SCREEN HAS BEEN SENT BACK TO THE PROGRAM, LINE 27                */
0005.00 /*     DETERMINES WHETHER THE USER WISHES TO PERFORM ANOTHER NET              */
0006.00 /*     SALARY CALCULATION. THIS IS DONE BY CHECKING THE VALUE OF THE          */
0007.00 /*     SCREEN'S STATE FIELD. IF THE USER HAS ENTERED A -1 IN THE              */
0008.00 /*     STATE FIELD THEN NONE OF THE CALCULATIONS BETWEEN THE DO AND           */
0009.00 /*     THE ENDDO STATEMENTS WILL BE PERFORMED AND THE PROGRAM WILL END.*/
0010.00 /* LINES 29 AND 30 SET PROGRAM VARIABLES EQUAL TO THE SCREEN VALUES.          */
0011.00 /* LINES 31 THRU 38 CALCULATE NET SALARY AFTER FEDERAL WITHHOLDING.           */
0012.00 /* LINES 39 THRU 47 CALCULATE NET SALARY AFTER NY STATE WITHHOLDING.          */
0013.00 /* LINE 48 SETS THE SCREEN'S NETSALARY OUTPUT FIELD EQUAL TO THE              */
0014.00 /*     RESULT OF THE CALCULATION.                                             */
0015.00 /* LINE 49 SENDS THE SCREEN WITH THE ORIGINAL INPUT VALUES AND THE            */
0016.00 /*     CALCULATED NET SALARY VALUE BACK TO THE WORKSTATION DISPLAY.           */
0017.00 /* WHEN THE USER PRESSES ENTER AND THE SCREEN IS SENT BACK TO THE             */
0018.00 /*     PROGRAM, LINE 50 SENDS CONTROL BACK TO LINE 27, WHERE IT IS            */
0019.00 /*     DETERMINED IF ANOTHER NET SALARY SHOULD BE CALCULATED.                 */
0020.00 /******************************************************************************/
0021.00 START:      PGM
0022.00             DCL       VAR(&NETSAL) TYPE(*DEC) LEN(6)
0023.00             DCL       VAR(&SAL) TYPE(*DEC) LEN(6)
0024.00             DCL       VAR(&STATE) TYPE(*CHAR) LEN(2)
0025.00             DCLF      FILE(PAYDSPF) RCDFMT(NETSALARY)
0026.00             SNDRCVF RCDFMT(NETSALARY)
0027.00 LOOP:       IF COND(&FLD002 *NE '-1') +
0028.00             THEN(DO)
0029.00                 CHGVAR VAR(&SAL) VALUE(&FLD001)
0030.00                 CHGVAR VAR(&STATE) VALUE(&FLD002)
0031.00                 IF COND(&SAL > 50000) +
0032.00                     THEN(CHGVAR VAR(&NETSAL) VALUE(&SAL * .65))
0033.00                 IF COND(&SAL > 25000 *AND &SAL <= 50000) +
0034.00                     THEN(CHGVAR VAR(&NETSAL) VALUE(&SAL * .75))
0035.00                 IF COND(&SAL > 15000 *AND &SAL <= 25000) +
0036.00                     THEN(CHGVAR VAR(&NETSAL) VALUE(&SAL * .85))
0037.00                 IF COND(&SAL <= 15000) +
0038.00                     THEN(CHGVAR VAR(&NETSAL) VALUE(&SAL))
0039.00                 IF (&STATE = 'NY') +
0040.00                     THEN(DO)
0041.00                         IF COND(&SAL > 25000) +
0042.00                             THEN(CHGVAR VAR(&NETSAL) +
0043.00                                 VALUE(&NETSAL - (&SAL * .10)))
0044.00                         IF COND(&SAL < 25000) +
0045.00                             THEN(CHGVAR VAR(&NETSAL) +
0046.00                                 VALUE(&NETSAL - (&SAL * .05)))
0047.00                     ENDDO
0048.00                 CHGVAR VAR(&FLD003) VALUE(&NETSAL)
0049.00                 SNDRCVF RCDFMT(NETSALARY)
0050.00                 GOTO LOOP
0051.00             ENDDO
0052.00 END:        ENDPGM
                *************** End of data ****************************************
```

2. Exit, save, and compile the member.

3. At any command line, type **CALL PAY** and press ENTER.

4. At the SDA-defined screen, type **10000** as gross salary and **FL** as the state. Press ENTER.

5. Notice that net salary is calculated and displayed (with a leading $) in the output field.

6. Enter other gross salary figures and states. Check that the validation is being done for the State field by entering invalid state codes.

7. When you have finished, enter **-1** in the State field and press ENTER.

REVIEW QUESTIONS

1. What is a display file?

2. Give three examples of system variable fields.

3. What are the two ways that data fields can be defined?

4. What is a display record? What is its relationship to a display file?

5. What are attribute characters, and where are they specified on a screen?

6. What are display attributes? Provide examples.

7. What is stored in a source physical file member with a type of MNUDDS?

8. Describe the fields that would be created by the following definitions:

+B(6)

+6(3)

+3(6)

+I

+9(3,2)

9. What other system utility allows users to define screens through an easy-to-use menu interface?

DISCUSSION QUESTIONS

1. Compare creating screen definitions by entering DDS specifications through SEU to specify screen definitions with SDA.

2. Describe the capabilities of the SDA test facility.

Index